Economic Analysis of Sub-Saharan Africa Real Estate Policies

Economic Analysis of Sub-Saharan Africa Real Estate Policies

Felix N. Hammond
and
Yaw Adarkwah Antwi

palgrave
macmillan

First published 2010 by
PALGRAVE MACMILLAN

Palgrave Macmillan in the UK is an imprint of Macmillan Publishers Limited, registered in England, company number 785998, of Houndmills, Basingstoke, Hampshire RG21 6XS.

Palgrave Macmillan in the US is a division of St Martin's Press LLC, 175 Fifth Avenue, New York, NY 10010.

Palgrave Macmillan is the global academic imprint of the above companies and has companies and representatives throughout the world.

Palgrave® and Macmillan® are registered trademarks in the United States, the United Kingdom, Europe and other countries.

ISBN 978–0–230–23231–0 hardback

This book is printed on paper suitable for recycling and made from fully managed and sustained forest sources. Logging, pulping and manufacturing processes are expected to conform to the environmental regulations of the country of origin.

A catalogue record for this book is available from the British Library.

A catalog record for this book is available from the Library of Congress.

10 9 8 7 6 5 4 3 2 1
19 18 17 16 15 14 13 12 11 10

Printed and bound in Great Britain by
CPI Antony Rowe, Chippenham and Eastbourne

Contents

List of Figures

List of Tables

Preface

This book examines how real estate markets in Africa work, the peculiar forces that drive its performance as well as those that impede the economic use and development of land and property which in turn undermine economic progress and sustainable poverty alleviation in these economies. Until comparatively recent times, there use to be a rather tenuous appreciation of the relevance of land and real estates in the pursuit of development and poverty alleviation in Africa and the rest of the developing world. Land, which formed the basis of real estates, was considered to be overly embroiled in emotive indigenous tenure rules and institutions, the analysis of which, it was thought, falls beyond the legitimate ken of economic analysis. As such, the immediate post-independence mainstream development ideologies which were widely adopted by many African nations sought to supplant indigenous land tenure arrangements by central land allocation mechanism. But as policy bulletins after bulletins, issued essentially by the international development community and often adopted by national governments unexpurgated, failed to produce instantly recognisable progress; as country after country presented continually appalling economic picture and as the disparity in the material standard of living between the developed and underdeveloped societies widened rapidly amidst widespread violent conflicts and deepening poverty in Africa in particular, apprehensions about the future of Africa and many developing countries surged. This caused persistent state of unease among the international development community. Several explanations for the state of affairs have been offered by various development experts. The problem is that not all of the explanations offered headed in the same direction. Many in fact were in conflict. This led to a significant rethink of economic policy frames prescribed for Africa and the developing world at the turn of the twenty-first century. A consequence of this is the emergence of the debate on the importance of land for the entire development process of Africa. It has been unequivocally established that omitting land and real estates in the development bulletins that have so far shaped the development path of Africa was a costly mistake. There is now a perceptible increase in the consideration given to the importance of land and real estates in the African development process.

Real estate markets in Africa are unique in that they are regulated by two parallel bodies of law – laws fashioned along the lines of European property laws on one hand and indigenous African land tenure laws on the other. To date, the actual economic potential of the indigenous tenure system remains little understood, even less understood is the economic impact of the joint operation of these two disparate body of laws. There exists still, in some quarters, pessimism and low regard for indigenous tenure frameworks and institutions and their capability to shape behaviours towards the economic use and development of land and real estate markets. The argument to smother and ultimately oust indigenous tenure through land policy has effectively collapsed as an ideology (albeit not necessarily in practice). Among researchers and international development agencies there are renewed calls for indigenous tenure across the developing world to be allowed a much wider scope than they presently possess in the development process. This new thinking has culminated in the 2003 World Bank publication of the pro-poor land policies.

The trouble is, to date the kind of land tenure systems and arrangements which might reasonably be expected to foster the needed economic development remains illusive. This is crucial, not least because the long period of state superimposition of laws on the indigenous tenure since the colonial era has resulted in a tenure regime that in most places lacks the resemblance, virtues and capabilities of pure indigenous tenure. Reversing government interventions entirely does not also appear to be a realistic option. If Africa is to benefit from the cross-border capital flows fostered by the increasing pace of globalisation and the rapid development of innovative cross-border real estate financing instruments such as REITS and real estate securitisation, it is essential that the currently tenuous link between real estate and economic development of Africa is strengthened. More so, if this link is well fostered, areas that require remedy will become clear and the system would become, if well understood, more tolerable and appreciated by the international development community and foreign direct investors with considerable equanimity. It is to this end that the book is aimed.

We wish to thank Professors Paul Olomolaiye and David Proverbs of the University of Wolverhampton for their support and encouragement in the course of writing this book. We also wish to extend further grateful appreciation to Alhaji Sulemana Mahama of the Ghana Lands Commission for his invaluable critique of aspects of the ideas expressed in this book. We accept that they cannot be held responsible for any errors in this work; errors contained in this material are of our own making even though we will not hesitate to blame each other for them.

1 Background

1.1 Introduction

Time was when economists blissfully ignored land/real estate in their propositions, considering it as a neutral element in the economic development process and hence warranting no serious attention (Hammond, 2006; Platteau, 1992; World Bank, 1975). Today, it is widely recognised that the omission of land/real estate in earlier development theories was a grave error that has derailed many otherwise sound economic policies (Hammond, 2006; Deininger, 2003). Perhaps the most critical dimension of real estate in the context of economic development is the policy and institutional arrangements that regulate the way it is acquired, owned, formalised, developed and used (Deininger, 2003; Antwi and Adam, 2003; Antwi, 2000). It is this dimension that ultimately determines the extent to which particular real estate parcels can be productively utilised, and that constitutes the main subject of study in this work.

The main thesis of this work is that real estate policies have a non-trivial causal relationship with poverty such that improvement in the way real estate is utilised is bound to have impacts on the poverty situation of the society in question. In pursuing this thesis, this book aims to examine the economic impacts of sub-Saharan African real estate policies with the view to proffering a role that such policies can or should play in support of the ongoing fight against poverty in the region.

With 80 per cent of their population living on less than $2.50 a day (Ravallion and Chen, 2008), it is beyond doubt that pronounced poverty together with its various derivatives constitutes the leading development challenge of sub-Saharan African nations today. The fact is, this appalling state of affairs is particularly inexcusable given that, since the twentieth century, the world at large has been experiencing what Henry George, writing in 1912, described as a 'prodigious increase in wealth-producing power'.[1] With the development of computer technology since the 1980s, there is no doubt that the acclaimed wealth producing power of the world has multiplied in capacity several times over in the last few decades. This has created better prospects for improving the well-being of individuals in society. It is quite curious to note that all the nations that have so far managed to capitalise on this power to deal with poverty tend to be grouped in one geographical area. Those nations for whom the opposite is true are similarly grouped together geographically.

Poverty is a concept of bewildering interpretations. In order to avoid unnecessary distraction to the aim of this present chapter, which is to set the scene for the coming discussions, a comprehensive definition of the term is deferred to the next chapter. Even so, we need to shape the contours of this present discussion with an idea of what is meant by the term poverty in this work. We therefore preliminarily define poverty as *a remediable but significant deficit in human well-being that causes hardship*. A person in such a state is classified as poor. The causes of such deficits are wide-ranging, as shall be discussed in Chapter 2.

Poverty is an all-pervading fact of life. It exists in both rich and less developed nations. What, however, makes the state of poverty in sub-Saharan Africa utterly worrying is its sheer spread and intensity as well as its bravado and capacity to defy all attempted policy solutions and interventions. So desperate is the quest for poverty alleviation in sub-Saharan Africa in particular that governments and the international development community have now developed obsessions with, and become very quick to draw attention to and commemorate, very marginal and often impermanent poverty alleviation achievements in the sub-Saharan region.

Justifiably, the alleviation of poverty is, by far, the most significant development concern of both national governments and the international community at large. This concern has persisted since the formative days of the postcolonial era and led, in the 1940s and 1950s, to the birth of development economics as a separate branch of mainstream economics. The principles of development economics were ostensibly tailored to the peculiar needs of less developed nations. Premised on this new brand of economics it was hoped, almost unanimously, that a poverty free sub-Saharan Africa, or indeed developing world, would soon materialise. Yet after nearly seven decades of experimentation, it is obvious that more faith was placed in the theories than they could actually deliver. The aspiration of a poverty free developing world is yet to be borne out in practice. Quite the opposite, the well-being of a great majority of the population of Sub-Saharan Africa continues to decline with speed and has now reached nightmarish proportions as relevant statistics show.

1.2 Poverty, a worldwide problem

In order not to create the erroneous impression that poverty is a problem exclusive to Africa, it is necessary first to provide a bird's eye view account of poverty as a worldwide phenomenon. Concerns about poverty are neither recent nor peculiar to sub-Saharan Africa; poverty is a worldwide problem, although its considerable scale in Africa gives cause for greater concern.

The earliest formal work on poverty dates back to the end of the nineteenth century. The two classics on poverty were by Charles Booth and Seebohm Rowntree. Charles Booth produced the first major empirical survey of the poverty conditions of the people of London between 1891 and 1903. Following Booth, Rowntree studied the level of poverty in York between 1897 and 1898 and published the results in 1901 in *Poverty: A Study of Town Life*. Though these works were based in the UK they have since generated international interest in the search for the real causes and nature of, and a cure for poverty across the world.

Following these works, interest in the fight against poverty across the world soared significantly, and has done particularly in the last six decades. The methodology employed by Rowntree continues to inform current techniques for measuring poverty by the World Bank. Some six decades after these initial works several international development institutions such as the World Food Organization in 1943, the United Nations Relief and Rehabilitation Administration in 1943, the United Nations Educational, Scientific, and Cultural Organization in 1944, the International Monetary Fund and the World Bank in 1944 and United Nations in 1945 were formed with audacious commitments to reset the post-Second World War economic order and to eradicate global poverty and conflicts. For instance, the preamble to the charter of the United Nations proclaims the determination of the United Nations to 'promote social progress and better standards of life in larger freedom'. Article 55 of the charter indicates that the United Nations exists to promote:

a. higher standards of living, full employment, and conditions of economic and social progress and development;
b. solutions of international economic, social, health, and related problems; and international cultural and educational cooperation; and

c. universal respect for, and observance of, human rights and fundamental freedoms for all.

On the strengths of these principles and with the expected support and assistance from these international development institutions, these newly liberated nations were rapidly to move up from their then primitive state to the status of important contributors to the growth of the global economy. As time rolled on, however, these aspirations turned into disappointments and the disappointments multiplied into anxiety and then in some areas into despondency (see further Sachs, 2005).

Despite the billions spent by these organisations collectively towards banishing poverty and spurring economic growth, about 65 years after their formation the aspirations of global economic growth and prosperity are yet to be meaningfully borne out in practice across the developing world. The case of sub-Saharan Africa is dire to say the least. This gives the impression that these monies are being thrown after a problem that is yet to be properly understood. The numbing statistics show that, across the world, but more so in sub-Saharan Africa, the poverty problem has become even more poignant than before.

Between the periods following the Second World War, when many of these international development institutions were established, and the present time, poverty has progressively worsened in most parts of the world. For example, in 1981 the number of people who lived on less than $1.00 a day the world over stood at 1.5 billion (Sachs, 2005). In 2001, the World Bank (2001)[2] estimates that, of the then 6 billion population of the world, 2.8 billion, representing almost half, live on $2.00 a day, and 1.2 billion (a fifth) live on less than $1.00 a day. At present however, nearly half of the people of the world (about 3.14 billion) survive on less than $2.50 a day, which essentially comes to the same thing as surviving on a medium size burger a day. In addition, only a fifth of the people of the world currently lives on $10.00 and above a day (Ravallion and Chen, 2008),[3]. It is in fact estimated that currently about 8 million people die each year because they are too poor to stay alive (Sachs, 2005).[4] It is estimated that over the last five years, the number of people living in chronic poverty has increased with the effect that between 320 and 443 million people are now trapped in poverty that lasts many years, likely for their entire life as well as those of their children (CPRC, 2008).[5] UNICEF (2006)[6] estimates further that on average more than 26,500 children under the age of five die each day around the world mostly due to poverty, hunger, preventable diseases and so forth. This equates to 10 million children dying each year (in 2006 annual figure dropped marginally to 9.7 million). Of these, some 1.8 million die each year as a result of diarrhoea (UNDP, 2006).[7] But, as said before, though poverty is a worldwide problem, its severity is most intense in the developing world, with sub-Saharan Africa being the most affected.

Such was the worsening global poverty situation that in 2000 the international development community made a frantic commitment to eliminate extreme poverty across the world. This commitment, enunciated by the United Nations through the Millennium Development Goals (MDGs) (United Nations, 2000), set 2015 as the year by which extreme poverty is to be halved, an obvious step towards the total annihilation of extreme poverty in the long run. Considering the focus of this work on sub-Saharan Africa, it is in order at this stage to delve a little deeper into the incidence of poverty in the sub-continent.

1.3 Sub-Saharan Africa's struggle with poverty

We now turn to the specific case of sub-Saharan Africa. The political decolonisation of African countries after the Second World War was accompanied by great economic and political aspirations and optimism. It was hoped that the political liberation of these nations would manifest shortly in very rapid and sustained economic growth and more prosperity than ever experienced. In particular, as Abernethy (1988) puts it, 'the overthrow of colonialism was perceived by the African population to mean the destruction of the barriers to development'.[8] These aspirations were to be delivered through the then emerging theories of development economics. Indeed, Fieldhouse (1986) claimed 'to have solved the problem of the origins and nature of poverty and to be able to provide formulas which could ensure its eradication'.[9] Yet after more than 60 years of development economics practice, sub-Saharan Africa remains riddled with abject poverty. Some few statistical examples are poignant here.

Table 1.1 below, retrieved from the World Bank's online poverty database *POVCAL* (2007), which currently provides the most extensive and up-to-date statistics on poverty, reports the proportion of the populations of respective developing regions that earn below the cut-off point for extremely poor of one US dollar a day.

The table shows that in 1981 sub-Saharan Africa had the third largest collection of extremely poor people in the developing world after

Table 1.1 Developing countries: Population living below US$1 a day (headcount, numbers of millions)

	1981	1984	1987	1990	1993	1996	1999	2002	2004
East Asia and Pacific	57.7	39	28.2	29.8	25.2	16.1	15.4	12.3	9.07
Europe and Central Asia	0.7	0.52	0.36	0.47	3.61	4.22	3.6	1.28	0.95
Latin America and the Caribbean	10.8	13.1	12.1	10.2	8.42	8.88	9.6	9.05	8.63
Middle East and North Africa	5.08	3.82	3.11	2.33	2.12	2.23	2.08	1.69	1.47
South Asia	49.6	45.4	45.1	43.1	36.9	36.1	35	33.4	31.1
Sub-Saharan Africa	42.4	46.3	47.5	46.8	45.7	48.0	46.1	42.6	41.1

Source: World Bank, 2007.

East Asia and Pacific region and South Asia. However, by 1999 when the MDGs were promulgated, sub-Saharan Africa had attained the unenviable position of the world's poorest region with 46.1 per cent of its population classified as extremely poor. Since then a lot has got worse. Sub-Saharan Africa is no longer the region with the third largest extremely poor inhabitants in the developing world. The region is currently top of the league table of poor regions of the world. Today, a great majority of the inhabitants of African countries, particularly those located south of the Sahara (excluding South Africa) live in horrid poverty and sanitary conditions amid rampant civil war. It is clear from the table that, with the exception of sub-Saharan Africa and South Asia, most developing regions are set to achieving the target by 2015. On the contrary, at current rates, it will take sub-Saharan Africa another 41 years from 2004 to eradicate extreme poverty.

It is important to draw attention once again to the fact that these statistics may present an overly optimistic view of the performance of these regions, as the cut-off line has not taken into account price changes that have occurred since 1993. Even the apparent good news of a reduction in the number classified as extremely poor might not be as unambiguously welcoming as first thought. For while the lifting or empowering of people to work their way out of poverty may reduce extreme poverty, the number of people classed as poor may also reduce not only through deaths arising from natural causes but also from conflicts, malnutrition, poor sanitation and hardships of all sorts.

In sub-Saharan Africa where conflicts are rife, life expectancy very low and ever reducing, child mortality very high and birth-related maternal deaths very high, a considerable proportion of the reduction in extreme poverty may be arising from deaths rather than actual economic uplifts. This would not be a cause for celebrations.

In the rush to meet the MDGs, countries and the international development community seem to be losing sight of the fact that poverty is indeed far more profound than just the extreme poverty (primary poverty) that is the main focus of the Goals. As the data shows, eradicating primary poverty completely cannot by itself resolve the poverty problems faced by a society; secondary poverty, which has plagued a lot more people, remains a major challenge. Table 1.2 presents data on the proportion of national populations that survive on less than two US dollars a day.

As the data show, even where less than 1 per cent of the population of Europe and Central Asia, for example, are extremely poor, as much as 10 per cent remain poor.

Indeed, with the exception of Europe and Central Asia with less than 10 per cent poor, 20 per cent of the population of all the developing regions is poor, with South Asia having the highest proportion (77.2%), followed by sub-Saharan Africa (71.96%). This shows that even when the MDG is achieved a great number of the population of the developing world would still be in secondary poverty.

Remarkably, while Europe and Central Asia have, for instance, managed to reduce the proportion of their population that is statistically

Table 1.2 Proportion of population surviving on less than US$2 a day (percentage headcount)

	1981	1984	1987	1990	1993	1996	1999	2002	2004
East Asia and Pacific	84.8	76.79	68.53	69.72	65.04	52.5	49.23	41.68	35.99
Europe and Central Asia	4.62	3.99	3.09	4.31	16.48	17.94	18.29	12.94	9.83
Latin America and the Caribbean	28.45	32.24	29.61	26.25	24.09	25.29	25.23	24.72	22.14
Middle East and North Africa	29.16	25.59	24.31	21.69	22.03	23.51	23.61	21.09	19.7
South Asia	88.52	86.95	86.59	85.63	82.2	82.12	80.44	79.7	77.2
Sub-Saharan Africa	74.49	76.88	77.34	76.99	76.15	76.79	76.05	73.81	71.96

Source: World Bank, 2007.

extremely poor, the number that are poor has actually increased between 1981 and 2004. In like manner, South Asia and sub-Saharan Africa made very little progress in reducing their proportions of poor people. The only region that made very rapid progress in reducing the size of its statistically poor population is East Asia and Pacific. This may indicate that, rather than confronting the poverty question as a whole, the exclusive concentration on the extremely poor has left the proportion of the poor only slightly improved, leaving the quest for poverty alleviation very far from achieved.

Rather than growing at a very rapid rate, many of these economies are shrinking and instead of making important contributions to the growth of global wealth, these nations have become significant drains on the wealth producing power of the world. The emerging prognosis of the economic future of these countries holds no comforting message either, prompting the world to unify global efforts to avert an evolving possible human catastrophe of nightmare proportions if things are permitted to continue as they have done in the past.

The African Commission estimates, in its policy document *Our Common Interest*, launched in March 2005, an additional US$75 billion annual investment in governance, public investment and social expenditure is required to kick-start the African economy. African governments were to contribute under these proposals over three to five years roughly US$12.5 billion (Our Common Interest, 2005). Further, the Group of Eight (G8) wealthiest nations agreed on 11 June 2005 to back a deal that calls for an immediate scrapping of 100 per cent of the debt (up to US$55 billion) owed by the 18 poorest countries.

Most of these nations are in sub-Saharan Africa. Massive campaigns by civil society and charities of the developed world dubbed 'make poverty history' are underway to call on rich nations to do more to help African economies. Indeed, never in the history of man have such global concerted humanitarian efforts been directed towards the eradication of extreme poverty in Africa. Debt cancellation will mark a major accomplishment considering that at present sub-Saharan Africa, the poorest of the poor regions of the world, pays US$10 billion in debt servicing annually to the rich countries of the world (Principal Voices, 2005). With debt cancellation, at least in theory, some extra money will be available to be spent on domestic African development programmes rather than servicing debts owed to rich countries.

Additionally, if the campaigns for rich countries to remove market protection and subsidies that have distorted the international economic terrain are heeded, a levelled economic playing field could be created on which developing nations can perform. To these extents, it is logical to conclude that debt relief, increased aid and equitable international trade are important and inexorable inputs to the development processes of sub-Saharan Africa. But such an assertion has to be made with some trepidation. It is important not to oversimplify sub-Saharan Africa's economic crises by placing too much hope on these international global efforts than they are actually capable of delivering. After all, these external supports offer no more than temporary reliefs. They have not and cannot provide permanent prosperity for the nations of sub-Saharan Africa. Thus, thrusting the whole development processes of Africa on international support will mean deferring the destiny of these economies indefinitely. Even so, it is questionable if these global efforts can really make headway when the internal forces that keep swallowing developmental gains, blocking progress and conditioning the state of sub-Saharan African economies are not restructured.

1.4 The place of public policy

The fact of the matter appears to be that an enduring and sustainable prosperity of Africa can only be achieved by 'building an investment climate that facilitates [private sector led] investment and growth and empowering poor people to participate in that growth' (Stern, 2002). According to Stern (2002, pp. 12–13) these embody the enactment of sound and sensible macroeconomic and trade policies; the installation of quality infrastructure including power, water, transport and telecommunication; efficient government institutions and behaviour (including limits on bureaucratic harassment, especially in administering taxes and regulations); the strength of financial institutions; the rule of law, including enforcement; and the control of corruption and crime.

All these conditions are internally generated, which reinforces the point that the development of Africa is, above all, the responsibility of African governments and the people of Africa. It is within Africans' grasp to deal with the internal forces that militate against these conditions while the international communities address the external forces. With heightened global commitment to abate the external bottlenecks underway, systematic inquiries into the internal bottlenecks that have led to the persistence of the African crisis is indispensable. This is an investigation whose time has come. There is no use clamouring for more external development support when the internal forces that are militating against development have not been properly identified and isolated. The question that should guide discussions around the African problem then is: what are these impediments, their nature, sources and panacea? In the 1980s Mabogunje (1980), like many of his compatriots, identified governmental systems and interventions as the impediments that created the less dignified and unsatisfactory conditions for a substantial proportion of the third world population. More recently, the United Nations (2005, p. 31) in exploring the reasons for the apparent failure of the MDGs establishes similarly:

> Economic development stalls when governments do not uphold the rule of law, pursue sound economic policy, make appropriate public investments, manage a public administration, protect basic human rights and support civil society.

This identifies again government and its governance machinery as the core of the formidable forces that impede the development of sub-Saharan Africa. It is therefore obvious that government has a role to play in the fight against poverty. What is yet unresolved is what this role should be. This is the grand issue at stake in the ongoing economic development dialogue with the effect that any consensus from it will certainly be fundamental to the successful execution of the war against poverty.

To know what the role of government action ought to be, particularly in the real estate sector, we must first understand what causes deficits in human well-being. This will be examined in some detail in the next chapter. It suffices at this stage, however, to note that a yet to be refuted theory of economics holds that human well-being is an *effect* that is *caused* by careful and united *use* of land (or real estate), labour, capital and entrepreneurship in the production, distribution and consumption of goods and services. Real estate is defined here to embrace land units together with whatever thing that is permanently attached to it, if any, whether situated in a rural or urban locality. A deficit in human well-being is therefore the result of inadequacy in the availability of these resources or deficiencies in their usage.

Looking at the scale of affluence and opulence of Western nations today, it is very easy to forget the fact that these now rich nations did not emerge from the start as such; they were all, once upon a time, similarly riddled with insidious and widespread poverty. Nonetheless, through successful leadership and effective leveraging of the wealth producing power of the world, the vast majority of their populations have worked their way effectively out of poverty. This accomplishment is an eloquent testament to the ability of humanity to deal decisively with poverty and its attendant menace, provided that what are needed to do so are correctly *known* and the *means* and *will* to do so are also adequately in hand. On the converse, sub-Saharan Africa's continuing struggle with poverty shows that the requisite knowledge, means and will to deal more decisively with the problem have not been available.

To make progress, there is the need primarily to focus inquiries on eliminating or abating development impediments inbuilt in African governmental systems. This also implies the need to subject the activities of these governments and their governance machineries in the various sectors to serious systematic and rigorous questioning. It would be naïve, anyway, to presume that these inquiries have neither been made before nor remedies attempted. However, the persistence of these problems as exemplified above suggests that the solutions proposed so far have failed to attack practices and systems that undermine development in these nations. The impediments still prevail. From the point of view of this study, the efficient utilisation of real estate resources has significant effects in reducing poverty but the solutions suggested have failed to attack impediments that prevent the effective and efficient utilisation of real estate assets in sub-Saharan Africa to contribute to the eradication of poverty.

It is possible that governments of sub-Saharan Africa would be persuaded if they were confronted with a sector-by-sector scale of the harm these impediments present in more practical and objective terms. The tradition of pointing out the overall gloomy economic picture rather than sector-specific issues may be making the problems look insurmountable to politicians and those in charge of affairs. They may thus see African problems as manageable rather than remediable leading them to renege on their efforts at addressing the problems. That said, such sector-based inquiries would be more useful if they were concentrated, for now, on the strategic sectors whose malfunctioning are likely to cause comparatively more damage to economic lives.

Significant progress appears to have been made in finding workable, though far from perfect, government actions to provide the framework for the use of labour, capital and entrepreneurship skills in most developing economies. Finding the right form of government actions for the real estate sector (real estate policy) remains a formidable challenge. Deploying the level of governmental involvement, the right mix of laws and institutions that regulate the ownership, use, exchange and formalisation of real estate together with the institutions that enforce these policies so as to eradicate poverty has eluded sub-Saharan African governments. The experiences of the West inform that appropriate government actions can produce very good effects on poverty alleviation and prosperity. At the same time poor real estate policy can cause considerable damage to the development of real estate markets and to the well-being of a vast majority of the population. The trouble is that the outcomes of policies are not self-evident. They can only be known through conscious acts of systematic measurement.

For several decades, a special body of law, regulations and government departments has been established in most developing nations to regulate the ownership, use, development, formalisation and transactions relating to real estate and the real estate market itself (see Chapter 4). Historically, government interventions in land and real estate markets have been applied for more than a century in much of sub-Saharan Africa since the colonial era. Postcolonial sub-Saharan Africa has additionally gone through about four and a half decades of social, economic and political changes during which real estate policy responses have been enacted. These enactments were aimed at remedying what were perceived at various historical times to be the problems of the real estate markets in the respective sub-Saharan African economies.

1.5 Analysing real estate policies

Real estate policy is a genre of economic policy. Its analysis therefore follows the way economic policies ought to be analysed. Appraising the performance of real estate policy is an endeavour in discovering its effects. The basic precept that underlies the assessment of effects is the law of causality,[10] which posits simply that to every effect (or outcome) there is an adequate cause. There is no known exception to this law. This means that certain causes map onto certain effects and vice versa. In other words particular causes give rise to certain and predictable effects. Consequent upon that, if we know the prevailing cause(s) we must be able to trace the effects to which they map onto or are in causal connection with. Conversely, if we know the effects we must be able to trace their causes. What this means further is that if we desire a certain effect, we must orchestrate the specific causes to which they are causally connected. If, for instance, we know that effect X is causally connected to a cause, Y, then, if we desire effect X, we must first bring about cause Y. A cause, in our case, may be a type of real estate policy in force or its mode of enforcement. The effects may be economic gains or damages to individual or societal well-being. Therefore, if we experience an undesirable effect we can trace the cause and then replace it with the appropriate policy or mode of enforcement that would be causally connected to achieving the desired effects.

Poverty, the central focus of development economics, is an effect that, accordingly, must have an adequate cause. Our task in this book is to draw attention to the extent to which real estate policy could be a contributory cause of poverty in sub-Saharan African economies and to suggest practical ways of organising these policies for better effects on poverty. We must start with a good understanding of the scale of poverty in sub-Saharan Africa.

Despite the long-standing general agreement between economists that development in real estate markets influences the rate and courses of economic development, earlier theories of development economics suffered from a momentous under valuation of the significance of real estate markets to the quest for the economic development of developing nations. Land and property were thus not incorporated into the early theories of economic development. As far as the early development economists were concerned, the crucial resources that mattered were capital and labour. In particular, the failure of nearly seven decades of development economic theory and practice to exert far-reaching impacts on poverty in sub-Saharan Africa has led to the realisation that, among other things, the non-incorporation of land and property into development theories is a costly omission calling into question the validity of those theories.

One of the costs created relates to the lack of economic attention to real estate policy in most countries. These policies increasingly became political instruments by which governments influenced decisions on who should be granted land rights and who should not (this is discussed in detail in Chapter 4). This realisation has brought sub-Saharan African real estate in particular to the centre of the development debate, prompting a wide range of research in this area.

Presently empirical studies surrounding sub-Saharan African real estate markets have generally taken four main routes. One group (Platteau, 1992; Mattingly, 1993; Larbi, 1994; Brandao and Feder, 1995) approached the issue using qualitative research design and methodology and hence were unable to measure, in quantitative terms, the impacts of these policies. Another group (McAuslan, 2000; Antwi, 2000; Quan, 2000) concentrated on the customary land sector without an evaluation of the economic costs and resource wastage associated with the government bureaucratic machinery responsible for policy implementation in these economies. Yet, others (Mattingly, 1993; Brandao and Feder, 1995; De Soto, 2000) have looked at the sector within the broader context of Third World or developing countries and hence have not provided a focused view of the sub-Saharan Africa real estate market situation. There are also studies that concentrated on the rural land markets per se and have not focused attention on the urban land and real estate market (Platteau, 1992).

The existing body of works have produced what may be classified as ideological polarisation. The works can be grouped into works by market advocates (Coldham, 1987; Feder and Feeney, 1991; Migot-Adholla et al., 1991; Sjaastad and Bromley, 1997; Payne, 1989; 1997; Toulmin and Quan, 2000; Quan, 2000; McAuslan, 2000; Okoth-Ogendo, 2000; Antwi, 1995; 1998; 2000; Antwi and Adam, 2003; Brandao and Feder, 1995; Kasanga, 2002) and interventionists (Asiama, 1984; Platteau, 1992; 2000). While market advocates blame government interventions for all the problems of the land and real estate sectors in these countries and have thus called for their outright removal, the interventionists view the customary tenure institutions as problematic, and have called for stringent state regulations and dominance over their operations. Most of these studies are largely qualitative and their findings have tended to be laden with value judgements, ideological orientations and the aspirations of particular researchers involved.

Besides, while many studies have attempted to evaluate the impacts of these policies the results have seldom been expressed quantitatively (Antwi, 2000; Ortiz and Bertaud, 2001, p. 240). Yet as Ortiz and Bertaud (2001, p. 24) observe, 'in the absence of quantification of the problem, measurement of effectiveness of any proposed remedy will be difficult'. This lack of quantitative measurement of the true impacts of these policies is doubtless a testament to the misunderstanding or understatement of the real impacts of these policies on economic lives and development prospects of these nations. The time has come for these policies to be subjected to objective and quantitative assessments devoid of ideological and value judgements. The purpose of this study is thus to attempt to ascertain, in quantitative terms, the true economic impacts of urban real estate policies in sub-Saharan Africa by comparing their social costs and benefits dimensions.

To be sure, both qualitative and scant quantitative studies agree on the fact that sub-Saharan African real estate policies present formidable constraints to the performance of real estate markets and the broad economy. This agreement belies the widespread land policy reform programs under the aegis of the international development community (see Chapter 5) currently being undertaken across sub-Saharan Africa. Yet many of these reforms are proceeding with very little empirical knowledge of the actual impacts of the policies that are being reformed.

The problem of such an approach is, if these ongoing policy reforms tend out to be inapt, as several decades of policy experimentation have been found to be, the affected countries in the end stand to lose the already scarce developmental funds and resources invested in promulgating and enforcing the policies. Beyond that, the generally impoverished taxpayers in these poor countries become obligated to repay these wasted and misdirected resources. In the end not only will the impoverished in these countries be cheated out of developmental benefits, they will be left to repay the resultant resources wasted in the process and bear the full brunt of the constraining effects imposed by inapt policies. This will inescapably aggravate poverty and slow down the development of the region immensely.

1.6 Summary

This chapter has attempted to set the scene for the ensuing discussions. It has provided a broad overview of the nature and scale of poverty in sub-Saharan Africa within a global context. Whether or not land and real estate can offer the requisite assistance towards the alleviation of poverty depends on the extent to which the policies that regulate land ownership, use and transactions make land accessible for the production of consumer goods or other higher order goods. The question is, are extant real estate policies able to play this role effectively? Are they causing damage or generating benefits to the poverty alleviation efforts of the nations of the regions? It is to address these questions that the ensuing discussions would be directed.

2
Primacy of Real Estate

2.1 Introduction

An attempt was made in Chapter 1 to unfold the chief object of this work: to contribute to the alleviation of poverty in sub-Saharan Africa via efficient real estate policies. In order to accomplish this stated objective, it is necessary, as a preliminary step, to take account of the primacy of real estate as a means for the reduction of poverty and for the pursuit of economic development. It is to this end that this chapter is directed.

We shall maintain in this discussion a clear distinction between poverty alleviation and economic development. This distinction is vital for a number of reasons. Firstly, though poverty alleviation and economic development are both concerned with improvements in human well-being, the causes of poverty are not necessarily the same as those of economic development. Secondly, it is now widely accepted by development economists that the attainment of economic development does not automatically imply, or even necessary result in, the attainment of poverty alleviation aspirations; the opposite is also true. No wonder incredible poverty still persists in highly developed and affluent economies such as the US and the UK. Thirdly, different standards and scales are traditionally used to calibrate the economic development and poverty status of a society respectively. Fourthly, poverty is a subsistence level issue whereas economic development is a national level issue. Fifthly, economic development indices, as shall be seen in due course, are merely proxies for gauging the well-being of individuals in a society whereas poverty indices represent the actual state of well-being of individuals as far as can be measured in monetary terms.

Thus there are important differences between poverty alleviation and economic development, making it necessary for any serious analysis to avoid a blurring of their intrinsic uniqueness. More importantly, these differences imply that policy measures required to tackle them may also be different.

Admittedly, because poverty alleviation and economic development are both concerned with the well-being of people, the paths of these concepts necessarily overlap in places. But such patches of overlaps do not, and should not be permitted to erase their distinctions, if suitable solutions are to be found for each.

Consequent upon these differences, the role of real estate in facilitating poverty alleviation may be quite different from its role in inducing economic development. Thus, if we wish to understand the economic significance of real estate, it is necessary to do so in the context of poverty alleviation and in the context of economic development respectively. We turn now to the significance of real estate in the fight against poverty.

2.2 Real estate and poverty alleviation

The scale of poverty in sub-Saharan Africa has already been described in Chapter 1. Our concern here is with the extent to which real estate can contribute uniquely to solving the problem of poverty in sub-Saharan Africa in particular. The law of causality as discussed in Chapter 1 suggests that poverty is an effect stemming from a cause. Solutions to the problem of poverty depend on its causes; after all, solutions are no more than rearrangements of things to eliminate or prevail over causes of a problem. This makes an investigation of the causes of poverty in any given society perhaps the most crucial endeavour in any attempt to solve it decisively. A necessary step in examining the significance of real estate in poverty alleviation is therefore to diagnose, firstly, the causes of poverty. Through adequate knowledge of the causation, we shall be able to determine the role that real estate can effectively play in support of the fight against poverty.

2.2.1 Causes of poverty

To know the causes of poverty we must understand its nature. As explained in Chapter 1, poverty is a complex phenomenon and has been defined differently by different authors and bodies. Poverty may be more formally defined as a *remediable* but *significant* deficit in human well-being caused by the non-satisfaction of economic wants leading to *hardship* and *misery*. We shall shortly strengthen this definition. It is the desire of every person to attain the highest possible level of wellbeing.

People attain their wellbeing when their wants are satisfied. Any shortfall or imperfect satisfaction of wants is thus generally regarded as an unsatisfactory state of affairs that must be improved upon. Importantly, a person is not poor simply because he or she has unsatisfied wants: almost everybody would be classified poor on this criterion. To be so classified by our definition there are two main conditions that must be satisfied.

The first condition relates to the significance of the shortfall. That is, the shortfall must be so acute as to leave no one in doubt of the appalling quality of life in which it inexcusably leaves the affected person. To reach this point, the shortfall must lead inevitably to *hardship* and *misery*. It is universally accepted that any shortfall in well-being that leaves a person surviving on the equivalent of less than $2.00 a day (the secondary poverty line – recall from Chapter 1) is regarded as significant enough to be classified as poverty. Where the shortfall leaves the person surviving on the equivalent of less than $1.00 a day, the poverty is considered as extreme. The second condition concerns the satisfaction, or the lack of it, of economic wants. The shortfall must be caused by the non-satisfaction of economic wants. The point is crucial because, to warrant any analytical consideration at all, the poverty must be solvable or at least reducible, using known methods and principles within the ken of economics. Economic methods and principles are designed to tackle problems associated with the satisfaction of wants of an economic nature. They are incapable of redressing wellbeing shortfalls stemming from unsatisfied exoteric, romantic and emotional wants for instance.

To be more specific, poverty arises from unsatisfied *basic* wants, not just any wants at all. Often, earnings or incomes are relied on as proxies for measuring the poverty levels of people. This is based on the understanding that with income people are able to procure their wants, thus if they have insufficient money to enable them procure all their basic wants then they are poor. Whereas this serves as useful shorthand, it tends to hide the real nature of poverty. It also hides the significance of real estate in redressing the problem. To appreciate the true nature of poverty we must therefore understand what basic wants are. Basic wants comprise those wants that are required for a mere decent standard of living. It follows that an analysis of the significance of real estate in the fight against poverty must focus on how real estate contributes to the satisfaction of basic wants.

While we may split hairs over what basic wants are, very few will disagree with the inclusion of food (including clean water), clothing, shelter, medical care, security and knowledge in such a catalogue. Even if we confine our discussions to these six basic wants, it is clear that poverty is a multidimensional problem. Indeed the term, poverty, can be construed in two main senses – collectively and specifically. In its collective usage, poverty may be used in reference to a shortfall in well-being arising from the non-satisfaction of all basic wants. In its specific usage, poverty may be used to mean non-satisfaction of a particular basic want. In that sense we can refer to shelter poverty, clothing poverty and food poverty. The term is collectively used when the poverty is caused by the combined non-satisfaction of all the dimensions of basic wants. It is specific when the shortfall relates to the non-satisfaction of a specific dimension of human want – say clothing or knowledge.

A person can be shelter poor, or health, clothing, food or knowledge poor. In each of these dimensions, real estate has a role to play. Money may be required to procure all these, but there is no guarantee that a person who has money will still find these to buy automatically. For instance a person who needs shelter may require land on which to erect it. If lands are not for sale in that society, then, though that person may have sufficient income, he or she may still not be able to satisfy his or her basic wants and hence may experience a significant shortfall in well-being. This is one of the reasons why focus must always be placed on unsatisfied wants rather than on incomes.

The crucial question is: how are wants satisfied? The answer to this is also the answer to solving the problem of poverty, for when basic wants are satisfied the problem of poverty is exterminated. With this knowledge we will appreciate the role of real estate in the fight against poverty. The straightforward answer is that people's wants are satisfied when they actually *consume* the specific goods and services upon which the satisfaction of these basic wants depend. A person's want for water is satisfied when he or she drinks water. Likewise, a person's want for shelter is satisfied when he or she is housed.

The term *good* is used in economics to signify any useful material thing. To that extent, real estate is a good. Judging from the way that wants are satisfied, it may be concluded that poverty is basically a *consumption* problem, leading to the further inference that making sure that people actually obtain and consume the goods and services upon which the satisfaction of their basic wants depend should be the preoccupation of all poverty alleviation efforts. But overstressing consumption could present a difficult challenge to finding practical solutions to poverty. If consumption is taken as the ultimate panacea to the problem of poverty, then, we will be forced by this criterion to consider as poor all those in possession of sufficient quantities of basic goods but who have freely chosen not to consume them to satisfy their wants. This would obviously be an odd classification. This, in practice, could create an almost insuperable problem for policymaking and analysis. For, as the old adage goes, 'a horse may be forced to the riverside but cannot be forced to drink from the river'; that is to say, people in possession of requisite goods can hardly be forced through policy means to consume the goods they own to satisfy their own wants. Hence, Carl Menger asserts:

> If a person has command of all the consumption goods necessary to satisfy his [or her] needs, their actual satisfaction depends only on his [or her] will. We may thus consider his objective as having been attained when he is in possession of these goods, since his life and wellbeing are then in his own hands'.

The analytical implication here is that poverty ought to be seen as a *command* rather than a consumption problem. With this point, there is the need to reconsider our earlier definition of poverty. Poverty may now more accurately be defined as a *remediable but significant shortfall in human well-being accompanied by hardships and misery, arising from a lack of, or insufficient command over basic good(s).* Command must be taken to consist of two elements: (1) secured property rights; and (2) the ability to make effective use of them. Property rights confer on a person the unassailable permission to use them productively. A person can however only make productive use of goods over which they have property rights if they are also equipped with what it takes to do so. Thus, conferring property rights over goods on the poor without also equipping them with the ability to make effective use of them to satisfy their wants will do very little to reduce poverty. Since, as shall become apparent in due course, real estate is a good of, arguably unmatched importance to all the dimensions of poverty, it is crucial that all poverty reduction policies involve measures to coffer command over sufficient units of real estate on the poor and this must be supported with the ability to make effective use of the allocated real estate to work their way out of poverty.

Let us now turn to the substantive matter of the significance of real estate. To appreciate the immense importance of real estate in the fight against poverty we must first grasp the *kinds* of goods upon which the satisfaction of basic human wants depend. Goods (useful things), in general, fall into two broad categories: (1) *first order goods* also variously called, final goods, consumers' goods or consumption goods; and (2) *original factors of production.*

Consumers' goods or first order goods are those that are directly consumable to satisfy human wants; they require no further processing, modifications or adjustments. These are the types of goods that the poor must have command over to enable them to work their way out of poverty. Factors of production on the other hand are those goods that must be used to produce consumers' goods; they are thus not directly consumable. Consumers' goods may be further classified into original consumable goods and artificial consumable goods. Original consumable goods are those bestowed on us by providence, needing no further human efforts. Examples include wildly growing fruits, vegetables, game and fish. Artificial consumable goods are those that are artificially produced or manufactured from existing things, mainly, from original factors of production.

To reduce the effort and time taken to produce artificial consumers' goods, certain *intermediary goods* are often required as tools or frameworks through which original factors of production may be transformed into artificial consumer goods. These intermediary goods are more commonly called capital goods or artificial factors of production and include things like equipment, office buildings, factories, warehouses, shops and so on that are not required just for their own sake but purely as a prerequisite to producing and marketing artificial consumers' goods. Capital goods are regarded as the *third* category of goods. Capital goods and original factors of production are together lumped together and called factors of production, producers' goods or production goods.

To sum up, the three main categories of goods needed to fight poverty are original factors of production (OFPs), artificial factors of production (AFPs) (capital goods) and consumers' goods (CGs). The most crucial of these, as far as poverty alleviation is concerned are however the CGs. OFPs and AFPs are imperative only because they are means to producing CGs.

Real estate is a unique good of immense complexity and importance, though often underappreciated even by analysts. It is important because it is as much an OFP, an AFP as it is a CG, cutting across all three categories of goods required to tackle poverty. After a long period of underappreciation researchers, particularly at the World Bank and other international development agencies, are now finding that land/real estate is an inevitable necessity in the fight against poverty.[1, 2]

2.3 Real estate as a factor of production

The importance of real estate in the fight against poverty stems from the fact that it is one of only two original factors of production, the other being labour. Land is real estate in its basic form. It is from these two OFPs that capital goods (the artificial factors of production) as well as artificial consumers' goods are ultimately produced. Without them, no artificial consumers' good or capital good can be produced in the manifold variety that we now have them. In other words, without real estate and labour, no human want can be truly satisfied and life will cease. Even original consumers' goods grow on or in land.

This very fact, by itself, underscores the overwhelming importance of real estate in the fight against poverty. The point of interest however is that, land/real estate by itself (that is, without labour services), is insufficient for the production of consumers' or capital goods. The opposite is true; labour by itself cannot produce anything without land. The two must be used in tandem to foster the alleviation of poverty. Real estate is perhaps the more crucial of the two. For, as Henry George avers:

> [L]and is the habitation of man, the storehouse upon which he must draw for all his needs, the material to which his labor must be applied for the supply of all his desires; for even the products of the sea cannot be taken, the light of the sun enjoyed, or any of the forces of nature utilized, without the use of land or its products. On the land we are born, from it we live, to it we return – children of the soil as truly as is the blade of grass or the flower of the field. Take away from man all that belongs to land, and he is but a disembodied spirit. Material progress cannot rid us of our dependence upon land; it can but add to the power of producing wealth from land.[3]

Whereas the labour needed to combine with available land to produce the consumers' goods upon which the well-being of the poor depend can be imported, land requirements of a nation cannot be imported. Further, a person with adequate command over land may borrow the capital required to pay for the labour services and capital goods required using the very land as collateral for credit if the land is located within a vibrant market.

Africa is the world's second largest continent with a land area of nearly 30 million sq km[4] representing about 20.4 per cent of the world's total land area of 148.94 million sq km.[5] Based on the 2007 sub-Saharan Africa population of 799,975,473,[6] the land per capita of sub-Saharan Africa works out to 0.19 square km. This means that if the land resources of the region were to be shared equally across the population each person would be entitled to 0.19 square km of land to contribute to the production of their basic wants. This idealism can only be achieved in theory. In practice however, land tenure rules, particularly those pertaining to original acquisitions of land have ensured that the total land area of a society is unequally shared across the population at any given time with the effect that some of the population may even be landless. Besides the availability of vast stretches of land in sub-Saharan Africa, the region has a wealth of natural resources, including minerals, forests, wildlife and rich biological diversity.[7]

The availability of land per se within the territories of a nation provides no more than a mere indication of the potential gains that can be made from it towards the alleviation of poverty. Without actualising the potentials from the available land, it will have an inconspicuous impact on the fight against poverty. Not too surprisingly, therefore, in spite of it having the second largest land cover, Africa remains the most ravished by widespread and incredible poverty as exemplified in Chapter 1. Land as we have said is a factor of production. It is a factor of production because it is capable of combining with labour and capital goods to produce consumers' goods. Lands that are unable to so combine with labour and producers' goods would thus not be classed as a factor of production. Only lands that can be classed as factors of production may be regarded as useful to the fight against poverty.

Even so, whether a given land would make meaningful contributions to the fight against poverty or not depends on whether their factors of production capacity can be actualised depends on three factors, namely: (1) what the available land is suitable for; (2) what it is actually used for; and (3) the effectiveness and efficiency with which it is used, if it is put to its most suitable purpose. Vast stretches of lands that are unsuitable for any productive venture are of no use as a factor of production and hence hold little potential to contribute meaningfully to the fight against poverty. Similarly, if suitable lands are left unused they will make no contributions to the poverty alleviation process. Additionally, unless the available lands are used specifically for what they are most suitable for, their full poverty alleviation potentiality cannot be unearthed. Even when the available lands are put to their most suitable uses, they will still not make their fullest contributions unless they are used efficiently and effectively. It follows that to appreciate the contributions of land to the fight against poverty we must appreciate not just the available land sizes, but also their suitability and extent of usage.

Broadly, the uses to which land can be put are typically categorised into rural land uses and urban land uses. Urban land uses comprise residential, commercial and industrial uses. Rural land uses consist largely of agricultural and forest-land uses. Agricultural land uses are perhaps the most critical of rural land uses.

2.4 Land and agricultural production

Food, medical care and clothing are perhaps the most critical of the six basic human wants listed above. Table 2.1 provides indications of the trends in food poverty across the developing world. As the table shows sub-Saharan Africa is the region with the highest level of food poverty (undernourishment). This trend has been projected to persist with the effect that by 2030 as much as 15 per cent of the population of the region numbering 183 million people would be undernourished.

Food is produced, at least initially, through agricultural processes. This makes agriculture a vital sinew in the fight against poverty in sub-Saharan Africa. Yet, while only 7 per cent of the population of developed nations are engaged in agriculture or depend on agriculture for a living, as much 51 per cent of the population of the developing world depend on agriculture for a living.[8] Actually, a whole 60 per cent of the population of sub-Saharan Africa depend on agriculture for a living. This affirms the unmatched importance of agriculture in the fight against poverty across the developing world but in sub-Saharan Africa in particular.

To the extent that land constitutes the most important input in agricultural production, we can further postulate that a nation's poverty alleviation prospect depends on the size and quality of its agricultural land relative to its population. The 2003–4 FAO *State of Food and Agriculture* computes the world's agricultural land area per capita to be

Table 2.1 Incidence of undernourishment, developing countries

	% population				**Million people**			
	1990–2	**1997–9**	**2015**	**2030**	**1990–2**	**1997–9**	**2015**	**2030**
Sub-Saharan Africa	35	34	23	15	168	194	205	183
Near East and North Africa	8	9	7	5	25	32	37	34
Latin America and Caribbean	13	11	6	4	59	54	40	25
South Asia	26	24	12	6	289	303	195	119
East Asia	16	11	6	4	275	193	135	82

Source: *FAO* World Agriculture: Towards 2015/2030.

0.0082 square km.[9] The corresponding figure for the developed world is 0.014 square km and that of the developing world is 0.0067 square km. The break of the agricultural land area per capita for the developing world is reported in Table 2.2.

As the table shows, agricultural land, consisting of arable lands and permanent crop lands represent 41 per cent of the total surface area of land in sub-Saharan Africa.

Since not every single individual in any given society is active in agriculture, a better view can be obtained by computing the land per capita using the economically active population in agriculture. This category of the population constitutes 44 per cent of the world's total population, 7 per cent of the population of the developed world and 54 per cent of that of the developing world. This represents 62 per cent of the population of sub-Saharan Africa. This gives sub-Saharan Africa an average agricultural land area per person of 0.053 square km. This makes sub-Saharan Africa the region with the largest agricultural land area.

It is inferable from this fact that the region has the best prospects of defeating food and agriculture related poverty, particularly when viewed in the context of the region's most conducive agricultural climate. Agricultural land per capita reported in the final column of the table is the average potential land area attributable to each member of the population. Thus, if the agricultural land resources of the respective regions were to be equally allocated across the population, each person's entitlement in square km is the region's agricultural land per capita as reported. Sub-Saharan Africa's agricultural land per capita is also the second highest after Europe and Central Asia. Thus, in an ideal world, it could be argued that, for a start, each member of the sub-Saharan African population ought to be allocated commands over 0.0123 square km to produce their agriculture based wants.

In reality, the size of available agricultural lands varies from country to country as shown in Figure 2.1. The first observation is that there is no sub-Saharan Africa country without agricultural lands. The figure also shows the variations in the sizes of agricultural lands across the nations of the region. As the table indicates, Sudan has the largest agricultural land area in sub-Saharan Africa, followed by South Africa and then Nigeria. Countries such as the Seychelles, Gambia, Comoros, Cape Verde, Mayotte, Mauritius, Sao Tome and Principe and Equatorial Guinea barely have agricultural land, though what they have may be significant relative to their respective surface area.

Having looked at the place of land in meeting the food and agriculture related wants of sub-Saharan Africa in relation to those of other

Table 2.2 Agricultural land per capita

	Surface area (sq. km)	**Percentage agricultural**	**Agricultural Land surface area**	**Population (2007)**	**Agricultural land per capita**
East Asia and Pacific	15,961,361.50	43.64	6,965,214.84	1,912,422,228.16	0.0036
Europe and Central Asia	23,939,400.81	27.70	6,630,825.74	445,641,258.71	0.0149
Latin America and Caribbean	20,420,996.38	32.70	6,678,630.52	560,647,820.16	0.0119
Middle East and North Africa	8,777,910.00	23.28	2,043,481.66	313,249,332.98	0.0065
South Asia	5,139,540.00	54.29	2,790,111.03	1,522,047,731.89	0.0018
Sub-Saharan Africa	23,739,325.10	41.34	9,814,183.14	799,975,472.88	0.0123

Source: Surface area, percentage agricultural land and population were extracted from World Bank Group's World Development Indicators Database, 2009. The remaining columns were calculated from these extracts.

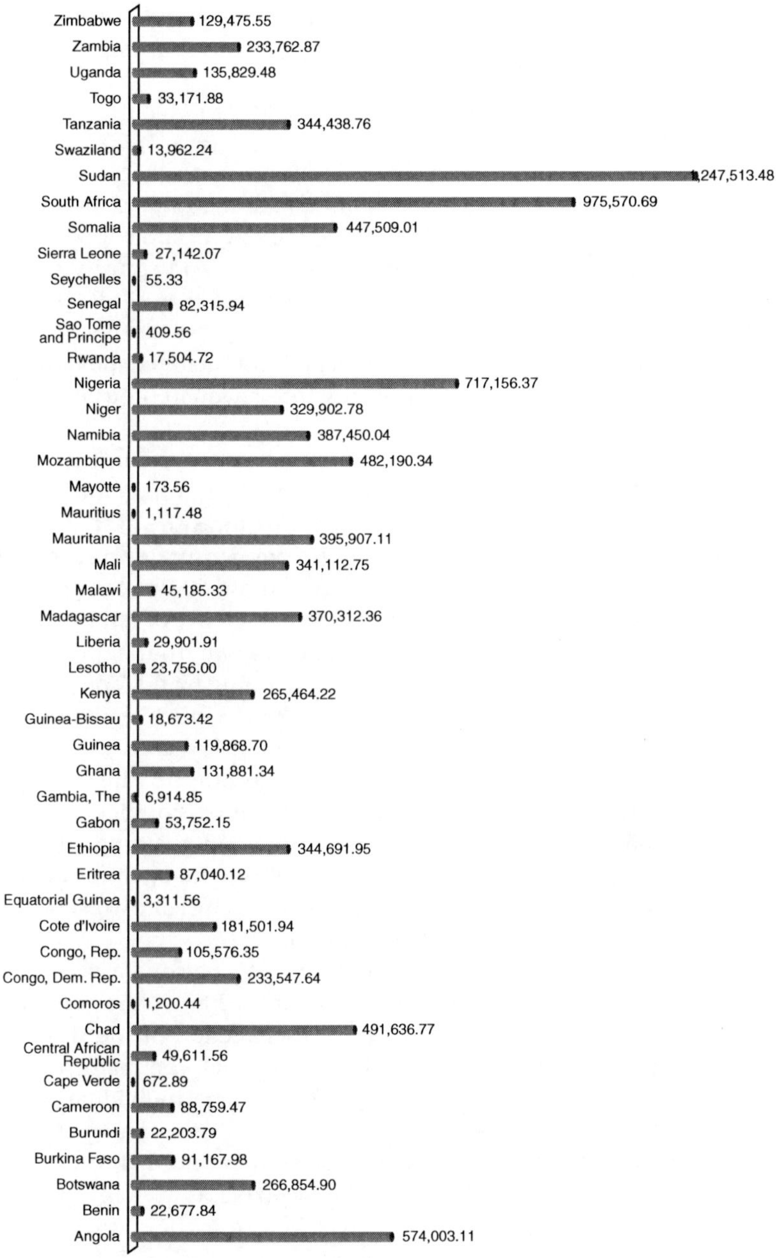

Figure 2.1 Agricultural land area in sq. km.
Source: World Development Indicators, 2007

regions, we shall now turn our attention to the role of real estate in satisfying other non agriculture based basic wants, notably shelter, at the subsistence level.

2.5 Real estate and shelter poverty

Shelter is one of the six key elements of basic human wants mentioned above. It is arguably the next most important want after food, medical care and clothing. Shelter provides protection and security against the vagaries of the weather, crimes and unwanted intrusions. It offers a stable locus for the family unit, a place to live, rest, sleep and enjoy family life, privacy, storage and protection for material possessions. Sadly, despite its necessity, the reality is that adequate housing is not guaranteed to everyone.

Shelter is largely a product of land. It is erected on land using mainly resources extracted from land – bricks, cements wood and so on. Meeting the shelter wants of the poor thus requires the availability of suitable, preferably non-agricultural lands commensurate with the size of the shelter wants in that society. With almost 60 per cent of non-agricultural land, sub-Saharan Africa has vast stretches of land available to meet the shelter wants of its citizens. This is a pattern that pertains in most countries, particularly those of the developing world. The problem is, according to the United Nations,[10] as at 2005, as much as 100 million people worldwide are without a place to live (homeless) and over 1 billion people are inadequately housed. This again buttresses the fact that, though land is the most important factor in the provision of shelter, the mere availability of even suitable land per se is no guarantee that the shelter needs of the poor will be met. Two options are open to the poor for the satisfaction of their wants. They could erect their own shelter or purchase or rent one from another landlord.

Where the individual wishes to erect the shelter personally, as is often the case in developing countries, he or she must first secure command over an adequate size of land needed for the erection of the shelter. If this is not possible, then the individual would lack the main resource requisite for the satisfaction of shelter. Even if the individual is adequately clothed with the requisite command, he or she must possess or be able to afford the labour and material resources needed to erect the shelter. Otherwise, though land may be available as a vital input, the end product can still not be produced. Likewise if the individual can afford the labour and materials required but not the land, the shelter want would still remain unmet. Perhaps the more interesting fact that often eludes analysts who are not very familiar with the social arrangements that regulate land transactions in sub-Saharan Africa is that merely because one can afford to pay the market value of a given parcel of land does not imply that one will be able to gain command over it. If that were the case, the solution to the shelter problem would perhaps be much easier to solve than it is presently. It depends most heavily on the prevailing land tenure rules. The tenure rules could forbid the transaction, which means that even where the parties are willing to trade in the land, the transaction cannot take place, and hence the party who is shelter poor would not be able to obtain the requisite land to satisfy the want.

Where the individual intends to buy or rent instead of erecting the shelter directly, the scenario is somewhat different. In that case, it will be the landlord from whom the individual intends to buy or rent the shelter who will be concerned with the issues mentioned above. For the individual seeking the satisfaction of his or her shelter wants, the most important factor is affordability – that is, the person's income relative to the market price or rent of the shelter. A person's shelter needs can only be met through purchase or rental if there are on the market suitable houses whose prices fall within their affordability limits. This depends most crucially on the income levels of the individual in question.

It is sometimes uneconomical for individuals to produce all the goods upon which the satisfaction of their wants depends. Besides, not all individuals in a society will have the resources and know-how to produce all of the goods upon which the satisfaction of their wants depends, such as medical care and education. This necessitates the production of certain goods on a larger scale for sale to those who are unable to produce for themselves. This takes us to the importance of real estate in economic development.

2.6 Real estate and economic development

Having examined, in broad terms, the significance of real estate in the fight against poverty, it is now time to examine its role in economic development. We define economic development or economic growth as sustained rise in the real income per person (per capita income)[11] in a given society.[12]

2.6.1 Measuring economic development

The per capita income, the universally accepted yardstick for measuring economic development, is simply a presumed real income per person in a given society. It is the income that each individual in the society would have earned were the total income earned within the nation or by its nationals to be shared equally across the population of the nation. Incomes are hardly shared equally across the population. This makes the per capita income measure of development more of a theoretical calibration of economic development. The per capita income of a society is measured by dividing the *national income* (i.e. the total income earned in or by the citizens of a society) in a given year by the size of the total population of that society for that year. National income is an economic index that indicates the performance of the economy as whole relative to the performance of other societies.

The real income per person is measured in two main ways. It may be measured using (1) the Gross Domestic Product (GDP) of that society or (2) its Gross National Income (GNI). GDP is the value of all the outputs produced within the geographical boundaries of the society in question. GNI on the other hand is the total value of all incomes earned by the nationals of that society in a given year, whether or not the incomes were earned within the geographical boundaries of the society.

Figure 2.2 shows the average Gross National Income (GNI) per capita (or per capita income) for the period 1991 to 2007.

As can be observed from the graph below, sub-Saharan Africa and South Asia are the least economically developed regions of the world,

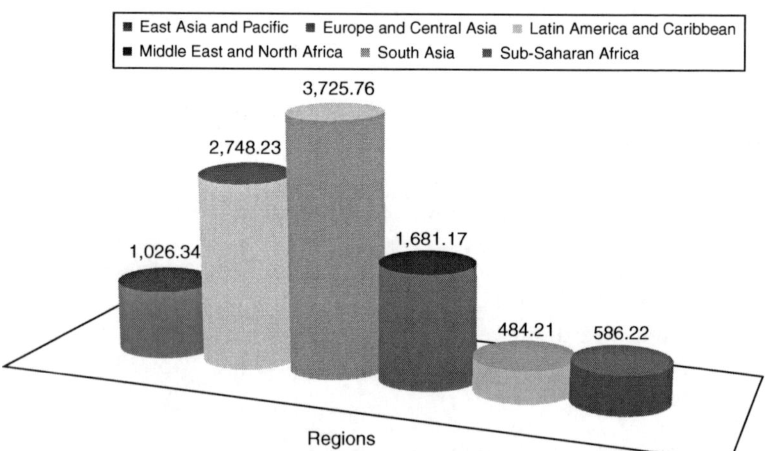

Figure 2.2 Average gross national income per capita (from 1991 to 2007)
Source: World Development Indicators, 2007

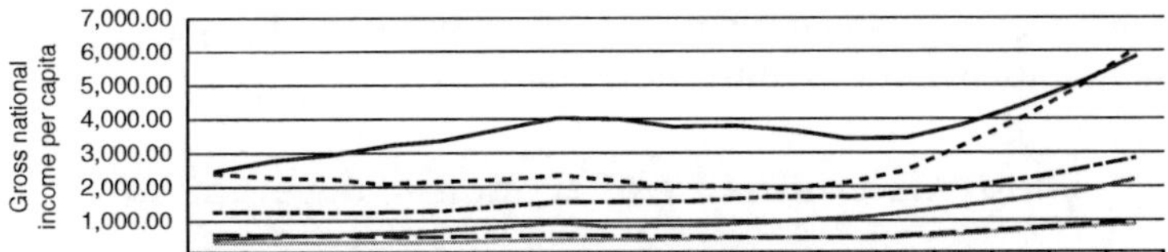

	1991	1992	1993	1994	1995	1996	1997	1998	1999	2000	2001	2002	2003	2004	2005	2006	2007
East Asia and Pacific	451.9	502.5	550.5	614.7	703.6	819.3	888.6	826.0	848.2	907.6	977.7	1,058	1,204	1,415	1,630	1,864	2,181
Europe and Central Asia	2,376	2,278	2,247	2,054	2,149	2,222	2,356	2,173	2,007	2,037	1,975	2,134	2,495	3,197	4,039	4,921	6,052
Latin America and Caribbean	2,455	2,761	2,925	3,197	3,365	3,694	4,000	3,978	3,740	3,788	3,648	3,387	3,431	3,815	4,352	4,994	5,800
Middle East and North Africa	1,244	1,263	1,223	1,250	1,290	1,441	1,537	1,573	1,588	1,640	1,675	1,663	1,772	1,951	2,192	2,452	2,820
South Africa	350.1	337.5	326.3	340.1	379.2	410.0	417.3	417.2	434.2	443.5	452.9	459.2	515.0	601.4	695.5	772.1	879.5
Sub-Saharan Africa	572.3	557.9	540.2	517.0	528.4	544.5	553.5	517.7	500.5	484.8	475.1	469.1	515.9	621.3	753.5	862.2	951.2

Figure 2.3 Gross national income per capita

with average per capita incomes of US$ 582.22 and US$ 484.21 respectively. Figure 2.3 shows the trends in economic growth in the respective regions from 1991 to 2007. It shows that while all other regions are making impressive headway in their economic development, economic development in sub-Saharan Africa has been sluggish and quite unimpressive.

The per capita income is a deficient measure of the state of well-being of individuals of a nation. Firstly, several assumptions are built into the computation of the per capita income of a country. This makes the measure quite subjective. It could therefore be a poor reflection of the true average income of individuals in particular societies, particularly with societies with very poor statistics. That notwithstanding, the average income of the vast majority of individuals in a country may bear very little correlation with the per capita income of that country. Indeed, a per capita income for a society would only be equal to the actual earnings per person in that society if incomes in that society were evenly distributed across the population. Equal distribution of incomes is something that is more likely to be encountered in books and theoretical discussions than in reality.

There is no society in which income is equally distributed; income inequality is a constant feature of every society. Thus, in some societies income could be so unequally distributed to the effect that only a few may be earning a larger chunk of the total income generated, leaving the vast majority impoverished. Thus, a nation could be doing well in terms of its economic development and still be overwhelmed with incredible poverty. This is yet another factor that distinguishes poverty from economic development. In order to show that real estate is significant to economic development we must first establish a causal relationship between the two. To do so we need to understand the basic determinants of economic development.

2.7 Basic determinants of economic development

To be significant, real estate must have adequate causal correlation with economic development. Thus to show that real estate is relevant we must show that it is not a trivial component of the determinants of per capita income. Income results from productive activities, that is, the use of productive resources to produce a valuable output. The magnitude of the income earned from a resource is dependent on the value of each output with the resource multiplied by the volume or quantities produced. From this we can infer that the main determinant of incomes and hence economic development is the use of scarce resources. Thus any factor that affects the use of scarce resources in any given society constitutes a determinant of economic development. The use of scarce resources is basically influenced by three main factors that we shall refer to, accordingly as the basic determinants of economic development. These are: (1) the type of available productive resources; (2) how effectively they are used; and (3) institutional rules and arrangements that constrain their productive usage.

We use the term productive resources here in reference to both original and artificial factors of production as described above. To enable a proper appreciation of the place of real estate in economic development it is necessary to reclassify these resources into five main categories. That is: (1) real estate; (2) labour services; (3) entrepreneurial skills; (4) money (capital); and (5) capital goods. Each of these generates its own unique income. For instance, land generates income in the form of rent. Labour services generate income in the form of wages. Money capital and capital goods produce income in the form of interest. Finally, entrepreneurial skills generate income in the form of profits.

It is the sum total of all these categories of incomes earned in a given nation or by the nationals of a given country in a particular year that constitute the GDP or GNI of the nation. In principle, it is this figure that is divided by the population size to estimate the per capita income of nations. To generate this income, the respective resources have to be put into productive usage. The magnitude of the income that each resource generates depends on a wide range of factors including the efficiency of the (labour, real estate and capital) markets in which they are traded as well as the price that people are willing and able to pay for what the resources are used to produce.

2.7.1 The availability of real estate

Thus for a nation to develop at all it must be in possession of all five resources in the right proportions. Acute shortage of a particular resource, say real estate or entrepreneurial skill, could adversely affect the economic development prospects of a nation. We have observed earlier that no sub-Saharan African country is without real estate or land space. That said, the availability of a resource by itself is of little help unless it is also of the *quality* required to produce the outputs needed to satisfy wants. For example, it is not so much the pool of labour that a country has that matters as its quality. A large pool of labour is of no use to the economic development process if they are all illiterates and diseased. Likewise, a vast real estate resource would be of no use to agriculture development if it is infertile and riddled with erosion. Thus, the real income per person may be low not because the resources are non-existent, but because they are of a less than adequate quality.

2.7.2 Utilisation of real estate resources

Apart from the availability of a resource such as real estate, the next factor that determines the real income per person in an economy is its effective utilisation with regard to its qualities. Again, a nation's per capita income could be low, not because of a non-existence of the requisite resources, but rather because of their under utilisation. Making effective use of land simply means putting the land to its highest and best uses. The highest and best use for a given unit of real estate is the use upon which the most *urgent* wants of people in the society depends. This use is also the use that is associated with the highest return. Where a real estate unit is not put to its highest and best uses society gets less than what it could get from it. The need to put land to its highest and best uses actually presents two crucial challenges to policymaking.

First is the proper identification of the highest and best uses of any given unit of real estate at any given time, without which society may be unable to gain as much as it could from its real estate resources. The second challenge pertains to the fact that the highest and best uses of land do not stay unchanged. Uses of real estate are in some ever-changing hierarchy or scale of significance with the effect that over time some are upgraded while others are downgraded. New uses also, occasionally, enter into the hierarchy at different levels, thereby displacing other existing uses. Thus the highest and best use of a given unit of real estate today may not remain so in a couple of years. The overarching task of policy is thus to push real estate resources persistently from one use to a better use until the highest and best use is reached. We shall return to this point in the next chapter. The very low contributions that agricultural real estate for instance makes to the average GDP of sub-Saharan Africa may thus be attributable, in part, to the use of the lands in less than their highest and best uses.

When resources are under utilised they yield less than their optimal income, which ultimately affects the per capita income of the society. Statistics on the extent of urban land utilisation in sub-Saharan Africa are scarce. Given that as much as 62 per cent of the labour force of sub-Saharan Africa is engaged in agriculture, perhaps agriculture land under utilisation constitutes a critical reducing agent on the real income per person in the region.

Let us take, as an example, arable lands. Table 2.3 shows that no region has so far managed to bring all of its arable lands into productive usage.

The data shows that the average arable land utilisation per region of the developing world as at 1999 is 56 per cent (calculated from the reported percentage figures per region). This is set to increase marginally by 2030 to 61 per cent, with Latin America and the Caribbean, and sub-Saharan Africa making the least uses as well as the most sluggish progress towards full utilisation of their arable land resources. Meanwhile, the extensive utilisation of arable lands in South Asia and Near East/North Africa is an indication that 100 per cent utilisation agricultural lands are possible. It also suggests the existence of impediments towards the effective utilisation of arable lands in sub-Saharan Africa, which may be absent in, or have been prevailed over in South Asia and Near East/North Africa.

Figure 2.4 shows the actual impacts of the above reported levels of usage of agricultural lands in the developing world. The graph places the average gross domestic value achieved by each of the comparable regions alongside the value contributed to it from agricultural activities. As the graph shows, sub-Saharan Africa represents the region with the least GDP. It is also the region in which agriculture makes the least contribution to its GDP. This is not surprising, considering that sub-Saharan Africa is the region that has made, and is predicted to

Table 2.3 Arable land in use as % of potentially arable land

Region	1997/99	2030
Sub-Saharan Africa	22	28
Near East/North Africa	87	94
Latin America and Caribbean	19	23
South Asia	94	98
East Asia	63	65
East Asia (Excluding China)	52	60

Source: *FAO* World Agriculture: Towards 2015/2030.

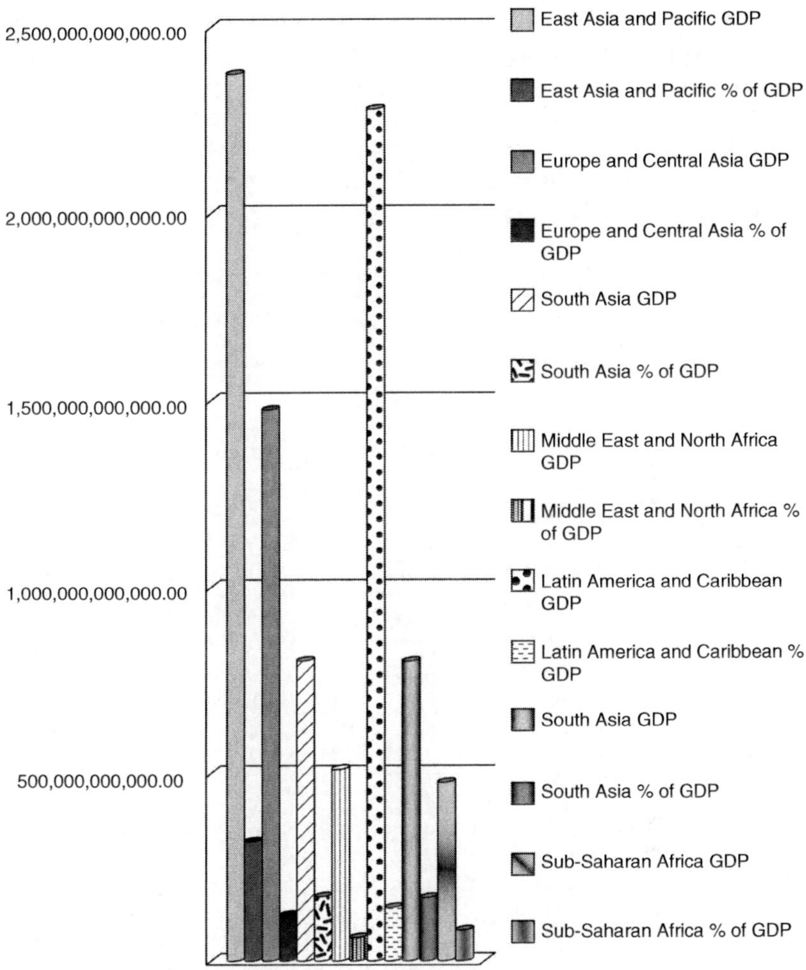

Figure 2.4 Agricultural value added as % of GDP (ten year average – 1997–2007)

make the least utilisation of its arable land capacity. These statistics buttress the point that agricultural real estate in sub-Saharan which is the source of income for the vast majority of the population have very little impacts on the economic performance of the region. Several factors could account for this underperformance.

To generate optimal results, the society must have in sufficient numbers the complementary resources needed to make effective use of the available real estate resources, namely capital goods, money, labour and entrepreneurs. Where those resources are non-existent real estate by itself is thus bound to make less than optimal contributions to per capita income. Labour is often in abundance across the developing world, judging from the vast amount of unemployed labour in these countries. Table 2.4 reports data on the labour force of African nations. As the table shows Africa is not at all in short supply of labour. The table shows that 40 per cent (388,532,305) of the total population represents

Table 2.4 Africa: GDP, Population and Unemployment – 2008

Nation	GDP per capita	Population	Labor force	unemployed	% unemployed
Equatorial Guinea	$16,507	616,459	246,584	69,469	28
Mauritius	$13,029	1,274,189	509,676	114,677	22
Seychelles	$12,135	82,247	32,899	1,645	5
South Africa	$11,035	43,786,115	17,514,446	8,070,806	45
Libya	$11,354	6,173,579	2,469,432	679,094	28
Botswana	$10,866	1,842,323	736,929	300,041	39
Tunisia	$8,223	10,383,577	4,153,431	1,453,701	35
Algeria	$7,095	33,769,669	13,507,868	4,727,754	35
Gabon	$6,977	1,485,832	594,333	212,025	36
Namibia	$6,658	2,088,669	853,468	187,980	22
Cape Verde	$6,287	426,998	170,799	69,670	40
Morocco	$5,765	34,343,219	13,737,288	3,434,322	25
Swaziland	$5,181	1,128,814	451,526	182,204	40
Egypt	$4,282	81,713,517	32,685,407	8,988,487	28
Angola	$2,829	12,531,357	5,012,543	1,503,763	30
Ghana	$2,601	23,382,848	9,353,139	3,107,427	33
Sudan	$2,417	40,218,455	16,087,382	7,641,506	47
Zimbabwe	$2,413	12,382,920	4,953,168	3,948,898	80
Mauritania	$2,307	3,364,940	1,345,976	672,988	50
Cameroon	$2,284	18,467,692	7,387,077	4,540,308	61
Lesotho	$2,163	2,128,180	851,272	544,863	63
The Gambia	$1,999	1,735,464	694,186	286,773	41
Guinea	$1,986	10,211,437	4,084,575	1,531,716	38
Djibouti	$1,957	506,221	202,488	55,187	27
Senegal	$1,914	12,853,259	5,141,304	4,055,434	79
Uganda	$1,817	31,367,972	12,547,189	8,783,032	70
Chad	$1,744	10,111,337	4,044,535	2,527,834	62
Comoros	$1,717	731,775	292,710	89,271	30
São Tomé	$1,638	206,178	82,471	11,247	14
Togo	$1,600	5,858,673	2,343,469	903,041	38
Côte d'Ivoire	$1,475	18,373,060	7,349,224	3,674,612	50
Rwanda	$1,431	10,186,063	4,074,425	2,546,516	63
Congo	$1,379	3,903,318	1,561,327	702,597	45

(*continued*)

Table 2.4 Continued

Nation	GDP per capita	Population	Labor force	unemployed	% unemployed
Mozambique	$1,335	21,284,701	8,513,880	4,044,093	47
Burkina Faso	$1,326	15,264,735	6,105,894	2,747,652	45
Nigeria	$1,188	138,283,240	59,313,296	38,719,307	64
C African Rep	$1,163	4,434,873	1,773,949	1,086,975	59
Benin	$1,147	8,294,941	3,317,976	1,244,241	37
Kenya	$1,125	37,953,838	18,181,535	9,347,536	51
Mali	$1,084	12,324,029	4,929,612	1,998,604	41
Eritrea	$917	5,028,475	2,011,390	1,511,390	75
Zambia	$911	11,669,534	4,667,814	3,251,290	70
Madagascar	$911	20,042,551	8,017,020	1,202,553	15
Sierra Leone	$901	6,294,774	2,517,910	2,069,701	82
Liberia	$900	3,334,587	1,333,835	1,000,752	75
Niger	$896	13,272,679	5,309,072	3,318,170	63
Ethiopia	$859	78,254,090	31,301,636	23,388,932	75
Guinea-B	$856	1,503,182	601,273	195,414	33
Burundi	$753	8,691,005	3,476,402	1,912,021	55
Tanzania	$720	40,213,162	16,085,265	11,661,817	73
D R Congo	$675	66,514,506	26,605,802	18,972,611	71
Somalia	$600	9,558,666	3,823,466	2,389,667	63
Malawi	$596	13,931,831	5,572,732	2,925,685	53
Average		17,995,958	7,330,798	3,935,987	47
Total		953,785,755	388,532,305	208,607,299	

Source: ICAfrica – International Charity for Africa.

the region's labour force. Of this number however about 54 per cent (208,607,299) are unemployed. With such a large unemployment rate, African can hardly be said to be in short supply of labour.

Now, what about entrepreneurship skills? Entrepreneurship skills are required to provide the leadership needed to make effective use of the land resources of respective nations. Where adequate entrepreneurship skills are available more profitable uses of real estate would be found and pursued leading to effective and extensive utilisation of the real estate resources available. The argument has, in the past, been that indigenous African entrepreneurship is less well suited for the entrepreneurial activities required for the advancement that African nations need. But doubt has been thrown over this assertion. Rather 'the evidence shows no dearth of ability among Africans to identify business opportunities and to act upon them – the two quintessential characteristics of entrepreneurship'.[13] There may of course be areas where specialist expertise may be needed that are non-existent internally. But if the conditions are right and affordable, expatriates could be brought in to provide the expertise required.

The next resource that is needed to ensure the effective use of real estate resources is capital. With adequate capital, the labour, capital goods and expatriate skills needed could be acquired to promote a more effective use of real estate. Table 2.5 reports statistics on the gross capital formation per region between 1991 and 2007.

The table shows again that sub-Saharan Africa has the lowest capital formation rate in the world, with an average capital formation rate of about 18 per cent per year. There is usually a trade off between the use of labour and the use of capital goods; capital goods and labour are used as substitute resources as much as possible such that where labour is in abundance and cheap, more labour and less capital are used. The opposite is also true. Sub-Saharan Africa is the region with the least gross capital formation and yet the region with the highest population growth rate. Capital is thus in shortage while labour is in abundance. This creates a conundrum in the sense that since the productivity of labour in agriculture for instance is widely acknowledged to be low

Table 2.5 Gross capital formation (% of GDP)

Country Name	East Asia and Pacific	Europe and Central Asia	Latin America and Caribbean	Middle East and North Africa	South Asia	Sub-Saharan Africa
1991	34.91	24.98	19.66	28.78	21.25	17.31
1992	35.49	24	20.18	29.29	22.85	15.78
1993	40.73	21.95	20.72	26.17	21.05	16
1994	39.41	20.89	21.3	23.87	22.77	18.06
1995	39.53	21.42	19.51	25.11	25.08	18.35
1996	38.36	21.46	19.7	25.73	21.73	17.84
1997	36.14	21.21	21.43	24.65	23.03	17.52
1998	32.25	20.36	21.16	25.95	22.13	18.34
1999	31.26	19.19	19.47	24.65	24.64	17.46
2000	31.55	20.77	20.01	24.45	23.45	17.27
2001	32.29	20.19	19.05	24.53	23.27	17.36
2002	33.46	19.87	17.72	25.51	24.05	17.52
2003	36.15	20.46	18.34	26.66	25.3	18.25
2004	37.64	21.42	20.28	27.16	29.15	18.91
2005	38.36	21.41	20.27	25.98	31.93	19.25
2006	38.6	22.85	21.6	25.72	33.54	20.51
2007	37.75	24.95	22.41	27.74	35.42	21.91
Average	36.11	21.61	20.17	26	25.33	18.1

Source: World development indicators, 2007.

relative to the productivity of capital goods such as large scale machinery, fertilisers etc., over-reliance on labour at the expense of capital goods is bound to lower productivity, and hence the contributions that real estate makes to the development process. At the same time, over-reliance on capital goods at the expense of the teeming labour would also lead to unemployment of labour and its poverty consequences – something that all underdeveloped countries are keen to avoid for pragmatic reasons. This could also exacerbate the acute income inequalities that are commonplace in underdeveloped societies.

2.7.3 Institutional rules and arrangements: Land tenure

While much has been written on economic development, it is only in comparatively recent times that this link between land tenure, urbanisation and development has been appreciated. In point of fact, the primary disposing function of urban land – a basis for shelter, workplace and space, factors of production and sustenance of economic life – is well known. Yet this recognition has all along been bolted on the presumption of abundant (Eicher and Baker, 1982) and problem-free (Falloux, 1987) land endowment across sub-Saharan Africa. Earlier neoclassical economic theory essentially perceived land tenure, the conditions under which land is held (Meek, 1949; Reyna, 1987), like all other social institutional forms (Bardhan, 1989) as a subject matter that falls beyond the ken of economic analysis (North, 1990). This derives from the fact that in earlier neoclassical economic theory 'there are no organisations or institutions except for markets that form the theoretical core of neoclassical paradigm' (North, 1981). To the earlier economists the land tenure subject was thus better taken as given (Warriner, 1964) as 'they can be ignored in economic analysis because they play no independent role in economic performance' (North, 1990).

With the economic imperative of land tenure so underappreciated, even lead International Development agencies as the World Bank and its compatriots avoided the land question in their development support programmes considering it to be 'too political' (Falloux, 1987). As a result, land tenure issues were often not mentioned at all or were given only cursory attention in economic development discourses (Platteau, 1992, p. 22). The fundamental outcome from this is the long dearth of an adequate economic analytical framework to tackle land tenure issues (Platteau, 1992). But all this was to change with the development of New Institutional Economics (NIE) as an institution-conscious economic theory in the 1970s.

This new economic dimension develops from the works of Coase (1937; 1960), Hayek (1945), Arrow (1963), Demsetz (1967), Davis and North (1971), Williamson (1971) and North (1990) among others. With these works, the prime importance of urban land tenure and institutions in general for economic development has now taken the lead in economic development issues (World Bank, 1975). The economic imperative of land tenure institutions derives from the fact that they define and limit the set of choices of individuals by constraining what individuals are permitted to undertake (North, 1990, pp. 3–4). They are thus in essence the 'nuts and bolts' that organise, guide, facilitate and strengthen the complex behaviours of actors to efficiently allocate land related resources, and to make legitimate choices about the ownership and use of land (see further Wunsch and Olowu, 1990). Accordingly, whether or not a country's land resources would be available or can be deployed productively to foster progress hinges directly on the compatibility of the applicable tenure system with economic development and poverty reduction.

The question, then, is should the land tenure vest rights in land exclusively to individuals as private people or should society as the embodiment of the nation or community be vested with these rights. Economic theory has long established that when the tenure system vests these rights in the nation or community represented by the sovereign, the maximisation of welfare quotients is removed from the arena of individual liberty and responsibility (Bastiat, 1850):

> The individual ... ceases to exercise free control over the satisfaction of his own wants, and, no longer having any responsibility for satisfying them, he naturally ceases to concern himself with doing so. Foresight becomes as useless to him as experience. He becomes less his own master; he has lost, to some extent, his free will; he has less initiative for self-improvement; he is less of a man. Not only does he no longer judge for himself in a given case, but he loses the habit of judging for himself. This moral torpor, which takes possession of him, likewise takes possession of his fellow citizens, and we have seen entire nations fall in this way into disastrous inertia.

To avoid this pattern, economists now widely concede that since only individuals, of all known agents, have the precise knowledge of their personal circumstances it is they alone who can tell what would best improve their welfare quotient. It is thus rational for these incentives and liberties to be entrusted to individuals so that they may be tasked to propel the deployment of their foresight, industry and experience and to channel their economic efforts into activities that would successfully maximise their own welfare quotients. This arrangement will provide the best grounds for economic growth. That said, when these liberties and responsibilities are vested in individuals without rules of coordination, cooperation and interdependency the desire to maximise surplus welfare quotients would invariably and rationally result in anarchy in its many dimensions of gross violation, externalities, overexploitation, waste and rent dissipation (Fisher, 1930; Gordon, 1954; Scott, 1955; Hardin, 1968; Demsetz, 1967; North and Thomas, 1973). To overcome this the tenure system must ensure that individuals are not simply vested with incentives and liberties but also exclusive rights to use their land (also their labour, capital and other resources) as they deem proper and they alone should possess the right to transfer their resources to other actors of their choosing on agreed terms (Coase, 1960; Demsetz, 1967; North and Thomas, 1973; Posner, 1977; Pejovich, 1997). To provide the right incentive to channel these liberties into productive activities, the tenure system must also facilitate cooperation, reward industry, creativity, productivity and success while penalising torpor through social and commercial relationships (North and Thomas, 1973; North, 1990; Drobak and Nye, 1997; Klein, 1999; De Soto, 2000).

For economic efficiency, the tenure system must additionally ensure the provision of a level playing field including fair and general rules for social and commercial relations. It must also lower the impediments to the full and productive deployment of these liberties by providing vital infrastructure and such services as roads, highways, water, telecommunications, police service, dispute resolution mechanisms, mechanisms for internalising externalities (Pigou, 1920), information supply systems (Simon, 1957) and others. These are so vital that, where the tenure system on its own is unable to provide comparatively cheaply, fairly and adequately, which is often the case, it will be the legitimate duty of government to step in with these provisions either exclusively or in partnership with the tenure system. When all these are in place, as Posner (1977, p. 10) explains, 'individuals will endeavour by cultivation or other improvement to maximise the value of land' (see also Alchian, 1965; Demsetz, 1967; Hardin, 1968; Becker, 1977; Ault and Ruthman, 1979; Feder and Feeney, 1991; Besley, 1995; Bromley, 1997; Payne, 1997; Cousins, 2000).

In sub-Saharan Africa, however, the conventional view is that the region's land tenure system promotes incentives for rent dissipation, externalities and gross violation, thereby constituting an imminent threat and constraint on productivity and growth. This review argues on the contrary that it is rather the land reform policies that were premised on this conventional view over time that are incentivising and rerouting the economic efforts of actors into activities that constitutes a threat to and constraint on growth and development. To establish this argument it is worthwhile to draw on historical policy events to establish the contributions they continue to make to the many policy issues that present themselves today. But first, a clearer view of the nature of the indigenous land tenure regime of sub-Saharan Africa will provide a solid basis for appreciating the consequences of these policy events.

2.7.3.1 The major land tenure theoretical positions

Many studies have enriched our understanding of the disposition of the land tenure system of sub-Saharan Africa. These studies have, however, progressed along divergent paths producing in the process an uneasy mix of consensus, contradictions and controversies (van den Brink, 2003). The two main positions in this dialogue are termed in this chapter the 'structural' and 'evolutionary' theoretical positions. Though these positions have so far been treated in the literature as contending theories, a critical look shows that they are indeed the two ends of a single continuum of land tenure evolutionary processes. The scenario that gives legitimacy to these theoretical positions and their policy consequences is briefly looked at in the light of the above discussions.

2.7.3.1.1 Structural theory of land tenure There is now a shared set of conceptions or doctrines that can be referred to as the structural theory of land tenure. This theory explains the land tenure system of sub-Saharan Africa in its basic terms and takes as its expository point, the model or structure of the pre-capitalist African tenure system as given. It takes the customary rules that govern the tenure system also as codified and immutable. Accordingly, the structural theory builds together, from this expository point, the intricacies between the spiritual and normative codes, behavioural and cultural beliefs, and organic structures of the pre-capitalist indigenous African era, to develop understanding and meaning of the region's land tenure system. It reaches this position by placing considerable weight on the kingship and lineage of communal structures and land relations of African societies (Bruce, 1986; Gyekye, 1998; Woodman, 1998).

A pivotal thesis of this theoretical position is that land in Africa is a sacred resource. It is regarded as 'a preserve of major deities, the sacred soil of the ancestors, an object of the most important rituals, the origin of royal power, the basis for health and prosperity; indeed, it was widely looked upon as the source of life itself' (July, 1975). Polanyi (1944, p. 178) for instance perceives land as an element of nature inextricably interwoven with man's institutions. Le Roy, É., Karsenty A. and Bertrand, A. (1995, p. 52, cited in Lund, 2001) argue further in reference to Francophone Africa that land 'is not only riches but also at times "a person" (in the traditional sense) which can be made to talk (like the dead). It was also (at least sometimes) a deity holding vital powers which should be dealt with with caution'. While it is very difficult to establish the origins of these sentiments, they invariably resonate with the view that land is more than a factor of production, basis for shelter or an economic good. Actually they reinforce the view that land is a priceless possession that no one individual could own as in the western sense (see further July, 1975). It is to be owned corporately by a group, clan, family or lineage including the dead, the living and unborn (see Nana Sir Ofori Atta, cited in Ollenu, 1962, p. 4; see also Meek, 1949). The dead or ancestors are part of this rather vertical corporate community as, it is argued, 'land [is] the sanctuary for the souls of the departed ancestors (Asante, 1975, p. 3) and hence 'belongs to the ancestors' (Busia, 1951, p. 44). The unborn generation are also incorporated into this community because, it is argued, to carry on life without land is much the same as being born without hands and feet since land is tied up with the organisation of kinship, neighbourhood, craft and creed – with tribe and temple, village, guild and church (Polanyi, 1944, p. 178).

The implication is that the living actors of society are essentially caretakers with beneficiary interest, not really exclusive owners. To make this position clearer, advocates of this position describe the land rights of the living actors as usufructuary rights (Ollenu, 1962), a term derived from Roman law, meaning 'the right to use a thing belonging to someone else or rent it to others but not to sell it or change its quality' (Pejovich, 1990, p. 28). Accordingly, rights in land in Africa are spoken of as co-owned (Doner, 1972; World Bank, 1975; Harrison, 1987) essentially by the vertical community or even 'as a regime not of tenure at all, and worse, one with no socio-spatial boundaries – that is, a regime of open, or public, not private access' (Alden Wily, 2000) with unrestricted rights (World Bank, 1993). The tenure system is thus presented as placing greater restrictions on the extent to which rights and liberties regarding land use can be entrusted in individuals for growth. Actually it reproduces the idea that the tenure system is prone to rerouting economic efforts into ventures that promote waste, rent dissipation, gross violations and mass externality.

To this position, the expected preoccupation of the living economic actors under this theory is to ensure that ownership of the land does not pass out from the community. Besides, the use and benefits from the land must also be restricted to the membership of the corporate community. It is therefore only the membership of particular communities alone who can capture benefits from the land (Pejovich, 1997, p. 4) either individually (Mol and Wiersum, 1993) or jointly (Lund, 2001). Accordingly, the tenure system, from this position, forbids commercial land transactions altogether either among the membership or between the members and non-members. This is because, according to Asante (1975, p. 4), in particular, land is 'the most valuable heritage of the whole community, and could not be lightly parted with' or sold (Gough and Yankson, 2001). Danquah (1928, p. 212) more forthrightly asserts 'an absolute sale of land ... [is] ... not simply a question of alienating reality, notoriously it [is] a case of selling a spiritual heritage for a mess of pottage, a veritable betrayal of ancestral trust, an undoing of the hope of posterity'. Thus the commercial relations that need to be promoted by compatible tenure systems are explicitly outlawed. This also reinforces the view that access to land cannot be determined under any circumstances by the forces of demand, supply, foresight, industry and entrepreneurial abilities but only by membership of the community (see further Migot-Adholla et al., 1991). This position is in reality toughened by the argument that to separate land from man and organise society in such a way as to satisfy the requirements of real estate markets is 'the weirdest of all undertakings of our ancestors' (Polanyi, 1944). The usual explanation for this position is that 'the creation of land market ... eliminates all claims on land originating in kinship or neighbourhood organization and could lead to landless peasant' (Mabogunje, 1989, p. 79). Such is the asserted proscription of commercial transfer of land rights that although families may have secure and inheritable land holdings, these are said not to be freely traded on the market (IIED, 1999). With this stressed inferior incentive structure it is little wonder that Africa is pervasively spoken of as 'a special case precisely because traditional land tenure systems which do not allow private land rights to be fully recognised still predominate' (Platteau, 1992, p. 83; Degnbol, 1996). If this theoretical position is valid, then the overwhelming conclusion is that unless the workings of the tenure system are fundamentally restructured to entrust individuals with liberties and exclusive rights to land use, transfer, benefits and costs, it will remain incompatible with economic growth.

There are very serious problems with this theoretical position and it is a wonder how it came to be a conventional wisdom. Examples of a few of these problems will suffice. Even if it is taken for granted that the arguments represent the truth, which is unlikely, the fundamental flaws in their underlying logic bring them into serious questioning. For instance, it is self-evident that if the living actors are to preserve the land in trust for the future generation they would require a means of sustenance. The land resource alone is not sufficient for that. It has to be effectively combined with capital and labour. So, where capital and labour are lacking it is naïve or illogical to expect the living actors to sit aloof, watch over the land resources for the dead and unborn generation and perish prematurely. Indeed if they do so, the unborn generation in time will also become the living and the present day living will become the dead and the cycle of premature perishing and destitution will be perpetuated in the region. How can it be that institutions evolved by men, not by the Creator, for themselves could be so constraining as to make poverty and underdevelopment a perpetual feature of society? Surely any doctrine, however emotive, that seeks to perpetually impoverish a group of people, is not only questionable and illogical but also illegitimate. Indeed if the position is correct then the living actors of Africa are caught between incompatible realities. On the one hand they are expected to sustain their livelihoods to preserve the land resources of the community for the unborn and ancestors, yet on the other they are denied the very means to do so. Surely, the maximisation of self interest will generously lead living members of society to so rampantly flout the custom that it will lose its meaning in no time. Possibly, the actual rationale behind this sacred characterisation of land is not to trap living actors in this sort of incompatibility of realities but to inculcate into the African society, by means of legends, a sense of sustainable and judicious use of land.

Then again, these theories originate from the pronouncements and writings of certain people and thus hold their validity to the accuracy and open-mindedness of these earlier writers. In reality, serious doubts have been placed on the credibility of at least some of the statements and works of these persons. A fundamental discovery of Berry (1993, pp. 39–40) for instance is that these earlier writers have not always approached the subject with neutrality and have constantly redefined these normative codes 'in order to take advantage of commercial or political opportunities'. Firmin-Sellers (1996) also studies the complex political processes by which property rights are defined and enforced in colonial Ghana using rational choice theory. The study found that prominent and politically influential, wealthy and mostly western-educated individuals in Ghana were the key players in the debate and renegotiated what constituted customary rights for their own benefit. These discoveries question the objectivity of the propositions under this theory.

Perhaps the greatest failing of the structural theory, from the economic perspective, is the exclusive reliance of the theory on almost fanatical non-economic parameters, spiritual myths, to make claims on an institution, the land tenure that is also economic in nature. Given that land tenure is a cultural as well as an economic institution, it is a reasonable expectation that, for objectivity, theories surrounding them both historically and presently are culturally and economically situated. The inability to do this demonstrates that this theory, if valid, explains only a part, the non-economic part, of the tenure system and thus lacks the merit to form the basis for economic analysis or policy. For a complete view there is the need to also situate the theory in economic principles as it exists in reality; an end to which the evolutionary theory is directed.

2.7.3.1.2 Evolutionary land tenure theory This theory illustrates clearly from empirical observation that the tenure system of Africa has incredible potential to offer incentives to channel economic efforts into productive ventures if permitted to evolve endogenously. The expository starting point is that, the world over, land was originally abundant and hence regarded as a resource of limitless supply for private exploitation by all and many. Land was thus owned by no one in particular (see further Hobbes, 1651; Demsetz, 1967; North and Thomas, 1973; North, 1997; Pejovich, 1997). This derives from the argument that

> if we are all here by equal permission of the Creator, we are here with equal title to the enjoyment of his bounty – with an equal right to the use of all that nature so impartially offers.
>
> (Henry George quoted from Ofori, 1992)

Karl Marx explicated in *Capital*:

> [T]he earth and the fullness thereof, were in the original state of nature, the common property of all mankind, so that every child born into this world had, ipso facto, an inalienable right to an equal share in the common inheritance.

Thus the cardinal element of man's relations to land was originally the right to use, usufruct, rather than ownership, and access was unrestricted.

Each member of the community had the right to use as much land as they could develop. This open access situation in the primitive state of society the world over including sub-Saharan Africa naturally led invariably to widespread capturing of resources. Each community or family developed or cultivated portions of the land until they abandoned the land or gave it out to another group. With time, land use became rivalrous in that if one individual or family captured and used a portion of the land, that portion would no longer be available for others. Thus individuals and families, in the bid to protect their investments and development in particular portions of the land, established an organic relation with the land. This helped in identifying members of a community and define their social or political importance (July, 1975). Self-interest maximisation expectedly encouraged overexploitation, which led to rent dissipation (Gordon, 1954; Scott, 1955). Every capture reduced the available land stock. Nonetheless, while land was still in abundance with no scarce value, supply problems were nonexistent and thus overexploitation was less problematic (Pejovich, 1990). In situations like that there would be 'no positive value to society of creating clearly defined property rights in land' (Johnson, 1972, p. 271). Any theory based on this stage of development of society is likely to arrive at conclusions analogous to those of the structural theorists. This confirms also that the structural theory and the evolutionary theory are not distinct theories as often portrayed but a continuum, explaining the initial and subsequent development of the land tenure system.

It soon became apparent that land was not to remain forever in excess of demand. Scarcity of land in Africa was occasioned by growth in cultivation of commercial crops, primarily oil palm, cocoa, groundnuts, cotton and coffee (Sender and Smith, 1986; Migot-Adholla et al., 1991, p. 158), population growth (Feder and Feeney, 1991; Binswanger et al., 1995), increased trade (Sender and Smith, 1986), social and economic changes, new technologies, natural calamities, migration, subordination, war and litigation (Field-Juma, 1996). This propelled the need for more precise demarcation of captured land holdings (Feder and Feeney, 1991; Brandao and Feder, 1995), which also came with widespread land disputes (see Meek, 1949) as was to be expected. As land became scarce the marginal costs imposed on other individual users as results of land capture by others begun to hurt the economic well-being of society. In every society, it is this condition that spurs the 'emergence of new property rights ... in response to the desires of the interacting persons for adjustment to [these] new cost responsibilities' (Demsetz,

1967, p. 350). This commences a transition from open access or group ownership towards a private property rights system (Demsetz, 1967). Eventually the goal of a private property system would be reached but over a considerable period of time, as the experiences of the western world demonstrates (Buell, 1965, p. 750; North and Thomas, 1973; De Soto, 2000).

As it happened, in Africa this transition commenced when those who first discovered (Bruce, 1987) and continuously exploited, maintained, defended and protected particular portions of the land together with the development thereon (Sarbah, 1897; Ollenu, 1962; Meek, 1949; Woodman, 1996; see also *Ohimen* v. *Adjei* (1957) 2 West Africa Law Report, 275) established for themselves use (*usu*), beneficial (*fructus*) and perpetual rights in those particular portions. The land rights so acquired have been noted for all practical purposes to be equivalent in every respect to private property rights or freehold interests in land as known to English land law (Bruce, 1987; Rimmer, 1992; for the nature of English freehold, see Megarry and Wade, 2000). The Chief or headman of the community exercises political (July, 1975) and administrative (Bruce, 1986) control over the pockets of unapportioned or uncaptured portions of land within the territories of the community for and on behalf of the entire group of which the Chief is also a member (Rimmer, 1992; Gyekye, 1998).

When the customary freehold in all the land within the territory of the community is completely taken up either by members or through sale, the radical or allodial rights held by the community in common and administered by the head are reduced to mere administrative rights over the land (for instance Pogucki, 1950; Okoth-Ogendo, 1982; Bruce, 1986; Dickerman, 1987; Feder and Feeney, 1991; Migot-Adholla et al., 1991; Platteau, 1992; Sjaastad and Bromley, 1997; Payne, 1997; Antwi, 2000; Cousins, 2000; McAuslan, 2000; Antwi, 2000; Toulmin and Quan, 2000; Quan, 2000; Platteau, 2000; Cousins, 2000; Gough and Yankson, 2001). At this stage in the development process it would be incorrect to describe land rights in Africa as an open access resource since it is only by the sanction of the community or original acquirer that access could be obtained (Berry, 1993; 1994; 1997; Sjaastad and Bromley, 1997; Alden Wily, 2000).

Perhaps what may have confused some observers is the fact that ownership boundaries over specific parcels were and still are usually physically non-existent except in some urban areas. These boundaries, however impermanent or invisible they may be, were known, accepted and respected by all in the pre-capitalist days and hence were sufficient to indicate limits of ownership. As Buchanan (1975, p. 20) explains, societies begin to consider precise definitions of rights and the drawing of the limits of ownership more carefully only when the tolerated limits are exceeded, when previously accepted boundaries are crossed. While this tolerated limit remained unbroken attention was focused more on building solidarity among neighbouring original acquirers to strengthen kinship ties and form communities. This solidarity served the indigenous Africans in many respects: social, economic and political. A fundamental objective for the formation of this community was to make it possible to pool together resources and redistribute risk in times of war, drought or pestilence (Field-Juma, 1996) and to provide common labour resources for agricultural cultivation (Bruce, 1986). Further, this solidarity according to Okoth-Ogendo (1994) was also

> meant to guarantee security of opportunity for all who had access rights to those resources. If there were a possibility that some of these rights would be taken away, the tenure system assured that these would occur only in exceptional circumstances, and only upon a collective decision made at the highest level of social organisation. Second, it was designed to ensure equity between and across generations. ... Third, [it] ... also determines important land use decisions ... and the nature of resource preservation or conservation measures, where these required collective action by the community.

As a symbolic gesture to cement this solidarity, the founding individuals or nuclei family units of the community agreed to a privileged association of their acquired land rights with their newly formed communities. The privileged rights that accrete to the community, the allodial rights, as Meek (1949, p. 179) establishes amount to what 'would be described in English law as a right of reversion – a right which cannot be lost by prescription'. The right to economic use and exploitation of the land remained vested in individual members of the community (Mabogunje, 1992). Thus when land in Africa is spoken of as commonly held it could only be in reference to this notional radical title in areas where the customary freehold has been acquired (Bruce, 1986; Woodman, 1996).

To date boundaries remain unclear in most areas. But these socio-economic changes and their accompanying fundamental changes in land prices led to some 'natives claiming ownership in the soil', which in turn increased the sale of land by one native to another and then from native to non natives as far back as in 1860 (Buell, 1965, pp. 761–2). This marked the break from the structural era towards the full fledged private property era. Initially, in keeping with the then value of the land, particularly during the pre-colonial era, the customary freeholds were sold for small symbolic gifts, such as 'a few yams or a tin of palm oil' (Berry, 1975, p. 95), locally brewed drinks (Ollenu, 1962), beer, produce or livestock (Kitching, 1980). With time, these symbolic payments transformed to substantial cash (Clark, 1980) or other forms of payments (Berry; 1975; Kitching, 1980, pp. 290–1) such as several years of labour (Woodman, 1996). Now, land rights in sub-Saharan Africa have taken on a more profound economic, social and political character. Thus though land is spoken of as inalienable under the structural theory, there is now sufficient authority to support the view that the sale of land was in fact common even before the introduction of government intervention.

2.8 Summary

This chapter has attempted to establish the primacy of land in the fight against poverty as well as in the quest for economic development. This has now set the stage for us to probe into the justification for government interventions in real estate markets as well as their impacts.

3
Rationale for Real Estate Policy

3.1 Introduction

An argument initiated in Chapter 2 is being developed to conclude that building an investment climate that facilitates (private sector led) 'investment and growth and empowering poor people to participate in that growth' (Stern, 2002) offers some answers to sustainable poverty alleviation in sub-Saharan Africa. This raises the obvious question: how does one empower the poor to participate in private sector led growth? Considering the pervasiveness of real estate ownership (generally defined) and transactions in the sub-Saharan region, creating an environment to provide the right incentives for the poor to utilise, via their own voluntary transactions, real estate assets efficiently may be part of the answer to the question. This chapter examines the parameters that determine what might be described as efficient real estate policy regimes that could garner the gains made by the poor, through real estate utilisation and transactions, to better their lot. The view of this book is that the poverty of appropriate real estate policy regimes in sub-Saharan Africa is a fundamental cause of why many of its inhabitants own real estate but are still hopelessly poor.

Establishing that real estate has a causal effect in alleviating poverty and economic development does not by itself justify the need for real estate policy. Why then are real estate policies necessary? Granted that they are necessary, what role should real estate policies be playing? There is in progress an important debate regarding the role that governments must play to ensure significant improvements in the standard of living of a vast majority of the population. This debate may be reduced in this book to a debate over the proper role of policy in the real estate sector. By knowing what roles real estate policies should be playing based on the need for them, it is possible to ascertain the efficiency and effectiveness of existing sub-Saharan Africa real estate policies.

Economists of all shades agree that government has a role to play in the fight against poverty. What is as yet unresolved is what the apt role or limit of the state ought to be. These are the grand issues to be discussed in this chapter. These questions can be addressed first by examining the conceptual foundations of policies and government actions. A useful starting point for such discussions is the economic concept of human action.

3.2 The concept of human action

Every acting person is naturally embedded with an overpowering drive to *live* and *prosper*.[1] To live means to exist without hardship and anguish; to prosper means to achieve a satisfactory level of happiness, comfort, welfare, security, safety, health and other interests. What is satisfactory is a matter for the individual in question to judge; what may be satisfactory for one person may be unsatisfactory for another. The phrase *to live and prosper* is often replaced with the word well-being or needs. These will be used interchangeably in this discussion.

It is the strong desire to achieve these twin ends of living and prospering that impels human beings to act *at all*. We are here referring only to deliberate, not involuntary actions. All deliberate human actions are directed towards achieving the ends of living and prospering.[2, 3, 4] No doubt, some people are also driven to act for the sake of the well-being of others.[5]

Ideally, we would all wish to achieve a perfect satisfaction of our needs. We all wish to exist without the slightest hardship or anguish, and to achieve the exact level of prosperity we desire. Any level of imperfect satisfaction of our needs is unsatisfactory and people would generally act in order to exchange a 'more satisfactory state of affairs for a less satisfactory' (Mises, 1996) one. For an individual to act there must be an incentive to change things. An individual who is content with his or her state of well-being will not act since there would be no incentive for him or her to change things.[6]

The incentive to act consists of three conditions. First the individual must feel *uneasiness* about his or her state of well-being.[7] Indeed, poverty may be looked upon as any state of well-being that causes a feeling of uneasiness and hence impels affected individuals to act. As observed above, development economists have devised a certain minimum state of well-being below which it is regarded universally uneasy, which is the $1.00 a day threshold. Secondly, to be impelled to act, the individual must be able to imagine a state of well-being that suits him or her better than the present state of affairs.[8] Thirdly, the individual must believe that his or her actions can bring about the desired state of well-being or remove the uneasiness.[9]

Where all these are present it is to be expected that the individual in question would be driven by his innate impulse to act to remove the uneasiness or bring about the desired state of well-being. Since it is only the individual who feels the uneasiness or knows his or her desired state of well-being, it is only him or her that can decide on the most appropriate actions that will most likely deal decisively with the uneasiness or bring about the desired state of well-being.

As argued in Chapter 2, human well-being, whether consisting of the removal of uneasiness or the bringing about of a better state of well-being is an end whose satisfaction depends on the consumption of goods and services. Different types and levels of well-being require the consumption of different quantities of different goods and services. The goods and services upon which the satisfaction of human needs depend are also called *wealth,* defined as '[1] useful material things, and [2] ... all right to hold, or use, or derive benefits from material things, or to receive them at a future time';[10] wealth thus defined is of two parts, the material (tangible) thing and its immaterial (intangible rights) aspect. Without the intangible rights the goods can not be consumed to satisfy needs. This means that to gain command over the goods needed for the satisfaction of wants the intangible rights over those goods must specifically be conferred on the individuals who need it most to satisfy their wants or the entrepreneur who is most capable of bringing these goods into their most productive uses.

To illustrate how human action works, take a two good and two individuals world in which the only goods available are goods *X* and *Y*, the two individuals in the world are *A* and *B*. Suppose that *A* owns good *X* even though the good he actually requires to meet his basic wants is *Y*. Suppose also that individual *B* is in the very opposite position in the sense that he requires good *X* to satisfy his wants even though he presently owns good *X* and not good *Y*. If the status quo remains unchanged, both citizens of our contrived world would not be able to satisfy their wants and would perish from the non-satisfaction of their basic wants. The well-being of the parties will improve if command over good *X* is conferred on individual *B* and command over good *Y* is conferred on individual *A*.

The act of transferring a good to a person or entity that did not own it immediately before the transfer is what economists refer to as *resource allocation*. A resource is efficiently allocated if it is transferred to the party who of all parties needs it the most or is most capable of generating the highest possible return from it. This conclusion is pretty obvious. But how can this transfer be best achieved, assuming that one of the goods involved is real estate. This is a policy decision that every nation must make as part of its efforts towards poverty alleviation and economic development. Broadly, there are two alternative ways of achieving this aim as alluded to in the previous chapter.

Firstly, the government may allow the parties to decide on the interchange at their own volition, voluntary trade (also called capitalism or the price system). The government may, in the alternative, take up the responsibility and first, override the will of the parties then allocate each available good to the party that is regard, according to some kind of a central plan, as most in need of it. This last approach has been called socialism. Allocation via central planning, or socialism, is currently a virtually dead economic ideology and therefore needs no further analysis here. We shall therefore now take a look at how the real estate price system works.

3.3 The real estate price system

Carl Menger (1871, p. 180) postulates that

> The benefits of mutual transfer of goods depend, as we have seen, on three conditions: (a) one economizing individual must have command of quantities of goods which have a smaller value to him than other quantities of goods at the disposal of another economizing individual who evaluates the goods in reverse fashion, (b) the two economizing individuals must have recognized this relationship, and (c) they must have the power actually to perform the exchange of goods. The absence of but one of these conditions means that an essential prerequisite for an economic exchange is missing, and that an exchange of goods between two economizing individuals is economically impossible.

It was observed earlier that all human beings act invariably to better their economic standing. Bettering economic standing consists of gaining possession of those goods and services upon which the satisfaction of ones needs and wants depend. Real estate is one such good upon which the satisfaction of human wants depends, as discussed in Chapter 2. For instance shelter, an example of real estate, is the basic need of all human beings. Real estate is also required as a higher order (or capital) good to support the production of other consumption goods. Such higher order real estate includes raw urban land, arable land, offices, shops, industries and factory buildings. To gain possession of the requisite consumption goods, whether they consist of real estate per se or other goods whose production requires real estate in the form of, say, offices, industrial units, etc., some form of trade and development activities may be necessary. Trade in its basic form entails the reciprocal interchange of goods and services.

Real estate trade may take, broadly speaking, one of two forms – direct sales or tenancy transactions. In the past (see Chapter 2), the vast quantity of real estate trade in sub-Saharan Africa involved the interchange of real estate on one hand and labour services and other goods such as drinks on the other. Most agricultural real estate tenancy transactions for instance involved the interchange of commands (rights) over certain specified real estate units over a given time duration for a share in the produce or proceeds earned from the economic activities undertaken with the real estate. In modern times, the rapid monetisation of sub-Saharan Africa, particularly in the cities, has ensured that, practically, all real estate transactions involve money. The money payments may take the form of periodic rents, in the case of tenancies, or lump sums, in the case of outright sales. In some rural communities, where the economy is not seriously monetised, interchange of real estate rights for other goods or labour services still occurs.

Real estate transactions – sales and tenancies – are coordinated by the price system. In the quest to better their economic standing, individuals are driven to interchange their relatively less valuable possessions, based on their own subjective valuation, for other possessions that they consider subjectively to be more valuable to their quest for better economic standing. Where such an individual comes into contact with another in a converse position, they will most likely agree, in pursuit of their self-interest, to exchange what they respectively regard subjectively as less valuable for what they regard as more valuable.

Nevertheless, because the parties are in a converse position, what one individual regards as less valuable becomes what the other sees as more valuable and vice versa. For instance if A has £100,000 which he values less than a two bedroom flat in a given location, then A would be prepared to exchange the £100,000 for the two bedroom flat, should the owner (B) of the two bedroom also value the property as less valuable than the £100,000. When a trade is affected, B would take command over the money while A takes command over the flat.

Both would have exchanged their possessions of goods that they value less for that of others that they value more highly. By so doing the price system has allocated the goods involved, in this case the flat and the £100,000 respectively, to those individuals that perceive them as most valuable (Balchin and Kieve, 1977; Balchin, Bull, and Kieve, 1995). Real estate markets are thus efficient if they perform these functions aptly.

Like any other market, the price system in the real estate field operates in response to the interplay of the forces of demand and supply (Farvacque and MacAuslan, 1992) to govern the exchange of real property rights. The price system is fairly active throughout Africa (see Chapter 1) and comprises the buying and selling of freeholds, leaseholds, rentals, pledging of property for credit, mortgaging, land pooling and other arrangements between individuals, private companies and public institutions (Quan, 2000). The price system works on the assumption that the free interplay of spontaneous economic forces could lead invariably to the full employment and efficient utilisation and distribution of resources thereby promoting the public interest better than any other means (Smith, 1776).

Though what constitutes an efficient allocation of resources may be fraught with uncertainties and debate, economists largely agree that an efficient allocation of resources turns ultimately on whether particular resources are put to the use that, of all the feasible uses, offers the most benefit to society (Harberger, 1959; Leftwich, 1973; Balchin and Kieve, 1977; Hallett, 1979; Arrow, 1985; Harvey, 1987).

This connotes the idea that an allocation of a resource is regarded as efficient if the worth (benefits) of the alternative uses forgone at all times fall below the benefits derived from the selected allocation (Coase, 1972, p. 313). For example, land employed in the production of housing is efficiently allocated if the worth of the foregone uses, say agriculture, falls below that of housing.

Economists usually adopt the Pareto criterion as a standard economic yardstick for measuring the allocation of resources in any particular society. As applied to real estate, the Pareto criterion posits an allocation of real estate resources to be efficient if it improves the welfare of at least one person in society without making another person worse off. By this index, an allocation of real estate resource is optimal if, beyond what has been accomplished, it is no longer possible to improve the welfare of any individual in society (in his personal view) without making another person in the society worse off (in his personal view) (Tisdell, 1974; Connolly and Munro, 1999). Pareto efficiency is not attained if, by providing housing for one person in society, another person is made homeless or deprived of health services.

Even so, the true state of a person's welfare is a subjective question. No one else apart from the particular individuals concerned can adequately tell by how much their welfare has been improved by virtue of a particular allocation of real estate resources (Hayek, 1944). Thus it is only when the individual or individuals in particular societies agree that their welfare has been improved or been made worse off by a particular real estate resource allocation or decisions that one can pass judgment on the efficiency of the allocation. The importance of individual decisions concerning real estate can therefore not be overemphasised in the quests to understand the impacts government intervention that regulate or enfeeble such individual choices.

What better way can there be to truly improve the welfare of individuals in any society than to equip them, remove all impediments and restrictions on their path and to allow them to select from a range of options the real estate resource allocation that in their own judgement will better improve their well-being. The price theory contends that, because humans are essentially rational and mostly influenced in their decisions and actions by their innate inclination to better their welfare rather than diminish it, when given the opportunity humans are likely to choose the option that offers them the best utility rather than those that in their judgment will give them pain and displeasure and hence make them worse off (Smith, 1776; Jevons, 1972–81; Arrow, 1985).

If real estate market participants are well equipped and unrestrained when confronted with such opportunity, they are likely to make such exchanges of their possessions (money or real property) that will be most beneficial to them. They are likely to desist with or discontinue particular exchanges they anticipate will most likely make them worse off. It is thus rational according to the price theory to expect real estate purchasers to pay just as much for a property as they perceive it is worth. Price thus serves as an index of the worth of a property to both the purchaser and the seller.

The price that a purchaser offers for a property, however, is a composite figure. Implicit in it are the prices of all the important attributes that contribute to the perceived aggregate utility that it offers (Balchin and Kieve, 1977; Hallett, 1979; Harvey, 1987; Antwi, 1998). The utility that particular real estates offers varies according to the variations in location, size, materials of construction and workmanship among others (Von Thunen, 1826; Isard, 1956; Beckman, 1957; Alonso, 1964; Mutt, 1969; Mills, 1972; Balchin and Kieve, 1977; Hallett, 1979; Miyao,

1981; Harvey, 1987; Kivell, 1993). So also are their prices. Thus for an urban property with utility influencing attributes of say: (1) location (*LOC*); (2) Neighbourhood (*NEI*); (3) Taste and Preference of purchaser (*TAP*); (4) Price of comparable properties (*PCOMP*); (5) the income of the purchaser (*IOP*); (6) the expectations of purchaser regarding future income prospects from the property (*EXP*); and (7) subsisting property rights (*PPR*) among others, the price that purchasers are willing and able to pay (demand price) can be represented functionally as:

$$D_P = f(LOC, NEI, TAP, PCOMP, IOP, EXP, PPR...N) \quad [1]$$

in which D_P represents the Demand Price.

Likewise, owners of real properties will normally sell their properties only at a price (supply price) equivalent to the value they place on the property (Coase, 1960; Buchanan and Tullock, 1962; Demsetz, 1967; Harberger, 1972; Hartley and Tisdell, 1981; Parsons, 2001; Harberger and Jenkins, 2002). Given that the factors that influence their decisions include: (1) the quantity of property available (*QAV*); (2) cost of construction of property (*COC*); (3) profit margin (*PM*); (4) investment risk (*IR*); (5) price of comparable properties (*POCP*); and (6) subsisting property rights (*PPR*), among others, the supply price function can be represented as:

$$S_P = f(QAV, COC, PM, IR, POCP, PPR...N) \quad [2]$$

in which S_P represents the Supply Price.

Ideally, equilibrium urban property prices E_p, the price at which real property resources are most efficiently allocated will be achieved through voluntary haggling and eventually bring equation [1] in line with equation [2] (see Smith, 1776; Coase, 1937; 1960; Tisdell, 1974; Arrow, 1985; Friedman, 2002). That is, demand price will ultimately equal supply price in the ideal world.

$$E_P = D_P = S_P \quad [3]$$

This is represented graphically in Figure 3.1 below. In the figure take *SS* to be the aggregate supply function for particular type of real estate and *DD* as the demand function. The equilibrium or stationary price E_P will be establish at the point where *SS* = *DD* and at that point the social optimum quantity (Q) of that particular property type will be produced and sold.

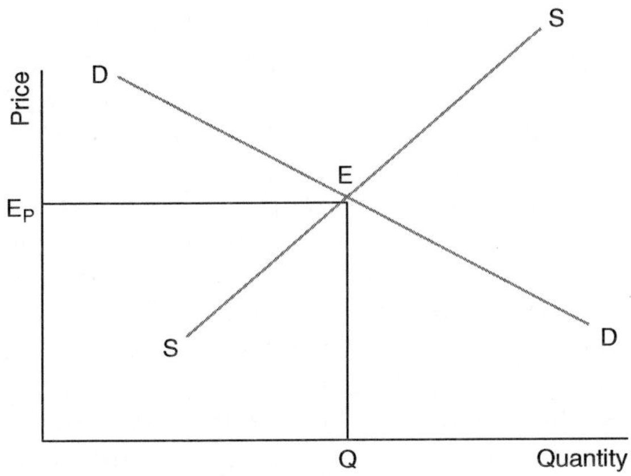

Figure 3.1 A Demand and Supply Model

At this point, the highest value or usefulness of the property to purchasers becomes equivalent to the highest value that suppliers place on the property. This equilibrium price indicates the highest value that purchasers place on the property. If the sale is concluded at this price, it becomes an indicator of the value that both purchasers and sellers alike place on the property. That said, in many economic fields, including the urban real estate field particularly in sub-Saharan Africa, the price system is vulnerable and highly susceptible to failure in many respects. It is this shortcoming of the price system that has given rise to the need for government involvement in real estate resource allocation.

3.4 Public policy in real estate markets

To begin with, the efficiency of the price system is contingent on an assumption of availability of full information equally accessible at no cost to all market participants (Friedman, 2002). As Simon (1957) however established, it is impossible in the real world for market participants to be in possession of perfect knowledge of all market events at the same time in view of the bounded rationality of the human mind as well as the cost differentials in procuring such information. Thus market transactions are inexorably carried out with incomplete information, thereby making it difficult for equilibrium prices to be accomplished. Moreover, in any market there are often income disparities between transacting parties and market bids may tend to be driven more by income constraints than by utility (Arrow, 1985).

In such situations the person with a higher income position usually assumes a position of strength and power and can easily influence the outcome of market transactions to the detriment of other less resourced transacting parties thereby reducing the chances of achieving equilibrium prices. Moreover, people may own property rights for non-economic reasons and may simply be unwilling to trade those rights away due probably to the strong emotional and sentimental ties they may have with particular properties, thereby withholding those properties from the market for non-economic reasons. Besides, the nature of the institutional framework within which land and real estate is held may allow the exploitation of owners of property rights by certain privileged and influential actors. In sub-Saharan Africa, for instance, traditional authorities owning land in trusteeship are spurred on by economic incentives to dispose of these lands at the expense of the beneficiaries who lose their lands and gain in most cases very little from the sale. This leads to social injustice and the exacerbation of income inequities.

Even so, without a well-clarified and enforced property rights system, urban real estate markets cannot function effectively. This is essentially because by definition urban property rights set the limits for the degree of freedom and liberty that a person has over particular property as well as the rules for trade (Davis and North, 1971). They prescribe behavioural rules, constrain activities and shape expectations of market participants (Keohane, 1988). Property rights also 'facilitate coordination among people by helping them form expectations which each person can reasonably hold in dealing with others' (Ruttan and Hayami, 1984). Urban real property rights thus offer property owners the incentive, opportunities and reward for productive use of urban land resources. However in sub-Saharan Africa, indeed the developing world in general, property rights in land are mostly ill-defined and ill-enforced (Feder and Feeney, 1991; Platteau, 1992; Brandao and Feder, 1995; Deininger, 2003) making the workings of the price system problematic. Finally, real estate markets, like most markets when allowed to operate unrestrained, tend to promote market monopoly, the production of negative externalities, the inadequate supply of public goods and the exacerbation of income inequities (Smith, 1776; Richardson, 1960; Pigou, 1962; Tisdell, 1974; Hartley and Tisdell, 1981; Williamson, 1986; Friedmann, 1987; Hodgson, 1988; Kivell, 1993; Sawyer, 1994; Denyer-Green, 1998; Connolly and Munro, 1999; Friedman, 2002).

The existence of these shortcomings of the price system has been conventionally adduced as justification for government intervention because their mere existence makes market competition improbable, significantly restricted, practically impossible or harmful (Richardson, 1960). These shortcomings cause not only a failure in the establishment of equilibrium prices but in addition cause instability in real property prices. When this occurs the price system is unable to allocate resources efficiently in the Pareto sense with associated telling consequences. As exemplified (Figure 3.2) instead of establishing equilibrium price P_D at point *E*, the existence of these elements of market failures ensure that either the demand prices or the supply prices or both constantly gravitate away from point *E* to such points as *b*, *c*, *d*, *e*, *f*, *g* or *h*.

If, for instance, the demand function D_0 is shifted to D_1 while the supply function (S_0) remains unaffected the equilibrium position distorts to, say, *c*, forcing the equilibrium price to move upward to P_2. The true magnitude of the distortion is indicated by $P_0P_2c\ M$. Accordingly, resource allocation efficiency is distorted that much. Conversely if the failure causes the demand function to shift leftwards of the equilibrium to, say, D_2, a distortion equivalent to, say, P_0MeP_1 occurs. On the supply side, if the failure resulted in a shift in the supply curve from its equilibrium position S_0 to, say, S_1 with demand remaining unchanged, a shift in the equilibrium condition equivalent to say P_0MeP_1 occurs, which will accordingly reduce the efficiency of resource allocation.

Moreover, if the elements of market failure cause a shift in the supply curve to, say, S_2 a consequential distortion in resource allocation equivalent to, say, P_0P_2aM will ensue. In extreme situations, these elements could precipitate a shift in both the demand and supply functions at

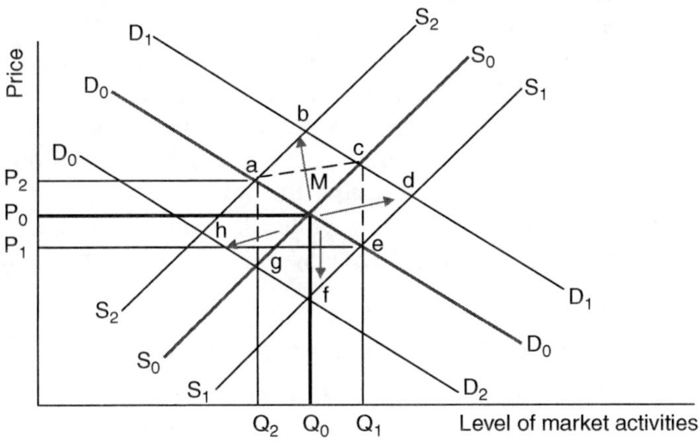

Figure 3.2 Market distortions

the same time and this could cause a shift in the equilibrium position to any point – say *b, d, f* or *h*. It is worthy of note that this is a highly simplified version of what pertains in reality. In practice, these elements of market failure could result in hundreds and thousands of points of distortion in the equilibrium position for particular types of real estate commodities. The further away these points of distortions are from the equilibrium point (*E*) the higher the degree of inefficiency that is introduced into the allocation of resources. Microeconomic theory suggests that if such market distortions occur or there is strong evidence to suggest that they are likely to occur, a means has to be found to either suppress them or eliminate them altogether by dealing with the shortcomings that are reproducing them. Such an improvement according to the Pareto criteria should improve the welfare of at least one person in the society without loss to anyone else. To implement such a change or improvement, it may be necessary to conjecture that the net gainers from the improvement can at least compensate the net losers (Buchanan, 1995).

The conventional view, associated with Pigou (1962), perceives government interventions as the most rational, potent and independent entity better positioned to deal with these problems. This view accordingly suggests that government interventions have the capacity to pull all instances of distortions to point *E* in Figure 3.1 without making any one worse off or with the guarantee that the sum of gainers will exceed the sum of the losers. To the extent that government interventions are directed towards and are able to accomplish this objective, the interventions are considered economically worthwhile and it is only by such criteria that government policies in real estate market in sub-Saharan Africa can be considered worthwhile from a microeconomic perspective. Successful government interventions must succeed in mopping up all existing deviation in the demand functions such as *abde* and *ahfe* respectively and that of the supply functions such as *cdfg* and *ghbc*. This will ensure that the aggregate demand and supply functions in these markets are pulled (see direction of arrows in Figure 3.3) permanently to coincide with and stick with D_0 and S_0, respectively.

3.4.1 Shortcomings of government interventions

The design of appropriate government interventions can be problematic to the extent that on occasions it brings into serious question the very suitability of government interventions as the only option in correcting market failures (see for instance Coase, 1960). The manifold

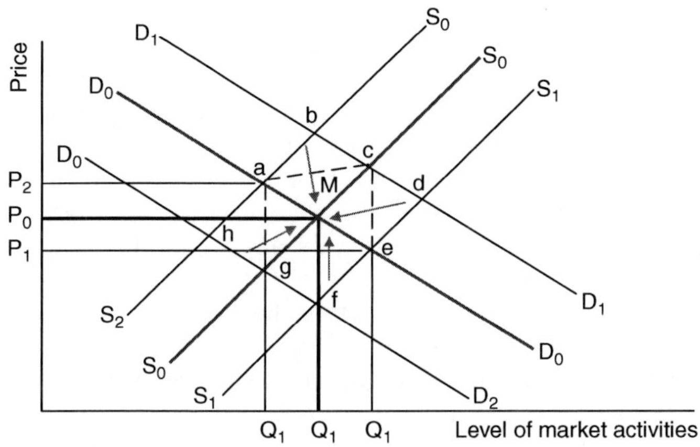

Figure 3.3 Removing market distortions

recorded instances of government failures in urban sub-Saharan African real estate markets, indeed those of the developing world (De Soto, 1989) bear evidence to this assertion. Brandao and Feder (1995, p. 191) have in fact come to the conclusion that, 'land market ... regulatory constraints ... significantly affect the operation of the market and equilibrium prices and sales, contribute to reduced efficiency and have negative equity implications'. Microeconomic theory provides insights into the practical events that undermine chances of securing optimal or appropriate government interventions in most economic fields.

Firstly, to be able to devise interventions that could induce a desirable shift in the points of market distortions there is the need for a vast amount of information (Simon, 1957). For instance in Figure 3.3 (see the direction of the arrows), information on all occurrences of market distortions – say points *b, c, d, e, f, g* or *h,* the precise location of these distortions in reference to the equilibrium position *E,* the measured extents of the deviations from the equilibrium *abde, cdfg, efha* or *ghbc,* the elements of market failures at play, and the avenues through which they distort the market.

The information requirements are vast and not easy to come by in practice. Moreover, the dynamism and spontaneity of human behaviour (Smith, 1776) imply that information in markets changes so frequently that they have very short life span. To be most useful, when the right information is procured (if at all possible), it is argued (see Parsons, 2003) that the information needs to be quantitatively and thoughtfully analysed in a way that would ensure that predictions of desirable future events on markets can be accurately foretold and undesirable future events pre-empted. For all that has been written about market failure, the literature is still devoid of any positivist or post-positivist means of achieving this information and analysis. This is because in practice, as Hayek (1944) and Simon (1957) point out, it requires the mind of omniscience to be able to accomplish that and, since governments are far from omniscient, there is very little reason to expect government policy experts to be able to devise rational policies to correct market failures in the Pareto sense.

Worse still, public choice scholarship (Buchanan and Tullock, 1962) has more forcefully confirmed in recent times that politicians who are the initiators and custodians of government interventions are often impatient in waiting for the rather long period of time required to gather sufficient information (even for what they are worth) for second best policy solutions to be devised (McNutt, 2002). Meanwhile public policies and government interventions emerge out of a complex decision-making process in which the respective participants have different and often conflicting ideological orientations, interests and values. They thus often disagree with what may be causing particular market failures or what indeed the solution should be. They each influence policies in the direction of their ideological orientation, interest and value rather than towards the correction of market failure per se.

Thus policies tend to be rarely value neutral, neither are they usually devised on pure economic considerations as expected of market failure oriented policies. Instead, they are often creations or instruments designed to meet particular interests or ideological ends (Buchanan and Tullock, 1962). When policies happen to be market failure focused, it may be because the most influential agenda setters in the policy process have rightly perceived market failure as an urgent problem for the government to tackle, or it may be mere coincidence. However, such occasions appear to be very rare in practice (Buchanan and Tullock, 1962). Thus it is more likely to be the case that policies emerge to serve private interests rather than to address market failure.

It is now well known in microeconomic theory that policies designed to serve specific private interests or based on doubtful information rather than addressing market failure often end up concentrating benefits on a few while diffusing the costs on the larger society (Hammond, 2006). This in effect leads to the divergence between the private and social costs thereby accumulating huge overall social costs rather than benefits. On this score, Coase (1960, p. 118) argues, 'direct government interventions will not necessarily give better results than leaving the problem to be solved by the market or firm'. Pigou (1962, p. xix) goes even further to state that

> The mere failure of private industry, when left free from public interference to maximise the national dividend does not of itself warrant interventions; for this might make things worse.

This potentially harmful side effect of government interventions is illustrated graphically in Figure 3.4. Take line *PMC* to represent the private marginal costs borne by the small (politicians, political parties, interests groups, voters, bureaucrats, etc.) in whose favour particular policies are designed to serve. In addition, *SMC* is the social marginal cost incurred by society on account of the policy. Line *MB* represents the marginal benefits of the policy. As Lipsey (1993) asserts, governments are slow in admitting mistakes even when they are aware of them. This is because it is often politically easier to go on spending money on a project that has turned sour than to admit fault. This often leads to the reliance on wrong policies or enforcement methods arising from initial mistakes in the choice of policy or methods of enforcement or because market conditions have changed while policies remain the same. The potential economic problems associated with this are illustrated in Figure 3.4. The costs of every improvement brought about by such policies exceed their benefits by the amount *BAD*. In such situation the result is worse than

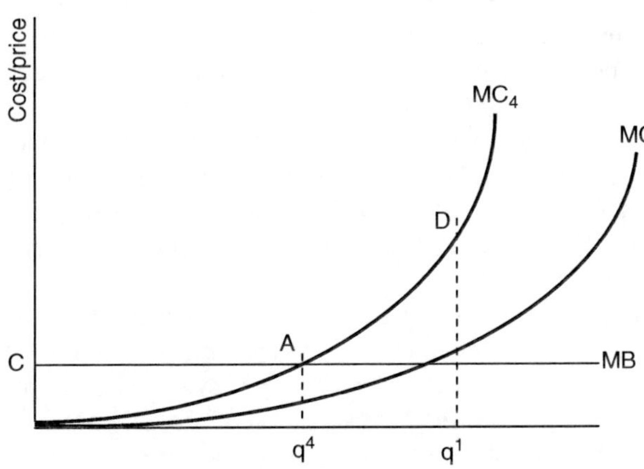

Adapted from lipsey (1993, p.416)

Figure 3.4 The potential effects of inappropriate policies

no intervention indicated by C_1CA. While the best possible intervention could have produced a net gain, wrong policy choice and methods of enforcement can produce a net loss.

Wrong policy choices could convert the gains from intervention into losses. *MB* represents the marginal benefit achieved from a particular policy. Assume that this is at constant prices. MC_1 represents the marginal costs of introducing and enforcing the policy. For all units up to q, marginal costs exceed marginal benefits. The optimal level of policy is thus q^1, where $MB = MC_1$. Total net benefits are $OCBq_1$. Suppose government specifies a method or policies that lead to a shift in marginal costs to MC_4 when costs shown by MC_1 could have been achieved using different policies or methods of enforcement; the optimal improvement in the market performance could reduce to q_4. The net benefits are then reduced to C_1CA1^4. This failure could be compounded if these high costs methods or policies continue to dictate proceedings on urban real estate markets.

The cost of every improvement brought about by such policies exceeds its benefits by the amount *BAD*. In such situation the results is worse than no intervention indicated by C_1CA. While the best possible intervention could have produced a net gain, wrong policy choice and methods of enforcement can produce a net loss.

3.4.2 Market improvement

Besides, public choice scholarship demonstrates that by far the most important causes of government failure arise from the nature of the government as a policy making and enforcing entity. Figure 3.5 depicts the way externalities can occur in policy formulation. The x-axis represents the policy levels while the y-axis indicates the benefits from policies. Functions *MB, PMC* and *SMC* represent the marginal benefits, private marginal costs and social marginal costs associated with policies respectively. Policy agenda setters seeking to maximise their private self-interest or accomplish particular ideological ends by securing a policy in their own favour could push for policies that would ensure their optimal satisfaction (P^0).

At this level the benefits of the policy to them is (B_1) while the private cost is (*c*). Yet the social cost borne by society in view of this policy could be as high as point *B*, which is far above the costs borne by the agenda setters as well as the benefits derived from the policy. The result is thus that benefits are concentrated on a few while the costs are widely spread on larger segments. The divergence between the social marginal benefits and the social marginal costs (*B–C*) provides an indication of the negative impacts that such policy is likely to induce.

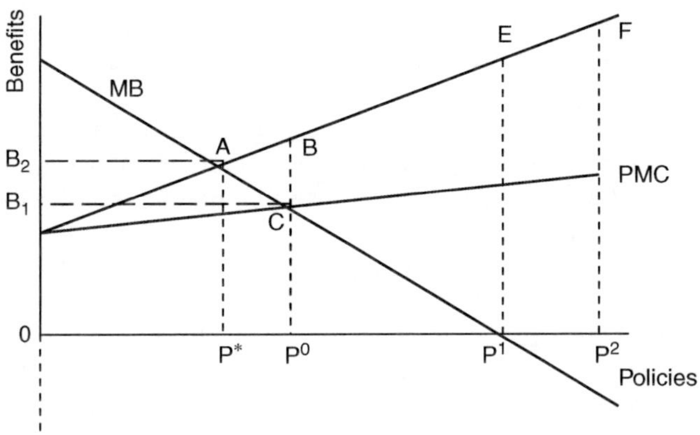

Figure 3.5 Policy externalities

Such policies are likely to result in a social welfare loss equivalent to triangle *ABC*, representing the externality associated with such private interest centred policies. Yet, if policies had been designed at, say, (P^1) the price system would have been able to ensure societal benefits of, say, (B_2), which would have been equivalent to the costs of the policy to society. The economic implication here is that by devising policies to serve the private interests of agenda setters (clients) as opposed to correcting market failure society is often made worse off by a margin of (B_1–B_2).

3.5 The Coase theorem

The Coase theorem controverts the conventional view that posits government interventions as the potential panacea to all forms of market malfunctioning (Pigou, 1920; Arrow, 1985). The Coase theorem was more coherently enunciated by Coase in 1960, even though its essential ingredients were first formally laid out by him in 1937. The theory has since been popularised and applied in many economic fields (see Stigler, 1966, p. 113; Calabresi, 1968, p. 68; Posner, 1993, p. 195). Transaction costs in this regard comprise the costs of discovering relevant urban property prices and ownership status, costs of negotiating and concluding separate urban real estate contracts (Coase, 1937), costs of policing and enforcement of contracts as well as surveying and measuring the valuable attributes of urban properties. It also includes the costs of protecting property rights as well as the opportunity costs of non-fulfilment of an efficient transaction (Dahlman, 1979, p. 148; North, 1990, p. 27; Rao, 2003, p. xvi).

Following its earliest formulation, various authors have reframed the theorem to place it in particular contexts. The theory states:

> In a regime of zero transaction costs [and rationality], negotiation between the parties would lead to those arrangements being made which would maximise wealth and this will occur irrespective of the initial assignment of rights.
>
> (Coase, 1992, p. 717)

In other words, if market dealers behave rationally, real estate markets would perform efficiently if the costs of real estate transactions are zero regardless of who owns property in particular societies. It is worth emphasising the point that the theory is not oblivious to the fact that in the real world transaction costs are rarely zero, certainly not in the real estate arena. Indeed, it recognises that on occasions transaction costs could be so high as to prevent transactions from occurring altogether (see Rao, 2003). The theory postulates instead that in every economic field, the lower the transaction costs the higher the potential for efficient outcomes.

This implies that rational commercial transactions are the single most important engine for economic growth such that the more frequently they occur, the higher the chances of realising economic growth and efficiency. Markets distort and slow down transaction because they are impeded by the existence of transaction costs in the real world. Thus to promote frequent transactions, societies must be in possession of means to drive down transaction costs as low as possible. Such a means could be from the private sector or governmental sources such as interventions or policies (Coase, 1966, pp. 442–5). From an efficiency standpoint the choice between the government and the private sector would have to be made purely on the basis of their abilities to make considerable progress in driving down transaction costs with regard to the transaction costs they also bring about in their strides. Thus the economic gains associated with the selected means are the extra transaction costs savings they engendered. Alternatively the economic gains can be in terms of the extra benefits they bring about.

That government interventions have a role to play in real estate market functioning within the ken of the Coase theorem thus derives from the common knowledge that on occasions they are better placed to drive down transaction costs in comparison to the private sector. Coase (1992, p. 718) for instance points out that government interventions could legitimately reduce transaction costs through the clarification of laws and by making legal requirements for market transfers less onerous. There is evidence that government interventions formed on this basis have infused trading confidence into otherwise problematic trading relations (see for example Goldberg, 1976, and Zucker, 1986). Williamson (1996, p. 268) also notes that provided the regulatory framework is appropriate, both the public bureaux and their customers 'would be able to make investment in specialised asserts on better terms than they would in the absence of such regulations'. To this view, such government interventions must neither be inconsistent nor replace the use of the price system (Hayek, 1944; Coase, 1966, p. 442) but rather prop it up for its smoother performance. As Coase (1988, p. 27) puts it, 'the aim of economic policy is to ensure that people when deciding which course of action to take [will] choose that which brings about the best outcome for the system as a whole'.

3.6 Framework for real estate policy evaluation

As applied to urban real estate policy analysis, three main lessons can be drawn from the above analysis. (1) Though the price system offer the best potential in allocating urban real estate resources more efficiently, it is not a perfect system and on occasions could experience failure with the attendant harmful consequences. (2) Government interventions, which are the only known panacea to such market shortcomings, are not perfect either. They are also prone to failure with the attendant undesirable consequences. Some economists have argued that government failure even causes more damage to societal well-being than market failure (Coase, 1960; Calabresi, 1968, p. 68). (3) The Coase theorem contends that markets can internalise their own shortcomings should transaction costs be zero. The presence of transaction costs in the price system presents a formidable impediment for markets to self correct their failures.

Thus changes in transaction costs on account of particular policies serve as the explicit proxies for estimating the economic impacts of particular real estate policies. In addition to the transaction costs mentioned above government interventions also come at costs, which also have to be factored in the calculation. The most notable costs associated with government interventions include the costs of establishing and running policy enforcement institutions (see Coase, 1960, p. 44; Arrow, 1969, p. 48). To test the validity of the Coase theorem in urban sub-Saharan African real estate policy, it is important to compare the change in transaction costs with the change in benefits associated with the policy. Accordingly, for urban sub-Saharan Africa real estate policies to be declared efficient, they should not push the extra transaction costs incurred on account of the policy beyond the extra benefits generated by the policy. Alternatively, benefits forgone due to the policy should not exceed the transaction costs saved on account of the policy (see further Harberger, 2002).

The benefits of particular policies are inclusive of the measure of the improvement in welfare of individuals affected by the policy. To evaluate urban real estate impacts, however, the three basic postulates of welfare economics (Harberger and Jenkins, 2002) can be deployed and made more relevant to real estate markets. The postulates stipulate:

1. The voluntary (competitive) demand price of an urban real estate policy represents the value of the policy to individuals affected by the policy.
2. The voluntary (competitive) supply price of a policy represents the value placed on the policy by the supplier of the policy.
3. To obtain a measure of net benefits or costs for an aggregate or individuals or for sub-Saharan African society as a whole, one simply adds up (across the individuals in the relevant group) the costs and benefits measured according to 1 and 2.

In Figure 3.6, the x-axis denotes the benefits that affected individuals derive from urban real estate policies, *P*. The y-axis denotes the transaction costs associated with particular urban real estate policies. *DD* and *SS* represent the demand and supply for policy *P* respectively. Assume that the level of transaction costs pertaining on particular urban sub-Saharan African real estate markets before the introduction of the policy concerned is TC_m with the associated benefits of B_m. If the policy raised transaction costs to say TC_1 the benefits derived from policy, *P* will be say B_1. Accordingly, the extra transaction costs attributable to the *P* can be measured as OTC_m minus OTC_1. The extra transaction costs generate a reduction in benefits from OB_m to OB_1.

The scale of the benefit forgone on account of the policy is equal to OB_m minus OB_1. At these levels of costs and benefits, since extra transaction costs brought about by *P* are far higher than the associated benefit (negative benefit), the policy is inefficient by the criterion of the Coase theorem. At such high transaction costs policy suppliers will be oversupplying policy at a level that should be generating benefits of B_{s1}. Since the actual benefits received from the policy, B_1, are far less than the expected benefit, B_{s1}, it implies that the resources used in the supply of the policy are not all translating into efficiency or tangible benefits.

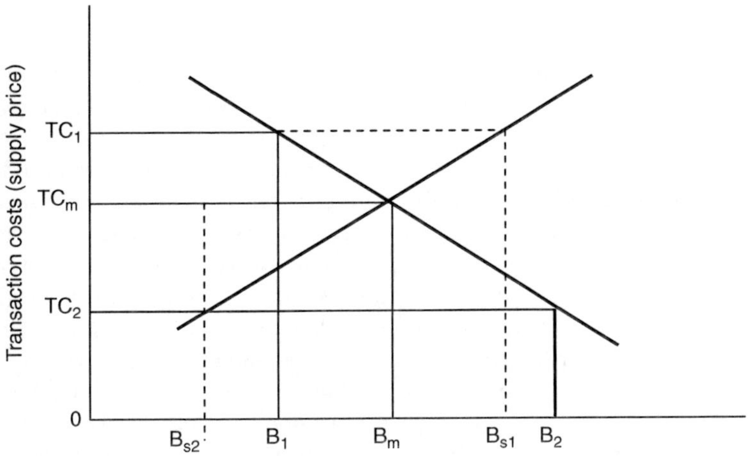

Figure 3.6 Transaction costs analysis of policy

Some level of waste of resources will thus be occurring in the course of supplying the policy. Conversely, if the policy reduced transaction costs from its original level of TC_m to TC_2 the cost saved on account of the policy is given by $0TC_m$ minus $0TC_2$. The benefit or demand price implication of this phenomenon is that an extra benefit of up to $0B_2$ is generated. The actual scale of the benefit can be measured as $0B_m$ minus $0B_2$. By the Coase theorem criterion since the policy induce savings in transaction costs as well as increased benefits beyond what existed before the policy, the policy is worthwhile. At this level rationality suggests that policy suppliers may be unwilling to supply in a sustainable manner, policies at this benefit and transaction costs levels. They will thus be most willing to supply at benefit levels B_{s2}. In a competitive environment the interplay of demand and supply forces will ultimately lead to a policy demand and supply level at which at least the transaction costs equals the benefits. That is at a level where supply price equals demand price.

Having outlined the conceptual dynamics a means has to be found to measure the actual demand and supply prices associated with particular urban real estate policies in reality. This will enable an understanding of the actual level at which the concerned policies are being supplied and consumed, together with their welfare implications.

3.7 Summary

The chapter has presented a proposition that provides a systematic view of the ends to which urban real estate policies in sub-Saharan Africa should be directed by specifying the relations between transaction costs and economic outcomes. Transaction costs are presented as the focal variable for measuring the efficiency of urban real estates. By employing insights from this chapter to analyse urban real estate policies in sub-Saharan Africa, an adequate understanding of the true economic impacts of particular policies can be gained. These insights would ultimately help in identifying urban real estate policies that are, in fact, to the best interest of particular sub-Saharan Africa economies. Before turning to the analysis it is vital that the real estate policies in question are examined in much more detail to establish their nature and intended objectives. This is the end to which the next chapter is directed.

4

The Political Economy of Sub-Saharan African Real Estate Policies

4.1 Introduction

As discussed in the first two chapters, the quest for poverty alleviation and economic development in Africa is now a matter of international concern. Yet, extant policies that continue to dictate proceedings in real estate sectors of most African nations have been constructed in a way that concentrate benefits and wealth on a few while spreading costs and poverty over a larger segment of the population.

These policies that continue to impose greater restrictions on poverty alleviation and economic development efforts have emanated from the peculiar political and economic history of Africa. An understanding of how these political events continue to shape the performance of land markets in these countries within the contexts of contemporary economic learning is thus key to understanding the policy directions required for success. This chapter employs insights developed in Chapter 3 to examine the historical political events that have led to the promulgation of such real estate policies. To aid the discussion it is useful to offer a brief overview of the classes of real estate policies currently operational in the region.

4.2 Taxonomy of sub-Saharan Africa real estate policies

The most commonly encountered classification of sub-Saharan Africa real estate policies in the existing body of research (Asiama, 1980; 1984; 1990; Kasanga, 1990; Brobbey, 1991; Platteau, 1992; Larbi, 1994; 1995; Sjaastad and Bromley, 1997; Okoth-Ogendo, 2000; Quan, 2000; Hatch Associates, 2002; Deininger, 2003) adopts broad labels or stated purposes of the policies. Thus real estate policies are classified as Land

Titling Policies, Deeds Registration Policies, Compulsory Acquisition Policies, Land Use Policies, Zoning Policies, Expropriation Policies and so on. Such classification provides a way of subjecting policies to individualistic and detailed scrutiny.

However, this approach is convenient to policy specific or micro level analysis. The approach becomes simply unwieldy at the macro level, the level of analysis envisaged by this chapter. For instance, Ghana alone (1 out of 40 sub-Saharan African countries) lists about 166 pieces of real estate policies in the 1999 land policy document of Ghana. The use of the conventional classification does not offer much help for macro level analysis. Indeed most research works that have followed this classification have suffered from in-exhaustiveness. For instance, Quan (2000) could only deal with Land Title Policies and Land Redistribution Policies in sub-Saharan Africa.

Furthermore, reliance on the purpose specific classification is fraught with technical limitations. Some of these limitations include:

(1) The variability of language and the multiplicity of meanings that could be associated with certain words used in particular policies, which may even be subject to change at different times and contexts, introduce significant ambiguities and uncertainties in identifying the true purpose of policies from its literal construction.
(2) As Slapper and Kelly (2001) point out, owing to the generality in their application policies they are invariably written in a way that ensure they can be effectively applied in various circumstances without the need to detail with those situations individually. This means in practice that it may be common to find ambiguities in the literal provisions of policies regarding how the policy envisaged particular situations to be dealt with when they arise sometime in the future.
(3) As Lindblom (1977) has maintained, policy elites prefer not to be precise in defining the goals of policies so that they can muddle through in the course of implementation to suit their changing personal ends. The Administration of Lands Act of 1962 of Ghana (discussed below), which empowers the state to manage Stool and other lands in Ghana and similar laws in other African countries is a good example. The Act made no attempt to define what constitutes management and left that decision in the hands of bureaucrats to determine from time to time. In addition, in Ghana what constitutes 'public interest' under the country's acquisition policies remains ill defined and uncertain (see Larbi et al., 2004). Reliance merely on

the literal provisions or labels of policies for classification in any analysis may thus be fraught with formidable impediments, which could lead to misleading conclusions.

It is accordingly indispensable in seeking to understand the true economic impacts of particular policies to go beyond the stated purposes or labels of the policies themselves and explore how the policies have actually been employed in practice. It is only in understanding how the policies have been used in practice that meaningful examination of their impacts can be ascertained. This forms the basis of the taxonomy devised in the next section.

4.2.1 The taxonomy

As discussed above, the taxonomy is based on the substantive way policies have been used in practice rather than their stated literal purposes. In general African policy makers have been concerned with the maximisation of two main utility variables, namely: (1) security of tenure; and (2) personal aggrandisement and the maintenance of strong client relationships. It is thus argued that the policies they enact, whether in the field of real estate or any other area, will be those that will enable them to maximise these variables. Enacting policies and laws that constrain and regulate the activities of those whose activities are considered threats to their security of tenure for instance can accomplish the first variable. These policies render such people and their activities helpless and ineffective, thereby posing very little threat to their security of tenure. This class of policies will hereinafter be referred to as *regulative policies*. In the real estate field, this regime of policies encompasses all policies enacted to regulate the activities of market participants such as land use policies, conveyancing and documentation policies.

The second utility variable can be maximised by enacting policies that will legitimise the distribution of material favours to policy makers as well as their clients. Such policies will give the incumbent free access to the largesse of the state, which they can distribute to their clients in exchange for political support. In the real estate sector, this can take two main forms. Firstly, the government could acquire land and real estate resources on payment of full compensation for distribution. These classes of policies are herein after referred to as *distributive policies*. In another vein, the government could confiscate or nationalise land without the payment of full compensation for distribution. Such policies are herein after termed *redistributive policies*.

Based on this analysis it can be concluded that real estate policies in sub-Saharan Africa fall into three main categories: (1) regulative policies; (2) distributive policies; and (3) redistributive policies. The institutional frameworks together with their internal procedures established to enforce these three main policies is considered a fourth category of policy and will hereinafter be referred to as (4) delivery policies. This is shown diagrammatically (Figure 4.1) below.

It is worthy of note that in this taxonomy the potential concentration of costs on a few under any policy does not necessarily make the policy unwise nor do widely diffused benefits necessarily justify the policy (see Lipsey, 1993, p. 410). The real merit of any of these policies depends on the net benefits they foster (see Chapter 3). As Kaldor (1939) and Hicks (1939) have illustrated, policies can be regarded as desirable when they meet the Pareto criteria or at worse when the net gainers could compensate the net losers to the extent that they would be no worse off after the implementation of the policy. This can only be ascertained through empirical studies, and the taxonomy provides a predictive analytic guide for such analysis. Thus this taxonomy devised will be employed

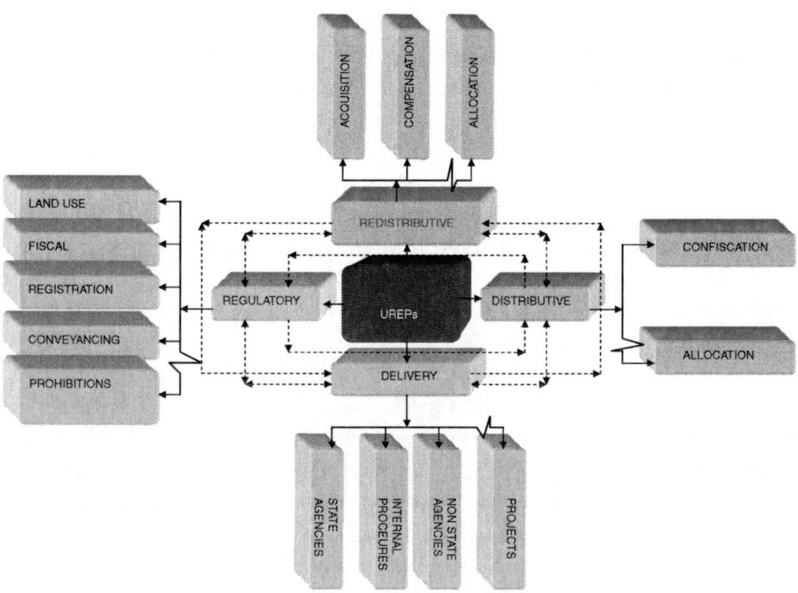

Figure 4.1 The real estate policy taxonomy

in the rest of the study to examine the economic impacts of urban real estate policies in sub-Saharan African.

4.3 The real estate policy process

We now employ transaction costs and public choice theories to examine the political influences that have shaped real estate policies in sub-Saharan Africa with greater emphasis on Ghana. The conditions that have given rise to poverty in Africa are manifold, ranging from corruption, political instability, unfair international trading rules, sedated policies and laws, poor social and economic infrastructure, weak capital and financial markets, poor human resource development systems, malfunctioning land and real estate markets, and so forth. While efforts by rich nations to rid Africa of poverty through debt cancellation and aid donations provide no more than temporary relief, they are appreciated, but only to the extent that they help remove the conditions that are giving legitimacy to poverty in Africa. Otherwise, they warrant no great confidence.

In recent times, perhaps as a response to learning in new institutional economics of the 1970s, there is growing concern about making land tenure contribute meaningfully to the quest for poverty alleviation in Africa. This has inspired a closer look at the workings of real estate markets and government interventions in the region (Quan, 1997; Toulmin and Quan, 2000; Quan, 2000; Platteau, 2000; Delville, 2000; Okoth-Ogendo, 2000; Cousins, 2000; Palmer, 2000; Alden Wily and Hammond, 2001; Deininger, 2003). It is well established in market economic theory that, from an efficiency standpoint, land policies, like all forms of government interventions, are desirable only on occasions of true market failures and excessive transaction costs (Coase, 1960; Pigou, 1962; Tisdell, 1974). Yet in reality, extensive research (Hogwood and Gunn, 1984b; Rose, 1986; Nakamura, 1987; Stone, 1989; Jenkins-Smith, 1990; Lindblom and Woodhouse, 1993; Stone, 1996; Dye, 1998; Sutton, 1999; Parsons, 2003) has established that policies, whether in sub-Saharan Africa or in advanced capitalists economies, are determined largely on political and bureaucratic considerations sometimes merely spiced with economic reasons. This implies that a prerequisite to understanding the prospects of these policies is an appreciation of the political and bureaucratic forces that have constructed them. The polar departure here is the usage of economic analysis; in particular, transaction costs theory to explicate the historical origins of the policies that are dictating proceedings on these land markets.

4.4 Pluralism, public choice and transaction costs

The processes by which policies evolve vary markedly between societies and political systems (Cobb and Elder, 1972; Jenkins-Smith, 1990; Rochefort and Cobb, 1994). These processes take two alternative forms – rationalist and pluralist. Many have suggested that the rationalist approach to policy making has very little practical application (see further Laswell, 1956; Simon, 1957; Mack, 1971; Jenkins, 1978; Hogwood and Gunn, 1984a; Rose, 1986). The sub-Saharan African real estate policy-making processes are thus better explained using the pluralist policy making framework.

Pluralists deem public policies as the outcome of free competition between ideas and interests of many actors (Parsons, 2003). The typical actors in the process comprise public opinion leaders (Hogwood and Gunn, 1984a), the media, experts and professionals including think tanks (Parsons, 2003), bureaucrats (Niskanen, 1971), interest groups (Sutton, 1999), and politicians and voters (Downs, 1957). The complexity in this process stems from the fact that each policy actor tends to hold peculiar ideologies, values and interests that may be irreconcilable with those of others (Dahl and Lindblom, 1953). The way forward in such a policy system is through mutual adjustment, consensus seeking and incrementalism (Lindblom, 1959; 1980; Nakamura, 1987; Stone, 1989; Sabatier and Jenkins-Smith, 1993; Lindblom and Woodhouse, 1993). Progress is thus made in the pluralist policy process only when there are means of resolving conflicts of ideologies, values and interests between policy actors in a way that makes the formation of Pareto efficient policies[1] possible.

Public policy studies (McKean, 1965, pp. 496–505; Haveman, 1976a, pp. 235–50) suggest that in a pluralist process as described above optimal outcome in policy formation is achievable when all actors involved are fully equipped with relevant knowledge and are willing to negotiate and build consensus on policy choices that offer the ultimate means of maximising individual and societal welfare. Additional requirement is 'a political process in which the full set of impacts of a decision on all citizens, the poor and minority groups as well as those with power, be somehow registered with decision makers' (Haveman, 1976b, p. 239). The ideal form of the pluralists' process thus can be likened to a 'smoothly functioning market system' in which the full costs and gains of any decision as experienced by individuals would be brought to bear on the decision maker (Jenkins-Smith, 1990, p. 30). Such an ideal policy process is based on the assumption of a widely diffused power structure in which each participant has equal influence on problem definition, agenda setting and policy choice (Parsons, 2003). It is nonetheless well established that such an ideal policy process is non-existent in reality (Jenkins-Smith, 1990) because unequal distribution of power between policy actors is a pervasive fact of political life (Brams, 1968, p. 461). Often, it is the government of the day that dominates the policy process.

Public Choice economics scholarship (see further Downs, 1957; Tullock, 1967; Niskanen, 1971; 1973; Buchanan, 1975; McLean, 1972; Mueller, 2003) presents a formal objection to the conventional welfare economics view that governments are benevolent and public interested actors with sacrosanct public policy roles. Accordingly, the mere fact that government is involved in the policy process is no guarantee that the policy outcome will be or is intended to be beneficial to the poverty alleviation and economic development aspiration of the society. Indeed the very involvement of political forces in the policy process could make matters worse. Whether or not the involvement of government in the promulgation of particular policies is likely to make matters worse or not can be understood from a patient study of the policy processes (Mueller, 1989).

The origin of Public Choice theory is credited to the works of Buchanan and Tullock (1962), Tullock (1965) and Downs (1967). These works laid the basis for the debate on the dangers of politicisation of the economic and public policy processes. Particularly, Tullock (1965) and Downs (1967), basing their argument on the self interest maximising behaviours of political actors, illustrate the harmful consequences of a government that would become ever more autonomous and sovereign in the policy process. The extent to which this latter proposition has manifested in the land policy processes of sub-Saharan Africa is examined shortly.

While public choice theory provides a powerful and convincing model for explaining policy processes from the economic angles they are difficult to test in any meaningful quantitative terms in reality (see further Parsons, 2003, p. 311). Besides, public choice theory omits an explicit treatment of how differing levels of transaction costs could produce differing behavioural patterns in policy actors.

This is exceptional, given that, following Coase (1960), there is now something of a general agreement among economists that transaction costs form the crucial determinant of the efficiency of any exchange economy (Williamson, 1979; 1981; 1986). Thus, without exploring the implications of transaction costs on the so-called political exchange economy, it is impossible to imagine how policy problems that presents themselves today can be traced to their real sources. The basic thesis of transaction costs theory is that higher transaction costs impede while lower transaction costs promote efficiency in any exchange economy. The relevant costs here include background information search costs, organising formidable and identifiable policy groups, costs of negotiating policy contents, costs of consensus building particularly in the area of problem definition, agenda setting and selection of alternatives as well as costs of monitoring and enforcement of policies when enacted. Other important costs include the costs of overcoming mistrust, uncertainty, duplicity and opportunism that may exist in the policy process. An attempt is thus made here to explicitly incorporate these costs in the analysis of the sub-Saharan Africa land policy processes.

Competitive policy process akin to the democratic political regime is conventionally argued to offer the best model for efficient policy formation (Dahl, 1961; Cobb and Elder, 1972; Rochefort and Cobb, 1994; Jenkins, 1999). This volume takes issue with this position and argues on the contrary, that both competitive and monopolised policy processes offer identical potential for efficient policies if transaction costs were nonexistent. Their relative efficiency depends on their inbuilt comparative transaction costs. Thus a competitive policy process could thus be even more inefficient than a monopolised system if their inbuilt transaction costs are relatively higher.

4.5 Pluralism in action

Persistently, the African political scene has witnessed the concentration of power in the hands of a minority through various mechanisms. Some of the most popular mechanisms by which power has been successfully heaped on the minority include forced invasion, as in the colonial era, the creation of a one party state, military interventions and despotism in the emergent democratic processes. These political events have culminated in exorbitant transaction costs in the policy processes out of which the region's land policies have emerged. These events are discussed in turn.

4.5.1 The colonial regime

Much has been written about the despotic rule of colonial administrations in Africa and how those arrangements influenced the determination and definition of problems, set policy agenda and led to policy choice (Harris, 1975; Sender and Smith, 1986; Mabogunje, 1989; Platteau, 1992). Suffice to point out in this analysis that, during this period, the exploitative objective of the concept of colonialism (Kaniki, 1985) became the driving force behind the autocratic governance structure instituted out of which much of the initial real estate policies in the region emerged. The 1895 statement by the then UK Prime Minister, Lord Salisbury (cited in Kaniki, 1985) to the UK Parliament exemplifies the main concerns of the colonial monopoly administration:

> It is our business in all these new countries to make smooth the path for British commerce, British enterprise, the application of British capital, at a time when other paths, other outlets for the commercial energies of our race are being gradually closed by the commercial principles which are gaining more and more adhesion. In a few years it will be our people that will be masters, it will be our commerce that will prevail, it will be our capital that will rule ... this is a tremendous power, but it requires one condition. You must enable it to get to the country where its work is to be done.

To accomplish this end there was the need to raise the costs of political opposition so that indigenous Africans who present an imminent threat to this agenda are precluded from the policy process. The political institutions during this time were made up exclusively of the white minority. Policy decisions were arrived at without reference to Africans and Africans could only oppose policies from outside the formal policy making arena. Conflict in policy formation was thus between the social system and the formal decision-making body. This meant that transaction costs faced by Africans in seeing that their views are taken care of in the policy process was enormous. It entailed the formation of viable countervailing forces with strong opinion leaders whose views could not be ignored even though they operated outside of the formal policy arena. Agenda building and policy formation thus turns on two principal transaction costs elements. One is the cost at which the countervailing forces could expand issues to gain the attention and support of a wider, even international, interested group and the second being the costs that the colonial powers were likely to incur if they ignored the views of that group.

If the cost of ignoring the views of the expanded audience or international interested group was regarded as insignificant in comparison to the gains, the administration had enough motivation to ignore them. However, where it was costly to ignore, the administration was bound to take note of the countervailing forces. As Cobb and Elder (1972) explained, in such a situation issues that are unlikely to be ignored comprise: (1) issues that are more socially significant; (2) issues that have long term relevance; and (3) issues that lack clear precedent. Although with regard to land policies all these conditions were present, the critical determinant of whether the views of the opposing forces would have to be taken account of was the ability of the opposing forces to bear the costs of expanding the conflict beyond the local formal policy arena. This was well illustrated when it came to the promulgation of colonial land nationalisation policies. In some Eastern, Central and Southern African countries where the opposing forces were unable to bear the full costs of issue expansion, their views did not represent a significant threat to the colonial administration and hence they were conveniently ignored. In these countries, the colonial administration successfully enacted policies that vested all property rights in 'vacant lands' in the government of the day for redistribution (Noronha, 1985; Platteau, 1992). This tallies with the public choice view of what harm an overbearing sovereign can fashion.

In particular, in these countries the main beneficiaries of land policies of the colonial regime were the minority white settlers and private firms favoured by the metropole (Glickman, 1988, p. 28). A case in point are the land redistribution policies in East Africa under the colonial regime, in which, contrary to the well-developed peasant agriculture found in Uganda and other African countries at the time of colonisation (Kaniki, 1985), the beneficiaries of the redistribution of lands by the administration were the white minority. Such was the generosity of the redistribution policy that at one time Lord Delamere, a European entrepreneur, owned more than 400,000 hectares of land in Kenya (Kaniki, 1985). Similarly, in Southern Rhodesia (now Zimbabwe), by 1911, Europeans owned about 7,700,000 hectares, and by 1925 they owned 12,500,000 hectares at giveaway prices (Kaniki, 1985). Kaniki in fact reported that in Southern Rhodesia 'in 1894 each member of the Victoria and Salisbury columns recruited to crush the Ndebele was promised 6000 acres of farm land'. These represent the origins of the violent clashes over land in present day Zimbabwe.

Rationally, citizens will incur such transaction costs required to oppose such policies when they envisage the potential benefits to be at least commensurate with the costs. In countries such as Ghana, Nigeria and Ivory Coast where the opposing forces incurred the full costs of issue expansion around the 1890s they (the opposing forces) were able, in the case of Ghana for instance, to go all the way to England to protest to the English parliament and monarchy (Rimmer, 1992). Having expanded the issue this much, the colonial administrations in these countries could only ignore their views at extraordinary costs. They thus could not be ignored in fact (Mabogunje, 1989) and the policy of outright land nationalisation that took root in Eastern, Central and Southern Africa could not be applied in these West African countries (Rimmer, 1992). But in countries where the transaction costs for opposing such policies were unbearable the citizens became essentially cordoned off from the policy process and the process of policy making became a game for those who could afford it. In such countries opposing forces were ignored and the colonial administration had a free hand in dissipating the land resources to the white minority and European merchants (Sender and Smith, 1986) as exemplified above. Where they could not be ignored the administration gained access only to those lands that they acquired at full market prices (Meek, 1949). These policy decisions enacted more than a century ago continue to impose economic repercussions on some of these societies many years after the colonial era.

As a result of these policies for instance, land ownership structure in Eastern, Central and Southern Africa is severely skewed in favour of a few whites or Europeans. This has engendered postcolonial clamour for more equitable redistribution of land resources by Africans, which are being honoured through policy reforms at great costs (Toulmin and Quan, 2000). In some countries such as Zimbabwe the clamour is being honoured through forceful takeovers of lands owned by whites leading to violent clashes, loss of lives, political instability and insecurity. Meanwhile in West Africa, the successful opposition presented by the countervailing forces prevented such skewed land ownership structure in these countries. Land ownership is thus more proportionately distributed in these countries and this has not specifically led to remarkable policy reforms and political events.

Interestingly, however, across Africa, when it came to policies that regulated the activities and land transactions of indigenous land owners without necessarily nationalising the lands, the opposing forces that had successfully subverted the earlier land nationalisation policies were benign and presented no opposition whatsoever. These later regimes of policies appear to be enacted to ensure state surveillance over the activities of land owners with a view to pre-empting and forestalling any activity or transaction that is likely to threaten colonial exploitation or breach of the peace which was vital for their exploitation. Generally, the central theme of these regulative policies followed the recommendations of the West African Committee set up to look into the causes of land litigations in parts of West Africa. The key recommendation of the Committee was that all transfers of interest in land by Africans to non-natives should be considered invalid unless it were by lease for a term of years and was made with the consent of the Governor[2]

(Meek, 1949). In Ghana, for instance, this recommendation was implemented under section 3 of the Concessions Ordinance (No.19 of 1939) as well as the Local Government Ordinance of 1951. In Kenya, the Crown Lands Ordinance of 1902 prohibited land sales between Africans and Europeans altogether (Platteau, 1992, p. 97). These regulations were intended to curb the emergent litigation emanating from the then rampant land sales between African landowners and European concessionaires (Platteau, 1992; Woodman, 1996).

Having expended many resources in subverting nationalisation policies, the West African countervailing forces appeared to have exhausted their resources and could not mount similar opposition. Another explanation could be that rationally, the citizens will only incur such transaction costs when they envisage the potential benefits to be at least commensurate with the costs. A great deal of the lack of opposition to such policies may also relate to the transaction costs faced by the African landowners and countervailing forces in obtaining the relevant information to be able to appreciate the full and long term implications of such regulations of their rights (see Alchian, 1965; Demsetz, 1967; Pejovich, 1997). In the absence of such information, opposing forces saw very little gain in incurring the costs of opposing as those in West Africa had done previously. It is highly probable given the supply of available land that at the time the restriction on their property rights did not reduce their earnings from the land significantly. As Meek (1949) reveals, most of the transactions were informal and purchasers were comfortable with any form of receipt or site plans, most of which had no bearing on the true triangulations of the land in question. Since these regulative policies were only enforceable when transactions were brought to the attention of public officials, very few of such transactions were subjected to these policies given the state of land documentation. Thus the practical impacts may well be very minimal and hence do not warrant the costs of opposition. Indeed it is possible that eminent opposing forces perceived these policies as more beneficial even, as they enabled indigenous landowners to retain ownership of their lands even after they had sold the land.

It is evident from property rights insights (Becker, 1977; Ault and Ruthman, 1979; Pejovich, 1990) that had power in the policy process been fairly distributed and the costs of transactions including costs of obtaining relevant information and the costs of opposition been low, landowners would have favoured openness to free markets. Thus they would have opposed such trade restrictions that evidently reduced their rights to free trade if they could have afforded to.

4.5.2 The single party postcolonial regimes

Contemporary researchers argue that the autocratic or monopolised policy process instituted by the colonial regime became a convenient legacy for the succeeding postcolonial regimes. Hameso (2002), for instance, argues, 'the post-independence leaders took over the political kingdom in its enticing state'. Yet at independence some five decades ago, all postcolonial African countries emerged as democracies governed by constitutions framed along the lines of what pertained then in the respective imperial countries of the colonial authorities (Bratton and De Walle , 1994). Power within the policy process was thus diffused and transaction costs were expectedly lower than during the colonial era. Soon, 'political plurality was decried as bottlenecks to the project of "nation-building" and national unity'(Hameso, 2002).

The new African leaders who had adopted the socialists' ideological stance (Sender and Smith, 1986) faced enormous transaction costs in seeking to impose their views and ideologies on society. But the notion that socialism was the desired objective does not seem to fit well. This is because Europe for instance has had several social democratic governments that have embraced socialism without resorting to dictatorship. As it turned out, the real rationale for the choice of socialism at the time was twofold. First was to meet the growing demands of the emergent African bourgeoisies who had contributed to the achievement of independence and hence were better placed to demand favours from the incumbent. Second was the urgent need for the new nationalist governments to consolidate their power over the nations' resources to be able to institute central planning and state direction of resource allocation in accordance with the then mainstream development economics ideologies in vogue (Sender and Smith, 1986). This second agenda also gained credence from the then favourable outlook of socialism and state interventions in the Soviet Union and UK (Sender and Smith, 1986). As Young puts it:

> development economists, sympathetic to state-led development and dominant modernisation theories readily acknowledged that economic development came first with democratisation expected to follow later.
>
> (Young, 1996, p. 54)

This second rationale also made it more convenient for the first rationale to be accomplished through the distribution of favours to the clients of the state after the state had gained a free hand in the control and allocation of vital resources. Transaction costs that the incumbents would need to incur to accomplish these two agendas were likely to have been very high in a pluralist environment, as they would entail reaching agreement with all countervailing forces on policy agendas and contents as well as overcoming uncertainties in the policy process as explained earlier. Nonetheless in a truly democratic pluralist system where public opinion and the media matter in decision making, the costs of maintaining strong opposition are on the contrary likely to be low. In Ghana, for instance, the disclosed intent of Nkrumah's government to take the nation on a socialist development course when in power after independence infuriated some sections of the public leading to uproars and disturbances of all sorts in the country. This culminated eventually in the formation of the NLM, a vociferous opposition party. The NLM proposed a federal system of administration, ostensibly to ensure that they gain control over the rich natural resources within their strongholds. These NLM strongholds incidentally happen to be the most endowed with natural resources including gold, diamond and timber. This would have atrophied Nkrumah's proposed socialist experiment. The then colonial administration agreed to a referendum to decide the question of the type of political system to be adopted on the grant of independence. This took place three years before the eventual date of independence. Fortunately for Nkrumah's government, the proposed federal system was defeated at the referendum. This emboldened the post-independence Nkrumah government to pursue their highly venerated socialist development agenda (Card, 1975).

The costs of formulating these so-called socialist policies from the perspective of the incumbent was thus mammoth and the options left for the government of the day were either to incur the costs of negotiating with the opposition or incur the costs of eliminating the opposition all together. The second option meant that the transaction costs of opposition were to be raised so high as to make it unprofitable to oppose. Since the outcome of any negotiation with the opposing forces was uncertain and potentially unfavourable to the incumbents the first option was unsustainable. The most plausible option left was to raise the transaction costs of opposition and to ultimately eliminate the opposition altogether (Rimmer, 1992). In Ghana the transaction costs of opposition were pegged so high that it became practically impossible for the opposition to partake in the policy process. Actually, the idea of eliminating opposition is really something that coincides with a desire for totalitarianism and megalomania, not socialism.

This was realised by transforming the multiparty democratic colonial political legacy in which transaction costs were relatively low to a single party system in which the opposition faced virtually all the costs of consensus building. To achieve this goal, in 1960s and 1970s most countries in sub-Saharan Africa transformed their political systems from a pluralist multiparty system to a monopolised one party system. Such was the commitment to power-hungry dictatorship that, during this period, 32 of the 54 African countries converted from a multiparty political system to a single party political system (Bratton and de Walle, 1994). By the end of this conversion period, the power to enact policy became almost exclusively concentrated in the hands of the incumbent with all opposing forces and pressure groups substantially cordoned off from the policy process.

Ultimately, in countries such as Ghana, this was achieved by removing the constitutional provisions that mandated decentralised government structures. This was followed by the rapid expansion of presidential powers in tandem with the removal of constitutional checks on the executive branch of government and then the imposition of a single party state (Daddieh, 2001). Nevertheless, this path to the single party state was rugged. The process commenced by discrediting political opposition. Indeed political opposition was viewed as despicable (Hameso, 2002). In Malawi the leadership argued: 'there is no opposition in heaven. God himself does not want opposition – that is why he chased Satan away. Why should Kamuzu [the then president] have opposition?' (Decalo, 1992, p. 10). Chinua Achebe painted the picture of the conversion process in Nigeria more succinctly as: 'all argument should cease and the whole people speak with one voice and that any more dissent and argument outside the door of the shelter would subvert and bring down the whole house' (Achebe, 1967, p. 37). These were only to prepare the ground for what was to come. Transaction costs of opposition were to be explicitly heightened. The costs of opposition in some countries eventually became literally equivalent to the price of human life and to incur it meant to choose death in place of life. In Ethiopia opposition was met with physical elimination and liquidation (Hameso, 2002). In Ghana, the process was more dramatic and extraordinary and in the event it led to the promulgation of land laws whose concealed agenda was to crush the opposition. Paradoxically these land Acts continue to form the thrusts of land policies in Ghana. The Ghana case is peculiar and needs further elaboration.

4.5.2.1 The Ghana case

Nkrumah, the first Prime Minister of Ghana, devoted the first nine years of his administration to eliminating the opposition (Card, 1975). At the time of independence, the main leaders of the opposition, the professional elites, had strong family or lineage ties with the Chiefs in Ashanti and Akim-Abuakwa communities of Ghana (Card, 1975). Chiefs were by custom political leaders of their respective communities as well as the custodians of all the land resources of their respective communities. They thus commanded great influence. Meanwhile their elevated status during the colonial era (Noronha, 1985) placed them in the position of a parallel opposing political power (Bretton, 1967; Rimmer, 1992; Firmin-Sellers, 1996). Given the land resources they controlled, the lineage ties that the Ashanti and Akim Abuakwa Chiefs had with the main political opposition parties and the parallel political power they represent, they presented an important obstacle to the socialist agenda of Nkrumah. Nkrumah could thus make meaningful headway only if the manoeuvres of the chiefs and their allies could be quelled or at least made too costly for them to engage in policy making or even to lend financial or other supports to other opposition organs.

Nkrumah vowed to make sure that some of those who constituted the main obstacle would 'run away and leave their footwear behind' (see Kasanga, 2002). Nkrumah pursued this agenda by first infiltrating customary law and practices with politics. During these periods, there were rampant destoolments (removals) of chiefs who were known sympathisers of the opposition in Ghanaian communities such as Kade, Abodom in Akim Abuakwa (Government of Ghana, 1959). These were followed up with legislation to remove for instance the Offinsohene (Chief of the Offinso community) to a place 30 miles' radius from his state while the Gyasehene of Akim Abuakwa was banned from the state and ordered to stay 60 miles away (Government of Ghana, 1959).

As a follow on, five years ahead of the launch of Nkrumah's first Seven Year development plan and barely a year after formal independence, Nkrumah launched an arsenal of enactments aimed evidently at crashing the opposition. Amid the series of enactments to crash the opposition, ranging from the Preventive Detention Act, under which some opposition members were jailed without trial and The Sedition Act and the Criminal Act, which provided for the death penalty for political crimes without trial by jury were two land Acts. These land Acts were the Ashanti Stool[3] Lands Acts of 1958 and the Akim Abuakwa (Stool Revenue) Act of 1958. These Acts indeed heightened the transaction costs of the chiefs and the opposition as it essentially took away the fiduciary role of the affected Chiefs over their land and thus stripped them of stool land revenue. Stool land revenue were alleged to be the main source of finance for the opposition. Such was the priority attached to these land

Acts that they were enacted under certificate of urgency. The motion for the Akim Abuakwa (Stool Revenue) Act, 1958 bill presents a telling example. The then Minister for Local Government in presenting the bill to parliament for debate and enactment into law stated as follows:

> Notwithstanding anything contained in the Standing Orders of this House if by 11.45 a.m. today the motion for the second reading of the Akim Abuakwa (Stool Revenue) bill has not been disposed of Mr. Speaker do put any question necessary to dispose of it. That the Committee stage be taken immediately after the second reading; that if by 12:40 p.m. the Committee stage has not been disposed of, the chairman do put any question necessary to dispose of it and report the bill forthwith; and that if by 12:50 p.m. the motion for the third reading has not been disposed of Mr. Speaker do put any question necessary to dispose of it.
>
> (Government of Ghana, 1958)

By this time the Criminal Acts that came along as a package with these land enactments had almost made opposition equal to accepting to be jailed or even killed. Such high transaction costs were evidently unbearable and the opposition could hardly subject the Act to any scrutiny. Such an important Act was passed by parliament in an hour and a half unexpurgated. Subsequently these Acts, together with other succeeding Acts relating to Stool lands, were eventually consolidated under the Administration of Lands Act, 1962. Under this new Act the principle was expanded to cover all Stool lands in the country. This Act is presently termed 'vesting policy' in Ghanaian parlance. The accomplishment of these vesting policies in Ghana has been phenomenal. They vest virtually all the ingredients of property rights in the affected Stool lands in the government of the day for redistribution. The rights expropriated from the affected Stools include the right to: (1) possess; (2) use; (3) manage; (4) alienate; (5) secure tenure; (6) bequeath; and (7) mortgage.

Table 4.1 depicts the Stool lands affected by the vesting policy in Ghana so far.

In its current form, the policy gives the government direct control over all incomes from the affected Stool lands as well as non-affected Stool lands in the country. To this extent Stools in the country have legal rights to only 22.5 per cent of all revenue from Stool land transactions. That is to say 77.5 per cent of gross Stool land revenue (capital and or rental) is deducted at source effectively as tax. In this context it is

Table 4.1 Stool lands vested in the government

No.	Location	Region	Instrument	Date	Size
1	Stool lands in Koforidua	Eastern	E.I.[4]195	1/11/61	19.47 km^2
2	Stool lands in Nkawkaw	Eastern	E.I.195	1/11/61	n/a
3	Efutu and Gomoa Ajumako Lands	Central	E.I. 206	21/11/61	n/a
4	Kumasi part 1 lands	Ashanti	Act 123	14/06/62	24.55 km^2
5	Winneba	Central	E.I. 83	6/6/63	1 mile
6	Accra-Tema	Greater	E.I.108	18/9/64	n/a
7	Inchaban	Western	E.I. 28	20/07/98	n/a
8	30 Stool lands in Brong Ahafo[5]	Brong Ahafo	E.I.46	18/2/61	n/a

Source: Field survey – compiled from the records of the Lands Commission, Ghana.

unclear the sense in which Asiama (1990, p. 247) argues that the vesting policy 'leaves ownership substantially in the landowner's hands'.

The Act actually made government through its agencies the managers of these affected Stool lands and it is empowered to allocate these lands to potential developers without reference to the expropriated owners and at the discretion of the officials in charge. These lands are allocated on leasehold bases at about 90 per cent rental subsidy. Thus, as a by-product of this Act it became possible for benefits by way of land allocation to be concentrated on the privileged few beneficiaries of the allocated lands at the expense of the expropriated owner and a larger segment of the non-benefiting Ghanaian taxpayer. It is now well established in the literature that the main beneficiaries of lands under these policies are the top civil servants and influential figures in the Ghanaian society (Asiama, 1990; Antwi, 2000). To underscore the full repercussions of this Act it is therefore pertinent that the costs imposed on landowners and the taxpayer as well as the benefits from the management of the revenue and the allocation of these lands are ascertained.

Nkrumah's particular interest in crushing the Chiefs to gain exclusive control over policy making has led to these policies that discriminated against Stools, as opposed to family, clan and individual land owners, thereby heaping costs on the stools. Apart from regulating their incomes, Nkrumah enacted policies that subjected Stool land transactions in particular to government surveillance and scrutiny. This regulative policy is referred to in Ghana commonly as 'Concurrence policy', which was fashioned along the lines of the recommendations of the

West African Lands Committee (see note 1). This can be explained in the light of the reasons for enacting the vesting policies against the Stools. The concurrence policy has now been given constitutional assent in Article 267(3) of the 1992 constitution, though with a somewhat different slant towards land use planning. By the time Nkrumah finished enacting these laws, the costs of opposition had been made practically unbearable and real opposition had vanished from the scene (Card, 1975). Nkrumah could thus now pursue the socialist agenda, which as mentioned was itself motivated by the need for self-aggrandisement (see further Card, 1975; Killick, 1978). An important land policy that underpins socialism is the policy that gives unhindered access to land (Buchanan, 1999). The colonial policy on expropriation was adequate as it had enough safeguards against abuse of government powers in compulsory acquisitions and unfairness in the acquisition process by insisting that all government acquisition must receive certification by the Courts. This however was too constraining for the Nkrumah regime as it made arbitrary use of power in the manner envisaged under Nkrumah's socialist agenda practically impossible. This meant that the transaction costs of implementing socialism in Ghana by the one party regime were high, entailing the payment of compensation for every piece of land required for the socialists' production and development agenda, or risk hostilities and revolts from the populace. The conundrum that such high transaction costs presented was made explicit in the speech by Nkrumah in launching the seven-year development plan (1963–70). Nkrumah notes

> The state will be controlling on behalf of the community the dominant share of the economy. This would have been accomplished without ever having to resort to such expedients as nationalisation, which if carried out with full compensation would only change the ownership of the means of production ... and if carried out without such compensation would inevitably incur such a large measure of hostility as to make our development plans very much more difficult to achieve.
>
> (quoted from Larbi, 1995, p. 42)

With the costs of overt nationalisation clearly unbearable to the government a clever and subtle approach to nationalisation had to be found if socialism was to succeed. This meant that a new law was required that offered reduced transaction costs in state land acquisition. The State Lands Act, (Act, 125) of 1962[6] was thus passed. The memorandum to this Act betrays the true intent of this policy. It established that

> The bill dispenses with the need to obtain a certificate from a court to effect vesting of land in the republic, and provides that a declaration by the president shall constitute the vesting instrument.

Though this Act did not specifically exempt the state from compensation payments, the requirement for compensation payment under the law has been so spuriously contrived to make compulsory acquisition without compensation legally possible. Under this policy it became possible to divorce compulsory acquisition from compensation in such a way that it was possible for government to acquire land and use immediately and pay the compensation at a time of their choosing. Apart from the lack of interest payments on delayed compensation payments, which is a serious problem in a country where inflation and poverty are endemic, it has been possible under this Act for government to place an embargo on compensation payments altogether since 1973 (Larbi, 1995). Thus while all expropriation under the colonial policy were paid for, there is a huge domestic debt arising out of unpaid compensation. The actual size of the debt remains unknown but is believed to be in the hundreds of millions of dollars (see Hatch Associates, 2001).

Thus during the era of single party political economy, the regulatory and distributive policies started by the colonial autocratic state widened and strengthened even in countries where, due to local oppositions, the colonial governments took a more cautious approach to land policy. The policies have also established a culture in which the distribution of vital resources, including land, during this era became the preserve of the dictatorial regime through coercion rather than consensus (Hameso, 2002). Thus with soaring transaction costs of opposing looming large in the sub-Saharan African policy process, the policies that emerged during this era, as insights from public choice shows, were those likely to serve the parochial interest of their originators at the expense of the wider society. What is more disquieting is that the policies enacted during this era have proved immutable and they continue to dictate real estate market proceedings in sub-Saharan Africa. Nonetheless a more far-reaching consequence of these political regimes is the insurrections and military takeovers that they engendered.

4.5.3 Military regimes

Events of the single party regimes engendered much anxiety among the citizens who had anticipated much welfare gains from the achievement of independence (Sender and Smith, 1986). If transaction costs were low, political opposition and pressure groups with the right incentives would emerge to present alternatives and compete for power. This would have led to a change of government at the next elections or even a vote of no-confidence. However, given that in most of these countries transaction costs of doing that had been made almost unbearable and that this had culminated essentially in the criminalisation of opposition, it was impossible for such a process to emerge. What followed was predictable. If frustration, dissatisfaction and grievances are sufficiently prolonged or sharply felt, aggression is quite likely, if not certain to occur (Gurr, 1993; 2003). This may have instigated a spate of military takeovers through force and violent means on the continent. Thus a culture of transfer of political power by force in the form of military coups, brutalities, warfare, insurrections, mutinies, severe riots and significant political assassinations (Zolberg, 1968) became the least expensive option. Such was the spate of force power transfers in Africa under this era that between 1960 and 1985 there were 131 attempted coup d'etats in Africa of which 60 were successful and three countries experienced six successful military coups (Bratton and de Walle, 1994).

Out of the 54 independent African countries, only six have not experienced attempted or successful coups since independence (Bratton and de Walle, 1994). By 1970, half of the independent African countries (all of which stated as multiparty democracies) had military governments installed through military coups d'etat (Bratton and de Walle, 1994). The costs of opposition in these regimes became even more unbearable than the two earlier models: colonial and single party regimes, discussed above. As Chauveau (1997) noted in the case of Ivory Coast, the state could choose at any time to invoke its overreaching rights and did not hesitate to enforce its wishes, with threats of prison if necessary when it was challenged.

Policies thus became what the sovereign desired and not necessarily what was good for the country. Like the previous autocratic regimes, the land policies enacted took two main forms: (1) those that gave the government of the day the rights to redistribute land resources by taking landownership away from the indigenous owners; and (2) those that regulated the free trade of real estate commodities. An example of (1) is the case of Nigeria where, like Ghana, the colonial government could not confiscate land in view of opposition, so the then military regime successfully enacted the Land Use decree of 1978, which was subsequently incorporated in the constitution of 1979 and 1999 respectively of Nigeria. The decree required certificates of occupancy to be obtained from the government for land held under customary and statutory rights and the payment of rent to the government. In another instance, one of the fundamental results of the Ethiopian Revolution was the nationalisation of all urban lands without compensation under the Government Ownership of Urban Land and Extra Houses Proclamation (No. 47 of 1975) (see Asiama, 1990, p. 242). In addition, in countries such as Ghana, at the time of the military interventions policies existed and continue to exist that gave the government virtually free rights to bring any land in the country under their control for redistribution. Many more lands were thus confiscated under these policies. By the end of these military interventions 20 out of the 40 countries in sub-Saharan Africa had nationalised lands and vested in the respective governments the power to redistribute these lands (see Mabogunje, 1989). These policies were passed without much opposition as a result of the prevailing soaring costs of opposition.

Though much of the regulatory land policies enacted under the previous regimes remained in force, some regimes had need to enact some more. For instance one of the fundamental outcomes of the 1966 military interventions in Ghana by the National Liberation Council (NLC) was the promulgation for the first time in the country a regulative land policy that discriminated against foreigners. The policy, which has now been given constitutional backing under Article 266 of the 1992 constitution of Ghana, restricted the length of time foreigners could own land in the country at any particular time to 50 years. This policy came as part of a range of discriminatory policies by the regime, which proscribed foreign investors from engaging in business activities such as retail and wholesale trade below certain turnover, taxi and trucking services, produce brokerage, baking, printing and manufacture of cement blocks (Card, 1975). The motive behind this policy appears to have been to prevent foreign competition in particular areas of the economy as a way of propping up local entrepreneurs to take up the running of the economy and to safeguard the country against piecemeal colonisation. Yet it imposed significant restrictions on the rights of landowners in the country to free trade. Also during the 1981–92, military intervention led by Ft Lt Rawlings in Ghana, the right of chiefs to grant freehold rights in land even to usufruct owners who want documentary evidence of their holding was taken away by the government under article 265 of the 1992 constitution of Ghana. These laws have significantly attenuated the rights of indigenous landowners and could be festering poverty.

4.5.4 Emergent democratic regimes

After a long period of monopolised policy process and high costs of opposition there was from 1985 a general trend towards democratisation of the policy process in sub-Saharan Africa. It was envisaged by the proponents of democracy for Africa, namely the World Bank and other international development agencies, that such a policy process would entail much lower transaction costs and formidable opposition would emerge to provide a check on the arbitrary use of government power over the years. In truth if this happens one expects that real estate policies will move towards redressing true market failures and excessive transaction costs. Inefficient policies would also be recalled to pave the way for the efficient functioning of a real estate market. Thus understandably the move was greeted with great optimism. Nzongola-Ntalaja (1997, p. 9) writes:

> Since 1988, the people of Africa have risen to replace one-party and military dictatorships with multi-party democracy. From its violent outbreak in October 1985, in the street of Algiers, this new social movement for democracy has manifested itself all over the continent, changing the rules of the political game and bringing about meaningful reforms in the institutions of the post-colonial state.

After more than a decade of experimenting with democracy in Africa, very little improvement has been achieved, particularly in the real estate policy environment. Rather, much of the autocratic policies enacted to crush the opposition and to impose restraints on opposing forces have now received constitutional backings. Large state institutions and bureaucracies have been established with full complements of staff and annual budgets to enforce policies that were ad-hoc measures to raise the transaction costs of political opposition.

The question then is why has democracy failed to achieve any meaningful outcome as envisaged? Some argue that multiparty politics is not the best fit for Africa, where socio-political structures and potent identification are more of ethnicity and less of classes (Hameso, 2002). Others have dismissed this idea as unfounded as the African culture admits of consensus building in decision making. Employing some of the insights of the discussions above it would appear that democracy has failed to yield a better outcome because the transaction costs of organising and maintaining viable opposition still remain high in most African countries despite the installation of democracy in these countries. Most of these so-called democracies are thus operating essentially without practical opposition. This has led to the emergence of despotism in democratic systems. Virtually all the then military regimes in countries such as Gambia, Guinea Bissau until the downfall of Nino Viera, Guinea Conakry, Burkina Faso, Niger under Maina Sara,

Chad, Togo, Ghana, Egypt, Libya, Mauritania, Sudan and Madagascar metamorphosed quickly to become civilian governments (N'Diaye, 2000). In addition, those who also gained monopolist control over the political system through civil wars and mutiny, as in Liberia, Ethiopia, Uganda, Mozambique, Angola and Zimbabwe, managed to get themselves elected as democratic leaders. Yet these leaders have openly declared their discomfort with democracy as a decision making process. Many of these governments have locked in on power and would do anything to remain in power.

It was logical to expect these leaders to find a way, if possible, to circumvent the transaction costs that they were not using to maintain a high transaction costs structure for the opposing forces. These leaders had one important opportunity to accomplish that. Being the 'last' autocratic regimes, the onus of drafting new constitutions for the incoming democracies was on them. This offered them the opportunity to set the 'rules of the game'. Many of them took advantage of this opportunity and entrenched policies that heightened the transaction costs of the opposing forces into the new national constitutions. In Ghana for instance all the previously enacted Land Acts to crush the opposition, namely the vesting policy and the concurrence policy, together with the socialist-motivated policies, found their way into the national constitution. The Nigerian Land Use Act of 1978 enacted by the military regime to nationalise all lands in the country also found its way into the 1999 Nigerian constitution. Casting these policies in national constitutions meant that the opposition and subsequent administration had huge transaction costs to confront if they wished to reform these policies.

Though democracies in Africa bear substantial traits of a democratic system as known in theory (see Dahl, 1989; Przeworski, 1991; Valenzuela, 1992), very few practical changes have occurred in land and real estate policies. The new addition to land policies during this era is the spate of land redistribution programmes initiated in Southern African and some Eastern African countries to confer on the state the power to redistribute land resources with the view to reducing inequities in land ownership (Quan, 2000). Substantively, however, land and real estate policies have remained largely the same as pertained under the previous despotic regimes. Governments retain a large measure of power to redistribute land resources and regulate the activities of land market participants.

Clearly, the policy process of sub-Saharan Africa out of which real estate policies have emerged is invariably monopolised by incumbent political forces. It remains to be understood the actual social costs that such a monopolised policy process could be imposing on society.

4.6 The social cost implications

What emerges from the preceeding is that land policies in Ghana and sub-Saharan Africa in general have evolved from a dictatorial policy environment. Economic rationality suggests that policy actors are maximisers of self-interest whose prime concern is to increase their personal gain from policies (Downs, 1957). The impact of this rational behaviour of monopolists is conceptually illustrated in the policy environment can be illustrated in. In Figure 4.2 take the y-axis to represent the price of policies and the x-axis to represent the efficiency policy outputs. *MB, MC, SMB* and *SMC* represent the marginal benefits of policy to the monopolists, marginal costs of policy to the monopoly policy actor, the social marginal benefits of policy to society and the social marginal costs of policy to society respectively. Q_C denotes the level of efficiency at which an unregulated real estate market is expected to allocate real estate resources between competing uses, while Q_E represents the optimal expected efficiency output of the concerned real estate market in the Pareto sense.

In a well functioning policy process with relatively low transaction costs, policies will be devised through competitive negotiation to push the market equilibrium of a policy from its temporary or initial location at point *C* towards the optimal location, *F*. At this point the highest level of efficiency in policy formation is obtained at a social marginal

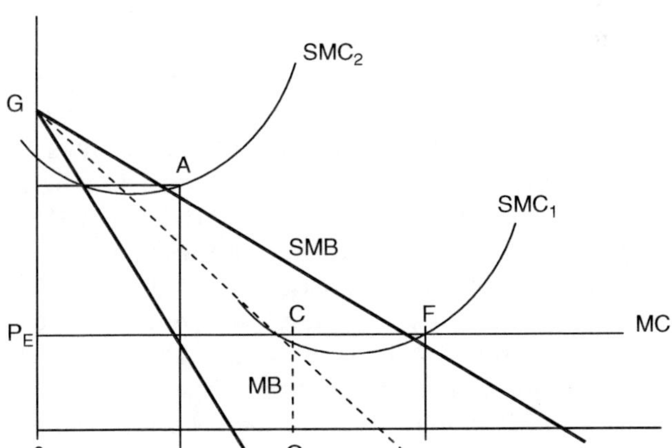

Figure 4.2 Self-interest maximising policy monopolist

cost of SMC_1. This social cost would be approximately equal to the social marginal benefits, *SMB* derived from the policy.

The marginal costs of OP_EFQ_E that will be incurred by the policy monopolist in securing policy at this level of efficiency will exceed the marginal benefits of OP_EBQ_M that he or she is likely to gain. Given the incentive structure of monopolists, self-interest maximising will lead them to choose policies that ensure that their personal (private) marginal benefits from the selected policies do not exceed their private marginal costs. Such policies will invariably maximise the interest of the incumbent monopolist. Incumbents and their compatriots will most likely choose policies such that the costs of the policies to them do not exceed the benefits they personally expect to derive from it. Thus policies under monopolist regimes are likely to occur at point *B* in Figure 4.2 above, where *MB* is the private marginal benefits expected to be derived from the policy by the monopolists.

Indeed, many of the policies enacted entrusted the allocation of land resources in the hands of the incumbent who according, to public choice theorists, are self-interest maximisers. Accordingly, access to these lands has generally not been dictated purely by efficient economic considerations but by the pursuit of the parochial interests of those in charge. For instance, as Rimmer cited by Killick (1978, p. 51) illustrates, the concerns of these administration were 'the enrichment of the government itself, (i.e. the ruler, of Ministers, of party leaders, of top civil servants, and possibly of numerous subordinate ranks of the public)'. See also Schtaz (1988). Thus access to these lands has tended to be heavily lopsided in favour of those who control the government in various ways rather than to those who are in real need.

Yet in sub-Saharan Africa in particular, efficient and equitable access to land represents an important plank in the quest for poverty alleviation. This is because in these countries a significant number of incomes are derived from agricultural activities particularly farming. Thus efficient and equitable access to land relates powerfully to the ability of the majority of the population of these countries to generate incomes, construct meaningful livelihood patterns for themselves and ultimately lift themselves out of poverty. Thus until this pattern of skewed access to land is corrected the potential for poverty alleviation will remain significantly atrophied. At this level the efficiency outcome of such policies is likely to fall short of what the market on its own would have produced, which would be, say, Q_M.

In Figure 4.2, the height of the marginal cost curve represents the social opportunity cost of the resource expected to be used in achieving efficiency output level Q_E. Yet while the true economic worth of resources likely to be employed to achieve the inefficient monopolist output level Q_M is OP_EBQ_M, the costs of inefficient behaviours of monopolists, which is referred to as X-inefficiency in economics discourse, is likely to lead to the use of expensive methods, lack of control and checks on the use of resources. This wasteful attitude of monopolists will force social marginal costs up from SMC_1 to SMC_2. This implies that under a self-interested monopolist policy environment, as in sub-Saharan Africa, policies enacted will most likely incur overall costs of OP_MAQ_M (which is > OP_EBQ_M) to generate an even more inefficient output of Q_M. Thu conceptually the difference between OP_MAQ_M and OP_EBQ_M represents the potential net social costs of real estate policies enacted under the various monopolist regimes in sub-Saharan Africa. This in itself creates a 'dead weight' loss represented by triangle ABF.

Transaction costs and economic rationality insights show that once such policies are evolved, regardless of their economic damage to society, it is improbable or at best very difficult to recall or even reform them. This is because in the first place these policies came through because the transaction costs associated with their subversion were too high. Yet since they offer the monopolist policy actors maximised utility, the monopolist has a greater incentive to retain them than to do otherwise. When the monopolist regimes that enacted those policies are removed and replaced by another monopolist policy actor, since African policy monopolists exhibit similar incentive structures, these policies are likely to become convenient tools with which they can maximise their utility. They are thus unlikely to recall such policies. In fact, if at the time of their assumption of office the benefits that are offered under those policies have been depleted by the previous regime, they are more likely to widen the remit of the policies or even pass new but similar laws so that more benefits can be obtained.

What is disquieting is that such land policies are much more difficult to reverse. This is because in the first place these policies materialised because the transaction costs associated with their subversion was too high. Yet, since they offer the monopolist policy actor maximised utility, the monopolist has greater incentive to retain the policy than to do otherwise. When the monopolist regime that enacted those policies are removed and replaced by another monopolist policy actor, since African policy monopolists have so far exhibited similar incentive structure, these policies are likely to become convenient tools with which they can maximise their utility. They are thus unlikely to recall such policies. In fact, if at the time of their assumption of office the benefits that are offered under those policies have been depleted by the previous regime, they are more likely to widen the remit of the policies or even pass new but similar laws so that more benefits can be obtained. Actually, even when the monopolist regimes are replaced by a regime that is mindful of the economy and wishes to reform these laws for better economic gains, the challenge may not be that easy because of the huge associated transaction costs. The relevant transaction costs in this case comprise the costs of providing information to convince the general populace of the need for the reform, the costs of seeking agreement on the way forward and more importantly the costs of convincing and seeking the consent of the existing body of beneficiaries, some of whom may be the clients of the incumbent, to consent to the reform of the policies. This existing body of beneficiaries includes politicians, bureaucrats, interest groups, clients and the influential and powerful in society, among others. It is likely that such consent may not be forthcoming leading to the possible continuous existence of inefficient policies even in 'democratic' systems.

4.7 Summary

The above discussion demonstrates that the power to enact real estate policies in Africa has for a long while been monopolised by a few. This is reflected in the institution of colonialism, single party policy process, military regimes and despotic policy processes within an emergent democracy. The discussion revealed that real estate policies enacted during periods of pure autocratic rule were no different from those enacted during the democratic era because transaction costs in organising and running a viable opposition, pluralism, negotiation and seeking consensus remained considerably high in both periods. Real estate policies were thus enacted with virtually no scrutiny and an absence of opposition to express indignation about inefficient decisions. Public opinion was of little concern, as political power was achieved not by the winning of votes.

Having made the transaction costs of opposition exorbitant to monopolise power, the monopolistic administrations faced very little or no transaction costs in policy formation, particularly in societies where the monopolisation of power was absolute. Policies thus emerged at the whim of the monopolistic government. Now with the policies now classified and their goals and basis appreciated the study proceeds with an outline for the processes for evaluating the impacts of these policies.

5
Real Estate Policy Reforms in Sub-Saharan Africa

5.1 Introduction

We have examined in the previous chapter the processes by which the real estate policies of sub-Saharan Africa have emerged, together with the types of real estate policies in operation in these economies. Over the years, the failure of these policies to bring about desirable economic outcomes has necessitated their reforms from time to time. In this chapter, we shall examine the ideologies that have driven these reforms. The difference between this and the previous chapter is that the previous chapter concentrates on the processes by which the policies have emerged while this chapter looks more closely at the ideological basis of the reforms.

5.2 First generation real estate policies

As discussed in the previous chapter, the first generation real estate policies in Africa were promulgated during the colonial encounter with Africa roughly between 1880 (Rodney, 1985) and 1956 (Morgan, 1992). Indeed, systematic research has established that all efficient economic outcomes from these policies were essentially by-products of activities intended to promote any of the threefold interests of the colonisers (Kaniki, 1985, p. 383; Fieldhouse, 1945–1980, p. 27; Mabogunje, 1989). The threefold interests were

> firstly ... to provide raw materials (agricultural products and minerals) to feed the machines of the industrial imperial power. Secondly ... to import manufactured goods from the imperial power and thirdly ... to be self-supporting.
>
> (Kaniki, 1985, p. 328; see also Fieldhouse, 1945–1980)

This necessitated the synchronisation of indigenous economic systems of Africa in line with these ends (Reyna and Down, 1988, p. 1). The key resources required from Africa to accomplish this were land and labour. However, since 'the strict definition of the ownership of land seemed to be the master key to African labour' (Lonsdale, 1985, p. 752 quoted in Sender and Smith, 1986, p. 22), land policy became the master key to the accomplishment of these goals. Perhaps the most significant disruption of the tenure system occurred when in the bid to mobilise land freely (Buell, 1965) for the intended large commercial farms (Bruce, 1987, p. 30) the administration sought to transfer land allocation authority from the community to the government.

This quest necessitated the application of 'legal, administrative and commercial rules already developed in European countries' in these African countries (Mabogunje, 1989, p. 83). For the British colonial dependencies, the received legal order was the 'Reception Clause', which made common law the doctrine of equity and statutes of general application already developed and applying in England equally applicable in British colonial dependencies (McAuslan, 2000). Similarly for Southern African dependencies (currently Botswana, Lesotho, Swaziland, Zimbabwe and Namibia) the received law was the Roman-Dutch law. The Portuguese laws were introduced in Mozambique and the French-speaking half of Cameroon (McAuslan, 2000, p. 76). The French Code Civil became the received law in French colonial dependencies (Delville, 2000). Backed by these laws, large indigenous land rights, particularly in Eastern and Southern Africa were forcefully taken over by the state (Munro, 1984; Kaniki, 1985; Delville, 2000; Okoth-Ogendo, 1982; 1994; 1998; 2000; McAuslan, 2000). It was only in West Africa that this free expropriation was largely checked by local resistance movements (Toulmin and Quan, 2000; McAuslan, 2000; Meek, 1949). Even so, in West Africa, although the administration owned only such lands as they actually acquired at full price (Okoin, 1999; Stamm, 2000; Meek, 1949), the conquered territories such as Benin in Nigeria and Ashanti in the Gold Coast as well as lands in both Northern Nigeria and the Northern Territories of Ghana were held by the administration in trust for the indigenes of the respective countries (Meek, 1949). These policies did not just disrupt the tenure process but rather replaced it altogether with government allocation systems in many African societies. Observance of the requirements of these European registration laws meant for instance that new regimes of transaction costs previously unknown under indigenous legal order came increasingly to bear on land market dealers.

The then simple and almost instantaneous land rights deals were immediately tempered with complex European legal requirements and covenants. As a consequence, transaction and information costs faced by landowners and indigenous purchasers increased rather than fell. This position has not changed since and indeed is now compounded, and has led to widespread informal land transactions in these countries (Noronha, 1985; Antwi, 2000).

This regime of policy reforms brought significant, largely irreversible, disruptive and material changes to the fabric of the indigenous tenure systems in particular and the economic systems of Africa as a whole (Frank, 1969). It is not surprising that to date the quest for remedial measures to deal with the inequities, injustices, inefficiencies, waste, unproductive client–patron arrangements, economic disruptions, market malfunctions and rent seeking activities originated by this generation of policies continues to dictate current policy thinking and debate across the region.

5.3 Second generation land policies

This regime of land policies occurred during the immediate postcolonial era. This era was a period of euphoria and great expectations and the newly liberated economies were poised to demonstrate their capabilities to manage their own affairs, oversee the undoing of the colonial era and rapidly make up for decades of lost development.

To accomplish this it was contended that a 'critical minimum effort' or 'big push' was required through a massive increase in the ratio of investment to national income (Killick, 1978, pp. 17–18). Premised on the principles of development economics that then venerated central planning (Leibenstein, 1957; Killick, 1978; Stern, 1989), this was to come by way of state directed modernisation (Harris, 1975; Arrighi, 1970) through industrialisation (Nurkse, 1953) since, 'after all, the process by which the countries of Europe modernized their economies is called industrial revolution' (Killick, 1978, p. 20; Sender and Smith, 1986). Since most of the import substitution industries that flowed from these policies were sited in the urban areas these areas attracted undue policy attention at the expense of the rural economy. This was soon to prompt internal rural to urban migration at a rate that the existing employment opportunities and land use planning systems could not accommodate. This led to a deteriorating urban poverty and a physical environment pattern that is flourishing today.

The indigenous economic system was thought inadequate to offer support for the big push as 'a ceiling existed on the level of attainable output per head' they could produce (Rostow, 1960). The agenda presumed however the existence of a large reservoir of unemployed labour (Lewis, 1954) and abundant land resources. As such capital formation was exclusively stressed as the only missing element in the big push equation (Killick, 1978, p. 19). This had theoretical support from the then dominant Harrod (1948) and Domar's (1957) capital output ratio (ICOR). But land and property development were disadvantaged as, while front heavy capital investment is required for property construction, the output was not empirically observable immediately to provide the input for these equations and hence was largely ignored. Yet the mobilisation of large tracts of land by the state was a key requirement for the successful execution of such a level of state-led and directed investment push as envisioned. Without the state owning large tracts of land, the vast industrial establishments, farms, industries and extensive bureaucracies could not be established and the vision would fail. Thus in the absence of any explicit incorporation of a land mobilisation strategy, the respective states had to decide their own land mobilisation paths.

This necessitated two main commitments by postcolonial governments that were to have far reaching implications for the land tenure system of the region. Both commitments meant in essence that the disruptions and reversals of the land market development process initiated by the colonial regimes were to be perpetuated together with their adverse consequences and benefits. First was the retention and expansion of the statutory controls inherited by the colonial administration, which subjected land transactions to a number of bureaucratic approvals, permissions, consents, regimentations and registrations (Hatch Associate, 2001; Brobbey, 1991). This provided a measure by which the government maintained constant control over the growth and expansion of the market to ensure that the state at all times outpaced the market in the development arena (see Rimmer, 1992). The second commitment was the consolidation of governments' grips on the large reservoirs of colonial public land holdings bequeathed to the new postcolonial governments (Antwi, 2000; Cousins, 2000; Delville, 2000; McAuslan, 2000; Okoth-Ogendo, 2000; Palmer, 2000; Platteau, 2000; Quan, 1997; Quan, 2000; Toulmin and Quan, 2000; Platteau, 1992; 1996; Bruce, 1986; Payne, 1997; Shipton, 1987; Meek, 1949).

This was followed by the adoption of the ideology and practice of gaining free or cheap access to land through compulsory land expropriation or nationalisation to support what some have described as 'propaganda projects' (Quan, 2000). It is however unlikely that all the projects supported by the mass land expropriation of this regime were propaganda projects. In the case of Ghana, for instance, this expropriation facilitated the development of mass social housing by the state housing corporation, the development of organised and well planned communities like Tema, hydroelectric facilities like the Akosomba Dam, and the creation of incidental communities and a host of industrial and farming estates, some of which continue to make immense contributions towards the development of the country. But the result of such massive expropriation is that, in countries such as Senegal, the State-administered property law of 1964 (Domain National) retained the principle of state ownership of all unregistered land introduced by the colonial administration.

In Tanzania following the colonial land policy, Land Ordinance 1923, which vested all unoccupied lands in the governor, the immediate postcolonial administration in 1962 expanded the domain of this policy to cover all lands in the country. In Uganda, the Land Reform Decree of 1975 sought to convert all land rights in Uganda into public land (Okoth-Ogendo, 2000). The situation is no different in Kenya, where lands are still held by statutory trustees rather than directly by indigenous owners (Okoth-Ogendo, 2000). In Nigeria, where the colonial government failed to nationalise vacant lands, the postcolonial administration passed the Land Use Act of 1975 to nationalise all lands in the country. In other countries where land has not been unequivocally nationalised by postcolonial administrations, such as Ghana, eminent domain policies and extensive statutory controls have been enacted to give government the power to freely acquire or vest lands in the government for all manner of purposes.

Following these commitments, it emerged that by the 1980s half of the countries of sub-Saharan Africa had nationalised lands and extinguished private property rights (Mabogunje, 1992; Gough and Yankson, 2001 p. 2487). As a result, in these countries, private property rights guaranteed by the indigenous tenure system remain largely abolished in favour of the state and the tenure system has become even more perverted than before.

5.4 Third generation land policies

The 1980s was an era of structural adjustments, reflected in the promulgation of third generation land policies in Africa. By the early 1970s the big push development approach adopted by the immediate postcolonial administrations in sub-Saharan Africa had combined unfavourably with the general international economic instability and rapid succession of global economic shocks to produce results that diverge starkly from satisfactory outcomes (see Dixon et al., 1995). These economic failures were blamed on the legacy of deep-seated structural imbalances, including poorly developed markets (World Bank, 1988) such as the land and real estate markets. The World Bank and IMF, together with other bilateral donor agencies, prescribed structural adjustment programmes and lending to facilitate the restructuring process (Cleary, 1989). The structural adjustment programmes were in essence aimed at, as Wardham (1989, p. 210) summarises: (1) getting prices right; (2) letting markets work; (3) reforming public institutions; (4) tight fiscal controls and financial discipline (Slater, 1993); (5) mobilisation of domestic resources; (6) policy reforms to increase efficiency; (7) the generation of foreign exchange earnings from non-traditional sources; (8) the establishment of the non-inflationary role of the state (Dixon et al., 1995); and (9) overcoming 'the asserted shortcomings of indigenous tenure' (Bruce, 1987, p. 35). (For details, see World Bank, 1981).

In the light of the structural adjustment programs, the World Bank exceptionally conceded that, 'improving land tenure/land use is a priority adjustment required in the economy of many [World Bank] ... borrower countries where the agricultural sector is predominant' (Falloux, 1987). Thus the Bank led a structural adjustment land policy campaign and approved between July 1987 and June 1999 a total of 156 land related structural adjustment projects, mainly land titling projects, 46 of which were in sub-Saharan Africa (Byamugisha and Zakout, 2000). The 1975 'Land Reform Policy Paper', of the World Bank published ahead of the disbursement of the structural adjustment loans in 1980 provided a blueprint land policy reform framework that was compatible with the tenets of the structural adjustment program. The policy promoted almost exclusively (1) the desirability of smallholder agriculture from an equity and efficiency perspective; and (2) the desire to facilitate efficiency-enhancing transfers of land to better users through commerce facilitated by land reform (Deininger and Binswanger, 1998). This is not without theoretical basis from the nineteenth-century theory of inverse relationship between farm size and productivity (Platteau, 1992). This theory suggests a relative level of efficiency of farm production by large numbers of small producers than for small numbers of large farm sizes. This theory is also compatible with the World Bank's agenda under the structural adjustment program for export-oriented agriculture to service the debts of these countries and improve their current accounts.

Rather oddly, the central thesis of this policy framework was predicated on the orthodoxy that land tenure systems in sub-Saharan African are impediments to the individualisation of land rights and hence the creation of markets in land (World Bank, 1975, p. 18; Deininger and Binswanger, 1998). Clearly the policy turned a blind eye on the land tenure evolutionary processes that had commenced over a century earlier, and this omission later became the undoing of the policy framework. Land tenure was evolving then into a fully private rights system comparable to the English private rights system from the then communal ownership system. The policy document proposed a conversion of the perceived communal tenure system to a form 'that would allow land to be dealt with as a commodity' (Bruce, 1987, p. 35) in order to improve land productivity and broaden the distribution of benefits (World Bank, 1975). In plain words, the goal was to promote the creation of private ownership using cadastral surveys, registration of titles and similar tools. The two main variants of land reform policies suggested under this rubric are: (1) land reforms that seek to individualise landholdings; and (2) land reforms that seek to nationalise landholdings to enable the state, the radical owner, to redistribute the land to individuals or groups of individuals (Bruce, 1987; Dickerman, 1987; Okoth-Ogendo, 1998; 2000). This, it was hoped, would clarify rights and make them more secure, ensure egalitarian land ownership patterns, facilitate access to credit, stimulate investment in agriculture (Delville et al., 2002), curb landlessness and contribute to flourishing land markets (Deininger and Binswanger, 1998). Thus private ownership was regarded as fundamental aspect of the market economy and common in most Western countries (World Bank, 1975, p. 11). True as this may be, there are clear dangers in reaching the goals of individualised land rights hurriedly. The problem is that the system of private ownership in the Western world, which was intended to be cobbled onto the land markets of sub-Saharan Africa, was not created by force as this generation of land reforms sought to do. It evolved in response to fundamental economic changes. As Buell (1965, p. 750) observed, while 'the Western world worked out its own destiny, unimpeded by an impatient taskmaster from without ... the people of Africa however do not have the same opportunity'.

Seeking to create such rights forcibly in sub-Saharan Africa is unlikely to yield the same premium as those of the Western world as their informing processes are different. The reason is that because private rights emerge in response to economic factors they must at all times be preceded by these economic factors. As a result, unless these preconditions are equally contrived, forcibly created private rights are bound to lack the requisite economic environment to flourish. Unfortunately these economic preconditions cannot be contrived given the scale of resources and information required to contrive them, making created rights inevitably unsustainable.

Better still, other studies point to the fact that land holdings in sub-Saharan Africa are already relatively equitable under indigenous tenure (Quan, 2000). Many of the reported cases of land concentration in sub-Saharan Africa stemmed from government interventions (Bruce, 1987) or ethnic conflicts and conquests as in Rwanda, Nigeria and some areas of Kenya (Dickerman, 1987; Shipton, 1987; Bruce, 1987). Nevertheless, Quan (2000) has lately noted that 'there is no clear correlation between the development of land markets and increasing concentration of land in few hands'. On the contrary, evidence abounds in countries like Kenya and parts of Uganda that land distribution has indeed become more equitable with the establishment of land markets (Quan, 2000). In another vein Migot-Adholla et al. (1991) employed cross-sectional data from Ghana, Kenya, and Rwanda in 1987–8 to explore whether indigenous land rights systems in Sub-Saharan Africa are a constraint on productivity as claimed under the World Bank blueprint policy. The study shows that very little empirical support exists for this view. Actually Bruce and Migot-Adholla (1994) show that the main purpose for people, particularly farmers, seeking formal title was generally to protect themselves and their investments from threats from the state (see also Sjaastad and Bromley, 1997, p. 549). So this generation of policies worsened the already policy-induced distorted land tenure situation. Likewise, the economic policy that provided legitimacy for their existence failed to deliver satisfactory outcomes.

5.5 The new path – pro-poor land policy regime

So far no land policy regime has given the indigenous tenure system the chance to evolve. It has either been disrupted or reversed. Yet both theoretical and empirical studies are showing that indigenous tenure offer more cost-effective solutions to land market problems in sub-Saharan Africa than freehold titles and subdivisions (Deininger and Binswanger, 1998). The new thinking from the 1990s as crystallised in the World Bank's current land policy blueprint published in 2003 (Deininger, 2003) is thus to allow the indigenous land tenure system larger scope to gradually flourish on its own with non-intrusive support from government. This is known as pro-poor land policy.

That is to say that 'rather than trying to replace local land tenure systems with a "modern" system of registration and title of ownership', local rights are to be recognised and controls of land handed back 'to local communities' (Delville et al., 2002). Many nations have embraced this new policy thinking and have followed that on with legislation across Africa (Alden Wily, 2000; IIED, 1999). Potentially this represents the very first attempt after more than a century of disruption to give the indigenous tenure system the opportunity to flourish and to confine government to its legitimate roles (Deininger, 2003), which are to provide of broad general rules within which the indigenous tenure must operate and to deal with adverse consequences. Judging from the distortions of past interventions and their failure to bring about desirable outcomes, it is legitimate to embrace this new liberal land policy ethos with great enthusiasm.

But this should never be perceived as an easy fix (and, in some cases, possible to achieve) in reality, not least because some of the fundamental distortions of the past are practically irreversible. The fine virtues of the indigenous tenure systems have changed violently. The normative codes that regulate the operations of the indigenous tenure system have so changed that the fundamental tenet of the tenure system that gives individual members of particular land-owning groups legitimate and free access to any unoccupied land of the group and to enter freely into commercial trade involving the particular land is no longer tenable, particularly in most urban areas of Africa. This is partly because of the elevated status of the trustees of these lands to de facto owner positions in most urban societies. This is also not helped by the abject dearth of records on lands that other members have previously taken possession of or that have been sold to other non-members. The insistence on this principle will necessarily breed litigation and confusion, which is obviously not an intended aim of any sensible policy proposition. Then there is the diminishing real influence of the indigenous tenure system in urban areas. The real influence of most indigenous tenure systems is felt most in primary land transactions. In secondary transactions very little reference is made, if at all, to the indigenous tenurial arrangements in practice. The evidence is that, in most urban areas, significant proportions of lands have already been subjected to primary transactions and many more of the diminishing residues are done so quite frequently. This implies that the residue of influence that the indigenous tenure system actually has on the land market in urban areas in particular is very small and, even so, fast reducing. This brings into serious question whether the latest propositions to leave a larger scope for the indigenous tenure system in urban areas will actually do anything to improve urban land markets in these areas. Of course in areas where the remainder of vacant lands abound this proposition could do more.

Further, as discussed above, the contrivance of chieftaincy institutions in many indigenous areas coupled with the elevation of chiefs to the status of landowners at the deprivation of the true usufructuary owners (customary freeholders) since the colonial era constitutes a fundamental and likely irreversible change that needs to be kept in sight. If the goal is to legitimise indigenous tenure forms then the focus must be on legitimising the rights of customary freeholders and their assignees while confining the Chiefs to their administrative functions under applicable customary law. In order words the right to transfer the customary freehold must be legitimised as the exclusive rights of the customary freeholders, and Chiefs and heads of land owning groups must be prevented from unduly interfering with these rights. The trouble with this proposition is that, apart from its in-built inequities and injustices, the elaborate bureaucratic mechanisms and procedures that have been put in place to execute the land allocation roles of these chiefs are not costless.

5.6 Summary

To keep the indigenous tenure flourishing as expected under the new policy pathway, there is the need for general macroeconomic stability, and for sensible and sound policies to provide the necessary preconditions for responsive evolutionary processes. Clearly, with government still in possession of large chunks of land holdings, particularly in countries where lands have been nationalised, poor macroeconomic environments across the region, and chiefs still in control over customary rights, there is no denying the fact that gains from these policies are likely to remain greatly restricted. The argument should rather be to promote the price system and not necessarily the indigenous tenure system.

There is considerable difference between the two. The price system accommodates market-devised solutions and ways of commercial dealings in response to changing circumstances. The indigenous tenure is by its very nature very conservative and slow in adapting to changes and thus could even constitute a drag on the market development process. It is in promoting the price system that the impediments imposed by the indigenous tenure structures as they exist today can be overcome. If, for instance, receipt and allocation notes obtained in respect of transactions emanating from those in possession of their rights is recognised without the need to obtain any further contract document from the paramount Chiefs, this whole social cost can be circumvented.

6
Economics of Real Estate Information

6.1 Introduction

Real estate markets function efficiently when driven by information regimes in which legitimate information is the same as the information that must count in market decisions. Where there are mismatches between legitimate information and the information that must count, gaps naturally emerge in the information order. If the conditions for the creation and widening of such gaps are not removed, tenure insecurity, real estate transaction constraints and social costs tend to be heightened. This chapter presents a view of the conditions that have created information gaps in some sub-Saharan African countries using the Ghanaian real estate economy together with their allied tenure insecurity and social costs. Propositions for alleviating these information gaps are consequently proffered.

The argument that transaction costs determine market efficiency is now widely accepted by economists and specialists in the field (Coase, 1960; Williamson, 1981; Turvani, 1997; Rao, 2003). As applied to real estate, transaction costs comprise the costs of ascertaining property ownership, relevant prices and available stock as well as the costs of measuring and monitoring the relevant attributes of real estates, negotiating terms of trade, together with the formalisation and enforcement of real estate contracts. Primarily, the relationship between transaction costs and market efficiency is discovered as an inverse one in the sense that higher transaction costs impede, while lower transaction costs facilitate market efficiency. For that reason, it is arguable that lowering transaction costs below the harmful threshold, or at least keeping them regularly within a tolerable limit, is an effective way of inducing efficiency in real estate markets. That said, it is now widely known that much of transaction costs, whether in real estate markets or in other markets, arise either from or relate essentially to the typical disproportionate distribution of relevant information between transacting parties – information gaps (Coase, 1960; Stigler, 1961; Geertz, 1978; Williamson, 1991; Platteau, 1992; Wyatt and Fisher, 1998; Feenan, 1998). What does emerge from these dialectics is that when information gaps in real estate markets are successfully blocked, transaction costs will fall and market rationality and efficiency will most likely increase.

That information is a critical determinant of market efficiency is not a recent discovery. Right through history the argument that reliable, accurate, relevant, verifiable, up-to-date, complete and intelligible information (Freenan and Dixon, 1992) promote efficiency in economic systems has been readily accepted by experts in the field (Feenan, 1998, p. 15). Yet seldom are economic systems in possession of the ideal quantities and qualities of information. For, invariably: (1) relevant data for efficient market decisions are scarce and disproportionately distributed among market participants (Stigler, 1961); (2) actors in possession of superior information are often incentivised to adopt opportunistic stance to increase their gains from trade to the detriment of other transacting parties (Williamson, 1981; 1986); and (3) actors have a limited capacity to absorb and process the requisite amount of data for efficient market decisions (Simon, 1979). Primarily, these conditions result in situations where different market actors hold different and possibly irreconcilable information about specific commodities or properties. This prevents the accomplishment of the notion of perfect information, which undergirds neoclassical market theory.

The fundamental questions that this situation presents for policy considerations are: in a situation where parties hold irreconcilable information, whose information is legitimate? Whose information is credible? And whose information must count? Efficiency demands that market information systems must ensure a strict match between the information that counts, and that that is credible and legitimate. This will help market participants to form their commercial decisions on reliable and unambiguous data regarding for instance, price signals, property rights, available stock and property identification criteria (Wyatt and Fisher, 1998). It is upon such information regimes that market participants are perceived as able to take rational decisions in the pursuit of their self-interest (Friedman, 2002). The existence of such good fits between the information that must count and that that is credible and legitimate largely explains why in rich countries market economies generate large-scale growth mainly because assts are exchanged with great confidence in large volumes (AMCAD, 1998; De Soto, 2000).

Where mismatches or gaps exist between the information that must count, and that that is credible and truly legitimate, confidence in trade is reduced and market transactions are constrained. Land transactions or credit based on land collateral are in particular constrained where there is a mismatch (or gaps) between what sellers/borrowers can provide as proof of property rights and buyers/banks will accept as proof. The reason being that such a perverse information order does not provide buyers/creditors with the confidence they need to rationally transact or provide financial credit to persons purporting to be owners of particular asserts. The immediate repercussion is that access to investment capital is greatly restricted, investment in land is reduced and the potentials of landed assets are less fully actualised, resulting in a loss of opportunities for growth. Then again, where there are no gaps in the information system, land buyers/creditors are better able to determine quite straightforwardly the credibility of ownership claims made by sellers/borrowers and are thus able to fairly easily formulate their purchase or credit decisions more rationally. In that case, access to investment capital is enhanced, investment in landed assets increases, the potentials of landed assets are realized in large scales leading to growth. Important, also, it ensures consensus between society and the law on whose rights or claims to safeguard and whose actions and interferences to emasculate. Legal actions turn out to be, as a result, largely predictable. Opportunistic behaviours become less rewarding and are thus considerably subdued as both the society and the law provide a solid defence and protection for the rights of true owners against opportunistic interferences. It is decisions made under such conditions that promote the efficient allocation of urban land and real estate resources.

This chapter argues from this expository point that tenure insecurity, social costs and market inefficiencies exist in real estate markets in sub-Saharan Africa primarily because information gaps are prevalent and have given rise to widespread opportunistic behaviours. Ghana is once again used as a case study. These information gaps and their attendant deficiencies in access to reliable land information, though they existed under the indigenous tenure system, have been compounded largely by the extant conceptually improper government land information systems. Instead of alleviating or eradicating information gaps, these government information systems have the tendency to mete out higher transaction costs and distort realities thereby aggravating information gaps, opportunistic behaviours and inefficient market decisions.

The fundamental result is a worsening of tenure security and market malfunctioning.

Over the years, attempts have been made in most sub-Saharan African countries with doses of donor support to provide information systems that will more appropriately capture and harness this information. Take the Ghanaian example for instance. These initiatives have come largely through the introduction of systems as Cadastral, LIS, Land Titling and GIS. Several international development funded projects such as the Ghana Environmental Resource Management Project (GERMP), Urban I and Urban II projects, Land Titling, LIM improvement strategies for the five major cities in Ghana (Williamson, 1991) and Land Record and Management strategy (Government of Ghana, 1998) were all efforts in that direction. These initiatives were not confined to Ghana. They were promoted across the developing world (see further World Bank, 1975; Deininger and Binswanger, 1999; World Bank, 2002; Byamugisha and Zakout, 2000). In particular, the World Bank and other international development agencies, since the 1980s (Williamson, 1991), have been devoting significant resources to research into the costs of land information, the importance of cadastral systems in the developing world (Doebele, 1983) and supporting technology for land information systems (Morgan, 1985). Quite surprisingly, in Ghana these projects have so far produced doubtful benefits.

A fundamental discovery of the World Bank (2005b) for instance is that, so far, these systems, together with the existing manual information, have struggled to capture just about 8 per cent of the land transaction information in the country. The earliest of the legislative frameworks for these systems was enacted about a century and half ago (Land Registry Ordinance (No. 8) of 1883, which was re-enacted in 1895 (cap 133) and revised in 1951) by the colonial administration. These colonial enactments were replaced in 1962 with the Land Registry Act (Act 122) and the Land Title Registry Law (PNDCL 152) in 1986. In addition a host of governmental organisations – the Lands Commission, Land Title Registry, Land Valuation Board and the Survey Department – exists for this purpose. As well, these systems have been able so far to capture just about 30 per cent of the information generated by the increasing urban land transactions in Ghana (AMCAD, 1998). Even the accuracy of the captured information has also been questioned (Brobbey, 1991; Antwi, 1996; 2000; Antwi and Adam, 2003).

Employing modern technology to capture and disseminate land information is important and cannot be left out of any real estate policy decisions in Ghana. Computers and information technologies are, however, simply tools. By themselves they offer little prospects for efficiency unless their use is underlined by an efficient and sound economic conceptual framework. Little merit thus exists in employing these technologies before their appropriate economic conceptual foundations are identified. In particular, if the conditions that created and continue to perpetuate information gaps in the Ghanaian real estate economy are not carefully and accurately identified and prevailed over by the systems installed, the subtle operation of these conditions will cause a resurgence of the gaps and the market will eventually relapse. The fact that these installed systems have done very little to improve the information regime of the real estate economy of Ghana suggests the lack of or weaknesses in the economic conceptual framework that has driven these information systems. To inquire further into this, there is the need for a brief insight into the origins of information gaps in the real estate economy of Ghana.

Before pressing this argument forward, it is important first to establish the urban real estate context of the paper and the important role of information in the development of real estate markets.

6.2 The strategy of inquiry

The empirical data used in this chapter was obtained from Accra, Ghana, using ethnographic research procedure, which is a research procedure that emerged from the field of anthropology (Creswell, 2003). The primary informants in this study are randomly sampled property market participants and officials of the Lands Commission and the Land Title Registry of Ghana. In all 54 market participants,made up of 40 property purchasers and 14 property sellers, were interviewed. In addition 10 senior staff made up of six from the Lands Commission and four from the Land Title Registry and 10 qualified real estate valuers were interviewed. Using ethnographic research methodology, the focus of this study is to gain a holistic view of the everyday experiences of the real estate market participants coupled with the nature, sources and consequences of real estate market information gaps in Ghana. The data for the study was collected from January through June 2004 with follow-up interviews from June through December 2005. This entailed interviews and review of administrative records and literature. The data analysis sought, in keeping with the ethnographic tradition, to identify and describe themes and explain events from the economic theoretical perspective. Descriptive analysis has been the vehicle for communicating the view of the nature, sources and consequences of information gaps in the study area.

6.3 The indigenous tenure system and information gaps

The essential features of the indigenous tenure system have already been discussed in Chapter 2. An interesting feature in the of the indigenous land rights system, a feature that distinguishes it from those of present day Western societies, is that critical information regarding, for instance, the limits and bounds of the groups lands, previous transactions, decisions and actions among others, are usually passed on orally from generation to generation (Brobbey, 1991, p. 49). Seldom do documentary records exist on such matters, with the exception of those necessitated by judicial proceedings in which the corporate land was involved. Knowledge of such important market information thus becomes the preserve of a privileged few who happen to be present at particular key events. More often this information is undocumented and stored in the memories of these privileged few who as a result attain privileged and opportunistic positions and could influence outcomes of market transactions enormously. Besides, as memories fade and those privileged few die, huge information gaps naturally emerge not only between buyers and sellers but also within the indigenous corporate groups.

One of the outcomes of these information gaps is that areas of land originally acquired, allocated to or taken possession of by individuals and subgroups turn out to be imprecise, imaginary and controversial, leading in many cases to rival claims and conflict. Properly, when such conflicts are resolved and the information relating to the outcomes are preserved and made widely available, recurrent conflicts that would lead to tenure insecurity are largely prevented. However, as this historical information is seldom kept in a widely verifiable form, its availability, reliability and accuracy depends largely on the candour of these privileged few. Whether it can be employed in market decisions also depends on whether affected parties will legitimately or opportunistically accept the information offered by those in possession of it. Where the information available is scant, absent or questionable, previously resolved conflicts and litigation become recurrent and endless at extra costs to disputant and social costs to the broad society. This also promotes widespread tenure insecurity in the communities.

More so, before the advent of government interventions and legislative controls, most indigenous land transactions were oral grants and were never reduced into writing, nor was writing in any form essential for validity in Ghana (Larbi, 1994; Woodman, 1996). Accordingly, for transactions between members of particular corporate land holding groups, it was sufficient that the requisite customary drinks and other rites had been performed in the presence of witnesses. In the case of transaction or grants to non-members of the corporate group, some modicum of documentation such as receipt and site plans in addition to other incidents required by the applicable customary law was sufficient. As Meek (1949, p. 171) described the state of documentation of land transactions in the colonial era in Ghana: 'no indefeasible title based on a Government survey can in fact be obtained but many landowners nevertheless waste their money on private surveys which are usually merely ground plans unrelated to the triangulation of the Colony. These worthless surveys are often regarded by their possessors as title deed'.

The general absence of accurate and sufficient documentation on transactions, boundary maps and proprietary plans indicating unambiguously the physical limits of the property rights of respective corporate land owning groups, meant that no systematically compiled information base existed to guide rational market decisions in Ghana. These created at the outset, even under the indigenous tenure system, serious information gaps, which continue to impose greater restrictions on tenure security and market efficiencies. Government interventions to redress these information problems have rather come to complicate matters and have become the prime source of information gaps in Ghana.

6.4 Sources and nature of information gaps

This section looks at the sources from which information gaps are produce in the contemporary Ghanaian real estate sector. These sources exist within both the demand and supply streams at both the capture and distribution levels of the information market. Curiously, in Ghana, the fundamental source of land market information gaps is not at all due to lack of information. As mentioned earlier volumes of land information are produced increasingly in Accra and other urban areas of sub-Saharan Africa with the current increasing trade in land and real estate that has emanated from rapid urbanisation. The real source of the gaps, strangely, derives from the polarised legitimacy of available market information. The government and market dealers are divided on the question: whose information counts as a reliable, legitimate and credible basis for market decisions? This has driven a wedge between the existing information order in these markets to create information gaps. The explanation for this state of affairs is presented below.

There are two categories of land information in Ghana as elsewhere in sub-Saharan Africa labelled here as *category-1* and *category-2* information respectively. Category-1 information is the direct transaction information. It is the information produced from original acquisition of land rights or from the exchange of property rights at either the first or second-hand property markets. By its very origin category-1 information is often immediately known only to the specific transacting parties. However, in the long run the relevant information becomes available to the neighbours and the community. Category-2 information is the officially processed, compressed, simplified and recorded version of category-1 information.

As argued throughout the paper, for any information to be effective in remedying information gaps it must have legitimacy, be credible and must count in the view of market dealers. Officially in Ghana only category-2 information is officially considered legitimate. In actual fact, if all category-1 information is, immediately after its production, transformed accurately into category-2 information, the only difference between them would be that category-1 information would be verbose, difficult to digest and assimilate while category-2 information would be simplified, intelligible and easy to digest. Nonetheless, in reality there is always some time lapse between the creation of category-1 information and its transformation into category-2 information. In the particular case of Ghana, this study discovered that it takes an average of 600 days for category-1 information to be transformed into category-2 information at the Lands Commission. Again, as at December, 2002 a backlog of 94,100 individual category-1 transactions were pending for transformation into category-2 information at the Land Title Registry. This implies that if transactions take place regularly in Accra as presumed, then the database on category-2 information could be some 600 days delayed.

This significant time lapse and the likely datedness of category-2 information notwithstanding, a major concern is whether indeed transacting parties perceive category-2 transactions as legitimate enough to induce confidence in real estate transactions. This can be measured from the desire of the market to convert category-1 information to category-2. To begin with, under the existing arrangement transacting parties are required to submit their category-1 information to the relevant agencies for transformation and legitimisation at costs to them. The main costs they face, in addition to official fees and charges, include: travel costs to the respective agencies; waiting time costs; expediting and unofficial gratuity payments. The World Bank (2005b) estimates the official fees and charges for the conversion process to average about 3.1 per cent of the value of the asset. Given these costs, and in the absence of any real compulsion, it is possible to gauge the willingness and scale of patronage for the conversion. If the patronage is high, all things being equal, category-2 information could offer potential for redressing the information gaps. Alternatively, low patronage indicates transacting parties' lack of support for the conversion process and a denial of the legitimacy of category-2 information.

As pointed out earlier, the World Bank (2005b) found that in Ghana only 8 per cent of category-1 information has so far been converted to category-2. This implies that only about 8 per cent of market dealers consider category-2 information as the information that counts and is credible for market decisions. Rather, 92 per cent of market dealers perceive category-1 information as the information that counts and is hence credible for market decisions. The problem is that often there are significant disparities between these two information categories. A typical case is the situation that has characterized about 70 per cent of government land holdings in Accra. The Sports Complex area at New Achimota, the atomic energy area at Haatso, and the area proposed for Military Training Grounds, Teshie, are examples of such areas in Accra. Whereas in all these areas the legitimate owner from official perspective is the government, market dealers acknowledge individual indigenous families as rightful owners and have felt comfortable dealing with them. These areas host some of the priciest properties in Accra developed largely by buyers not from government but from these recognised individual families on the ground. Even intermittent threats by government over the years to demolish these buildings do not seem to have deterred market dealers from recognising these individual families as legitimate owners. Herein lays the gap in the land information system in Ghana. The information that counts is not legitimate and the officially recognised legitimate information does not count from the perspective of market dealers.

This is a clear evidence of almost unanimous lack of support or patronage for the conversion process, an indication also of a lack of sufficient benefit from the system to warrant the costs of patronage. The worrying question is why would 92 per cent of transacting parties prefer to hold their transaction information in an illegitimate format rather than in a legitimate format? Perhaps an important reason for this stems from the limited secondary property transactions as most property owners regard real property largely as a consumption and inheritance good, rather than as an investment good in the classical sense. Many are also unwilling to use their property as collateral for credit for the fear of losing their inheritance through force-sale. Uncontested physical possession is thus to them more important than documentation and formalisation. This is a far cry from what pertains in the developed world such as in the UK, where on the average each property is sold every 14 years, with many under mortgage. Though this position is changing, the change process is rather slow. This could be attributed to the wedge that exists between what information must be legitimate and what must count.

Having looked at the sources and nature of the information gaps in the Ghanaian system, this chapter turns now to the implications of these gaps on tenure security and social costs.

6.5 Information gaps and tenure security

The importance of tenure security to efficient real estate market functioning has long been appreciated by international development agencies involved in land issues such as the World Bank (1989, p. 87) and other experts in the field. The fact that in such countries as Ghana 800 new land litigation cases are filed at the high court each month (Hatch, 2001) shows that the quest for secure tenure in at least that country is far from successful. Conventional orthodoxy postulates that, as far as Africa is concerned, the transformation of communal tenure to freehold rights will automatically ensure security of tenure and market efficiency (World Bank, 1975; Deininger and Binswanger, 1998). The accuracy of this thesis has now been extensively questioned (see for instance Antwi, 2000; Quan, 2000; Larbi et al., 2003).

Even so, to date the question of tenure security has not really been perceived as an outcome of information gaps in land markets in sub-Saharan Africa. Instead, it is perceived as a technical and legal issue remediable by the issuance of land Title Certificates or other similar documents endorsed by public officers and declared indefeasible by law.

Such a conception of tenure security is misleading, and until security is perceived as an outcome of information gaps in real estate markets no solution will in the long run be able to redress the problem substantially. Tenure security is not land litigation. Indeed some form of land litigation is required for the effective definition and clarification of property rights in land (see Demsetz, 1967; Platteau, 2000). Though this type of litigation may on occasion generate social costs on society, it is not by itself a source of tenure security in the true sense of the term. Tenure security is simply the insurance against unlawful eviction or dispossession of legitimate property rights.

This implies that for tenure security to occur, the rights in question must have been previously created, well defined and clarified. Accordingly, in a market democracy where rights to assets are already created and well defined, tenure insecurity can only occur essentially when the true information about the property rights in question are not so well known by society or gaps exist in the information framework that opportunistic actors, including the government, can clandestinely and successfully exploit for profit. To exploit these opportunities particularly in a democracy where rule of law and human rights virtues are extolled, it will be in the interest of opportunistic actors to hide their opportunistic nature to obviate serious social condemnation or outright prohibition by the law. This means that they must also be in possession of some form of information that at least superficially appears credible to support their rival ownership claims. This cannot be achieved where there are no gaps in the information order, where the information that counts, that is credible and legitimate is widely known and accepted. On the basis of this opportunistically contrived irreconcilable information, they can commence ownership contests with the rightful owner. Since rightful owners will normally not give up their rights without contests, land litigation is likely to ensue.

Now, when this litigation protracts, at some point, there will be the need for adjudication or legal action. The job of the adjudication procedure is no more than ascertaining which of the two conflicting ownership information presented for adjudication must count. Which is credible? And which is legitimate? Where there are no gaps in the information order, the adjudication systems will address these questions by reference to a single generally accepted credible and legitimate information source. Where such a source exist, the results of adjudication or legal actions will be easy to predict by the parties even before the commencement of the litigation. It follows that opportunism will have no merit and truly credible and legitimate tenure will remain secure. Nonetheless, where no such information source exists the outcome of litigation becomes largely a matter of chance, or becomes dependent on how well the disputant (or their counsel) argue their case. There will thus be as much chance that the adjudication procedure or legal system could answer the questions correctly as answering them wrongly. The results will largely be unpredictable. When the adjudication system or courts answer the questions wrongly, they themselves become sources of tenure insecurity. This shows how simplistic the clamour for adjudication as the means for redressing tenure insecurity can be.

There is no shortage of conflicting land judgements in Accra, Ghana. These demonstrate how in a regime of information gaps even the courts can promote and aggravate tenure insecurity. Take the judgement in civil appeal number 49/80 delivered in 1982 (otherwise referred to as the Numo Nmashie family judgement) for instance. That case relates to a 25-acre parcel of land acquired by the government of Ghana for the Ghana Broadcasting Corporation for a television station. The government received three rival claims to the compensation due from The Osu, The Berekuso and the Numo Nmashie family. The court of appeal on the matter gave judgement in favour of the Numo Nmashie family. In the course of the legal proceedings the appeal court requested for a survey plan to be prepared to enable the court to identify the villages being mentioned in the trial and their relationship to the land. The idea it appears was to give judgement in favour of the owners of the villages in the closest proximity to the land in question. This situation would have been unnecessary but for the existence of information gaps in the system.

On the basis of this plan, the court entered judgement in favour of the Numo Nmashi family. The judgement accordingly became officially interpreted and recorded as a declaration of the Numo Nmashi family as owners of all the land connecting all the villages indicated on that survey map. This land covers several hectares stretching from the northern end to the southern end of Accra engulfing several existing historical villages and towns. The judgement rather curiously conflicts with a number of judgements that have previously declared portions within this area for other families,[1] some of which date as far back 1933 and were delivered by higher courts, and the adjudged owners have also remained in effective physical possession since. Moreover, the judgement overlaps with some 25 major government acquired lands. Accordingly the apparent tenure securities that these previously adjudged owners who are also in physical possession of the lands together with the government enjoyed are now threatened by this judgement. Potential exists also for other subsequent judgements to conflict with the Numo Nmashi judgement and the cycle of insecurity could be perpetuated. On the ground, this judgement expectedly has generated intermittent violent clashes between the existing owners and the newly declared owners.

Such a perverse situation provides a recipe for opportunism to flourish as it improves the likelihood of gains from opportunistic behaviours. It is clear from this argument that when information gaps are blocked, the incentives for opportunistic behaviours are removed; opportunistic rival claims and title contests will be considerably curbed, thereby improving tenure security enormously. It needs to be noted that in societies where property rights are still evolving, however, genuine litigation and ownership contests will continue until all titles are fully evolved and clarified.

The chapter now turns to the second element in the thesis, the social costs of information gaps.

6.6 The social costs

In any situation in which information is disproportionately distributed among market participants, possessors of land rights often have more knowledge about the extent to which their rights to the land are defective or even are likely to become contested than other individuals, especially those from other communities (Brandao and Feder, 1995). In the same way borrowers tend to be better equipped with current and accurate knowledge about their ownership details and defects in titles used as collaterals than credit suppliers. This leaves a large room for opportunistic behaviours (see further Williamson, 1986). Those with superior information have the incentive to suppress or hide defects in their ownership details and rather hype the quality of their rights to augment their profits. This leads to market malfunctioning, as transactions concluded on such a skewed information structure are likely to result in inefficient outcomes with wider systemic repercussions with attendant social costs.

Figure 6.1 illustrates how such information gaps leads to overpricing or under-pricing of real estates with the attendant social costs. In the figure the vertical axis is taken to represent the price of particular category of urban real estate property; say property class *X*, while the horizontal axis as the likely quantities of property class *X* associated with particular prices. Take d_0, d_1 and d_2 as the optimal, underpriced and overpriced demand scenarios respectively for class *X* properties. In a regime of perfect and equally distributed information, the equilibrium price is P_0 for class *X* properties and the equilibrium or optimal quantity is L_0. This price and quantity arrangement represents an informed purchaser's decision point and it will be the point at which the market will be said to be performing most efficiently and land is put to its optimal use. Typically few, if any, urban real estate markets operate within a regime of perfect information to permit this always to occur. As Senior (1854, cited in Rose (2002)) avers 'the details of commerce are so numerous, the difficulty of obtaining early and accurate information is so great, and the facts themselves are so constantly changing that the most cautious merchants are often forced to act upon very doubtful premises'. This is especially so in the developing world where, as Geertz (1978, p. 29) argues, 'information is poor, scarce, maldistributed, inefficiently communicated and intensely valued'.

When information gaps persist they engender one of two or both possible outcomes. The d_1 scenario occurs essentially when the available level and quality of information leads to an overestimation of the utilities and an underestimation of the defects in land and properties, whether legal, technical or physical. This results in overpricing of land and properties. Alternatively, the d_2 scenario occurs when the available information leads to an underestimation of the utilities and an overestimation of the defects in land and property. This conversely results in underpricing of land and property. Both scenarios come with social costs.

Real estates have inherent ability to skew information in favour of property owners. They own the property and are better informed than purchasers about say the subsisting rights, defects in title or physical conditions and any rival title claims affecting the property. Moreover, property suppliers could deliberately exacerbate this skewed information situation by withholding information from purchasers.

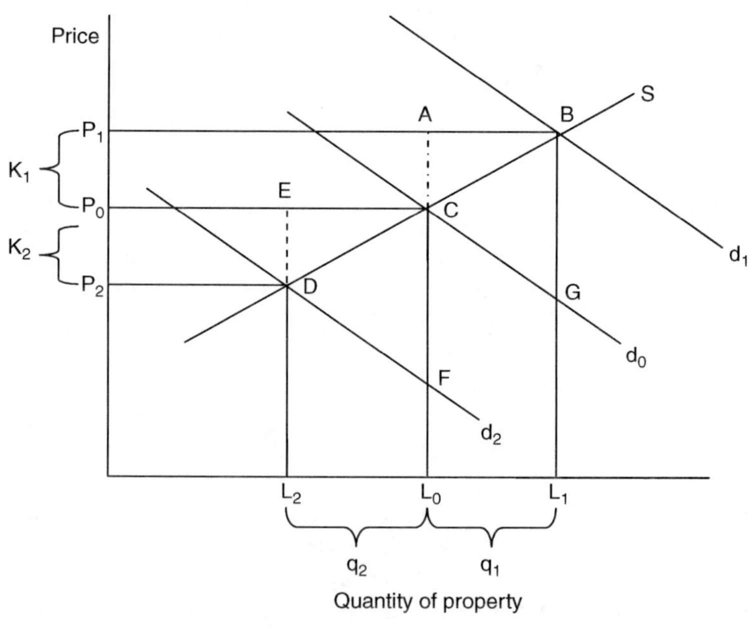

Figure 6.1 Information induced pricing

This is most likely simply because the very presence of information gaps in economic systems creates rents or windfall returns. Relying on such faulty information in market decisions could result in purchasers overpricing the intrinsic utilities of particular properties and bidding higher than the actual worth or optimal price. Such purchasers will be forced to operate along d_1 instead of the d_0 optimal scenario at which L_1 quantities of class *X* properties will be purchased at unit price of P_1. In this (d_1) scenario where land is overpriced, there is an efficiency loss as land is presumably taken out of its current use to a new use that will produce returns that are less than the price offered for the land. For example if residential lands are overpriced to the levels of commercial lands, the optimal returns produced by this land will match the optimum for residential lands and will be likely to fall below those of commercial lands. Thus purchasers who acquire properties above the optimal level suffer social costs given by [P_0P_1AC] + [ABC]. Arithmetically, $P_0P_1AC = K_1(L_1 - \Delta q_1)$ and $\Delta ABC = \frac{1}{2}(q_1 \times K_1)$. Harberger (1964) shows that $\frac{1}{2}(q_1 \times K_1) = 0.5\eta(K_1)^2 P_0$ (see also Posner, 1975). This implies thus that social costs associated with scenario d_1 can be expressed as:

$$S_1 = 0.5\eta(K_1)^2 P_0 + K_1(L_1 - q_1)$$

In which S_1 = total social costs, K_1 = change in price associated with the d_1 scenario and η = the elasticity of property. It needs noting that this expression measures only the social costs due to the distortion in the purchaser's decisions concerning the quality of class *X* properties to be purchased. Changes in property prices also distort property choices by inducing a substitution effect in favour of properties with financial advantages. Thus estimating social costs exclusively by the above expression leads to underestimation. However, to simplify the discussions in this chapter this expression is focused upon. Accordingly the total social costs aggregated over all class *X* properties under scenario d_1 will be:

$$S_1 = \sum_{i=1}^{n}(0.5\eta(K_1)^2 P_0 + K_1(L_1 - q_1))$$

In which i = number of class *X* properties and n = last class *X* property.

Yet this scenario (d_1) at the same time creates a rent or windfall return of the same magnitude ([P_0P_1AC] + [ABC]) for landowners. Thus motivated by the higher windfall returns or rent associated with overpricing, land and property owners are likely to firstly ensure that the rent associated with overpricing persists, and secondly that where possible they grow by hyping the utilities of their properties and downplaying the defects in their properties to compel purchasers to overprice their bid and operate along d_1.

Essentially this is accomplished by withholding information, for instance regarding defects in their property. This requires the expenditure of real resources to provide such an information blockade through, for instance, the preparation and dissemination of false or inaccurate boundary maps and documents, the employment of personnel to peddle misinformation and even to maintain some form of physical presence on the land in the form of land guards, among others. These expenditures are incurred by moving resources away from other productive sectors or uses just to prevent accurate information from getting to purchasers with the sole aim of maintaining a sub optimal condition d_1. Indeed if land owners do not protect this rent induced by the information gaps and hence overpricing, they can be sure that other suppliers (erstwhile purchasers who have now gained the true position of the information and thus realise they can gain by operating as suppliers) will attempt to enter the market and increase supply, thereby forcing prices downward towards P_0. Eventually, property market transactions under scenario d_1 will lead to inefficient outcomes as willing and able purchasers are denied the opportunity to make the most efficient use of real estate. Creditors are also put at risk as they are denied the right information to determine the true collateral values of properties used to secure credit and hence are likely to overvalue such properties.

As mentioned earlier and reflected in the d_2 scenario, misinformation that leads to an overestimation of defects or underestimation of the utilities of properties, is likely to lead to underpricing. Such information lowers purchasers' opinion of the value of the property concerned. As a consequence purchasers offer lower prices of say P_2, and reduce the quantity L_2. This again is a sub optimal decision level and landowners who accept prices below the optimal level suffer welfare costs given by $[P_2P_0ED] + [ECD]$. Based on the above analysis and equations the social costs S_2 associated with the d_2 scenario can be expressed as:

$$S_2 = \sum_{i=1}^{n} (0.5\eta (K_2)^2 P_0 + K_2(L_2 - q_2))$$

Purchasers also gain by the same magnitude. In this d_2 scenario, where land is underpriced because of information gaps, landowners will continue to supply land between L_2 and L_0 in its current uses because the returns from that land use (discounted over time) as given by the area under the supply curve ($DL_2 L_0 F$) exceed the price that is available in the market. As a consequence there is an efficiency loss as compared with a situation of perfect information because that area of land is not being put to its most valued use as given by the triangle (CDE). Then again, since purchasers need the right information to take rational market decisions, they will draw resources from elsewhere into acquiring extra information from sources other than the landowners to support their decisions. Undoubtedly disclosures of the true information would most likely cause purchasers who would have otherwise acquired the properties (for higher valued uses other than the current one) to become aware of the defects and make them especially reluctant to proceed with the purchase or at best offer a lower price to reflect the defects in the title (Brandao and Feder, 1995, p. 194). Knowing this, opportunistic suppliers seeking to market their stock will also most likely, in the absence of any unfair trading rules, expend resources to peddle untrue and damaging information about the land and properties of their competitors. This, if successful will force prices down to P_2. In that scenario, purchasers will gain from underpricing the properties. Conversely, debtors will also lose as creditors will also undervalue the potential worth of their properties intended to be used as collateral for credit.

What emerges from this analysis is that all deviations from the perfect information scenario d_0 results in social cost arising out of a loss of producer surplus (the triangle between the supply curve and P_0 (DEC)) because some landowners would be willing to sell some quantity of land at a price between P_2 and P_0, and of consumer surplus (the triangle between P_0 and the demand curve d_0 (ABC) as some buyers would be willing to pay more than P_0 for some of the land. In the long run unless prevented by artificial barriers such as government interventions and legal impediments, private economic agents will emerge to take advantage of the accompanying arbitrage opportunity created by gaps in the information. Indeed the work of real estate brokers, valuers, agents and solicitors among others is precisely to specialise in the acquisition and supply of such withheld accurate information to get the market going not at d_1 or d_2 but at d_0. Where in a particular society private actors are sluggish in stepping in to supply the requisite information the job of government intervention is to identify and remove the impediments that are preventing private actors from acquiring and supplying this information. Alternatively government could evolve institutions to capture and supply credible and legitimate information. But such government interventions must be founded on a sound understanding of the factors that are responsible for the existence of information gaps in Ghana. However to effectively close these gaps, there is the need to grasp an understanding of the sources of these information gaps.

Though evidence of a d_2 scenario exists in the country in the form of adjoining landowners or even members of the same landowning community discrediting the authenticity of the rights of particular landowners or Chiefs, this does not appear to have affected the prices of land in any significant way. Prominently, the information gaps have lead to a widespread d_1 scenario in Ghana. Accra land markets are currently full of land agents peddling lands for which they are no doubt aware of rival claims and litigation to unassuming purchasers. Indeed, as is the case in the Nungua locality of Accra, individuals and families from Teshie, adjoined neighbourhood adjoined to Accra, have managed clandestinely, with the help of officials from the government agencies, to register large tracts of lands involving thousands of building plots in the Nungua traditional area in the name of Teshie indigenous community lands since the 1970s. This travesty persists to date even though it is widely known by both communities and relevant government officials that under indigenous tenure arrangements the affected lands belong to the Nungua rather than Teshie community.

Since the registration was not published, this did not come to the notice of the true owners of land in Nungua. Physically, Nungua landowners are in effective possession of the lands in the area and market dealers acknowledge them as such. Yet, to date, from the official perspective, the legitimate owners of lands in those areas are the Teshie families, but the true owners recognised by market dealers on the ground are the Nungua landowners. This gap that is opportunistically created has led to the creation of an unearned rent for the Teshie families. Market dealers who rely on category-2 information for their transactions are compelled to deal with the Teshie families and pay the full market price for the land (which sometimes, for obvious reasons, is lower than the market price). But since the Teshie families are not the legitimate owners according to the category-1 information on those lands, these buyers will again have to buy the land at full market price from the Nungua landowners, the accredited owners based on the category-1 information. Thus as a direct result of the information gap the price of the land in this area is generally doubled. To give an impression of the social costs of this information gap in this particular neighbourhood, a random sample of data on market prices of land in the neighbourhood was compiled. The total sample size is 40. Table 6.1 reports the frequency distribution and displays the number and percentage of cases for each land value.

Table 6.1 The frequency distribution of land values in Nungua

Land values		Frequency	Per cent	Valid per cent	Cumulative per cent
Valid	50000000	1	2.5	2.5	2.5
	55000000	1	2.5	2.5	5.0
	60000000	1	2.5	2.5	7.5
	65000000	6	15.0	15.0	22.5
	70000000	3	7.5	7.5	30.0
	72000000	1	2.5	2.5	32.5
	75000000	5	12.5	12.5	45.0
	80000000	2	5.0	5.0	50.0
	82000000	2	5.0	5.0	55.0
	83000000	1	2.5	2.5	57.5
	85000000	5	12.5	12.5	70.0
	90000000	5	12.5	12.5	82.5
	95000000	3	7.5	7.5	90.0
	97000000	1	2.5	2.5	92.5
	100000000	2	5.0	5.0	97.5
	110000000	1	2.5	2.5	100.0
	Total	40	100.0	100.0	

Source: Field survey.

Figure 6.2 presents the histogram on the distribution together with a fitted normal distribution curve showing that the distribution is a normally distributed.

The figure also reports the mean land value to be ¢79,650,000.00. If price paid to obtain documents from the Teshie families is conservatively put at 50 per cent of the typical land values (that is about 40 million Cedis) and elasticity of land in the area is assumed to be 0.5 then from the social costs equation for the d_1 scenario deduced above, $K_1 = 0.5$; $\eta = 0.5$; $P_0 =$ ¢80,000,000 and $K_1(L_1 - q_1) =$ ¢40,000,000.00. Conservatively the social costs per transaction on a typical residential plot in the area associated with this particular information gap are:

$$0.5 \times 0.5(0.5)^2 \times ¢80{,}000{,}000 + 40{,}000{,}000.00 = 45{,}000{,}000.00$$

This converts to about US$5000.00 at October 2005 prices. The total social costs for the affected portions will be the sum of this marginal social cost across the number of affected plots. Thus, again, if a conservative figure of 1000 is assumed for the number of affected transactions in the area, the total social costs will turn to US$5,000,000.00. Though this social cost excludes for instance the social costs of the land litigation that is usually associated with this problem, it gives a good feel

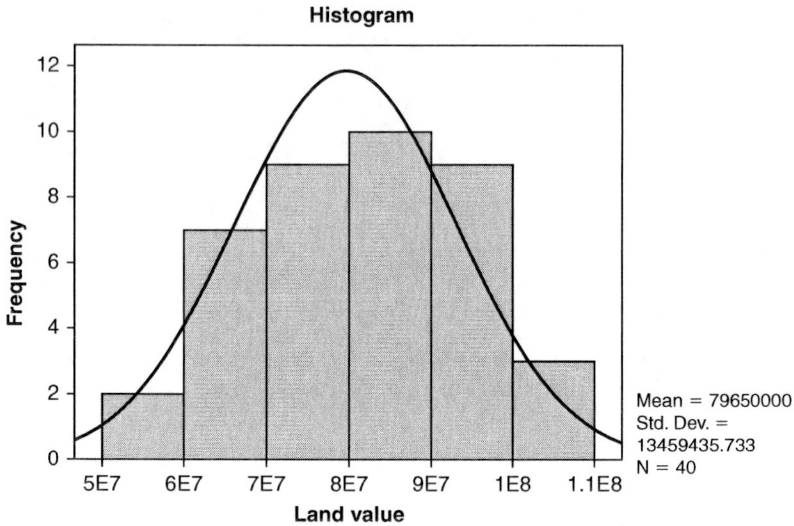

Figure 6.2 Histogram of land values frequency distribution

of the likely order of the magnitude of the overall social costs across the country.

To prevent such social costs, the way forward is to alleviate the market of the information gaps that have produced them to ensure that all distortions to d_1 will be removed and cause the equilibrium to gravitate to d_0. The next section proffers some remedial policy actions.

6.7 Rectifying the gaps

What emerges from the foregoing is that, to make significant inroads into the alleviation of information gaps in these markets an information system that is capable of aligning or harmonising the land information that counts with those that are perceived legitimate and credible needs to be established. Perhaps the difficulties lie with how this can be accomplished and debate on an option for aligning these three attributes of information would be a healthy development. The position of this chapter is that, since 92 per cent of market dealers perceive or rely on category-1 information as the information that count in their market dealings, placing much premium on category-1 information as opposed to category-2 information would offer better prospects for alleviating the gaps. This implies the need first for category-1 information to be accorded official legitimacy. This will ensure that what is perceived as legitimate by a majority of market dealers tallies now with what is officially recognised as legitimate information. The next stage would be to place this now legitimised information onto the official information system in a manner that would make it easy to digest and assimilate by a larger segment of the Ghanaian population. This new information would then have to be reconciled with the 8 per cent that already exists in the official information systems to remove all anomalies and to reinforce the integrity of the information in the system.

To this end, as a way of capturing the category-1 information that is currently outside the government system, a systematic nationwide property by property tenure census is proposed as an effective way of capturing this information in urban areas of Ghana. This has to be conducted in a manner similar to the periodic national population census exercises. This method is not without precedent. The Domesday survey of William I in England and the modern cadastre of Napoleon I in France and many parts of Europe, are prime examples (Williamson, 1994).

The idea is not to create a Domesday Book but to facilitate a closure of the information gaps in the system by establishing a comprehensive dataset based on category-1 information to form the pedestal on which a viable national land information system is to be built. With the rapid advances in technology the feasibility of this undertaking is not in doubt, and given the sheer size of the attendant social costs there can also be no doubt that the process would, if successful, be most likely socially and economically viable. This solution obviously entails huge resources and considerable time. But whatever the costs, it will be nowhere near the social costs, tenure insecurity and market inefficiencies that the current system is exuding. At least the costs of rectifying the information gaps that are generating social costs in the Nungua area of Accra discussed above will be nowhere near US$5 million. This fact coupled with the general high level of poverty and the need to ensure comprehensive coverage, makes it economically wise for government to meet these costs out of the public purse. Perhaps there would be the need for a review of the US$55 million allocated for the ongoing Land Administration Project (LAP) in Ghana with the view to making ample allocation for this task. While it is proposed that government should sponsor the programme, it does not imply that the programme has to be implemented by government bureaucracies and agencies. Perhaps a team of private sector consultants, adjudication experts, local opinion leaders and relevant government departments could be set up to discharge this programme.

To ensure success and data integrity there will be the need for careful development of a data collection strategy that has an inbuilt, workable, onsite adjudication system, openness, incentives and disincentives for candour, and timely registration of category-1 information as well as subsequent dealings.

6.8 Summary

Alleviating information gaps constitutes a key issue in the quest for improved real estate market functioning in Ghana and elsewhere in sub-Saharan Africa. The insights in this chapter call for a reappraisal of the workings of existing government information systems employed in practice to supply information to real estate market participants to ensure the legitimatisation of the credible information that market dealers rely on in market transactions.

7
Performance of Real Estate Bureaucracy

7.1 Introduction

This chapter provides a testing of classical public choice ideas about the propensity of public bureaucracies to maximise their budgets at the expense of efficient and economic provision of public services. It tests these arguments in a quantitative analysis of budgetary allocations in five government land related services delivery bureaucracies in Ghana. These bureaucracies are chosen because firstly they are representative of public bureaucracies in Ghana generally in terms of their budgetary, governance, salary and employment attributes. As well, Ghana presents an interesting story of a developing country struggling since independence to contrive for itself a workable and efficient land related service delivery bureaucracies. Presently, the World Bank and other development partners such as the DFID are sponsoring US$55 million towards improving land service delivery Ghana dubbed the Ghana Land Administration Project (see Hatch, 2001). It is anticipated that lessons learnt from the Ghana experience will inform other initiatives of the World Bank and other international development partners in other developing societies with social structures and land tenure systems that are similar to those of Ghana.

That said, a study of the scoping report and blueprint of the Ghana Land Administration Project (Hatch, 2001) reveals that, despite its considerable costs and scale, the project is not underpinned by rigorous and possibly quantitative testing of the extent to which widely accepted economic theories of bureaucracies explain the state of affairs in Ghana. Rather, perceptions, suspicions, speculations and sometimes superstitions have largely provided the impetus for the proposed reforms.

The essence of a study like this is illustrated by the point that public sector bureaucracies, the world over, bear immensely on the economic outcomes of policies (Grindle and Thomas, 1990; 1991). As a result, researchers and managers have, over the years, demonstrated growing quests to understand the efficiency of public sector bureaucracies. A resulting school of thought from these quests is the public choice theory, which perceives public sector bureaucracies as 'basically inefficient' (Tullock, 1965, p. 151). To this view, bureaucracies are 'malignancies destined to fail' (see also Beetham, 1987; Finer 1945, p. 110). The central thesis of the public choice argument is that public bureaucracies are invariably prone to excessive costs and waste (Niskanen, 1973) relative to the private firm faced with the same demand conditions (Mises, 1944; 1962). They have the tendency to enlarge their budgets and outputs above the social optimum thereby generating waste at social costs to society. In order to test this claim, most authors have set out to compare the costs and outputs of public and private sector organisations providing similar services (usually, but not always, in the same country). So there are, for example, such studies on airlines, banks, bus services, postal services, hospitals, refuse collection, nursing homes, insurance companies, oil tankers or utilities (for a review of this huge literature see Mueller, 2004, pp. 373–8). The tests have so far not been applied to land sector bureaucracies of the developing world despite the millions of dollars of donor funds and aid poured into these countries to improve the performance of land and real estate markets in these regions.

That said, for two reasons, comparison between the private and public sector in this sense might not readily be possible nor the results thus obtained always convincing. The first reason is the general difficulty in identifying identical private sector comparables to facilitate such comparisons. This is because by tradition or law the services offered by public sector bureaucracies are often services designed for exclusive delivery by the public sector. These services include provision of public goods, regulation of externalities, regulation of unfair trading and market monopolisation, defence and in many countries land registration services. The second reason is that at least part of the demand for the goods and services supplied by public bureaucracies is invariably transmitted through political mechanisms (McNutt, 2002) that are not applicable to the private firm. Accordingly, the demand and cost conditions they respectively face are likely to be significantly different from those of private firms in competitive markets. This makes comparison odd and questions the validity of testing the efficiency of bureaucracy by comparing with the private sector.

Given that both reasons given above are applicable to the land sector bureaucracies under review, an alternative approach to examining the efficiency of these bureaucracies is presented. The approach proposed here is to scrutinise the levels of the inbuilt waste of the bureaucracies in question to provide indications of their potential efficiency. This, theoretically, necessitates the explicit dichotomisation of the absolute costs of these bureaucracies into pertinent and extraneous costs. The extraneous costs represent those costs that can be saved by avoiding certain modes of conduct without compromising efficient outputs. This offers good indications of the scale of inbuilt waste and hence the potential magnitude of the internal inefficiencies of the bureaucracy. Pertinent costs on the other hand are the unavoidable costs if efficiency outputs are to be achieved. They thus represent the costs required for efficiency outputs. A review of the public choice literature provides an apt context for this examination.

7.2 Economics of public bureaucracy

The long quest for an optimal organisation form for policy delivery has produced contending views of efficiency of public sector bureaucracies and much less consensus so far. Neo-Weberian scholarship associated with Max Weber (1964) contends that bureaucracy is the most rational organisational form necessary for capitalist production and development. It is, it is argued, apolitical and capable of attaining the highest degree of efficiency and hence most suitable in policy delivery (see further Weber, 1964, p. 337). As further contended, it is 'superior to any other [organisational] form in precision, in stability, in the stringency of its discipline, and its reliability ... both in intensive efficiency and in the scope of its operations' (Weber, 1964). It is accordingly less prone to extraneous budgets as its inbuilt rationality and impartialities enable it to circumvent such budgets and costs. Nonetheless, it is condoned that it accumulates extraneous costs and budgets when it becomes aimless and inattentive to its real task or to changing economic and technological contexts (Goldsmith, 1999). Thus, from the Weberian standpoint, the possible aimlessness and inattentiveness of public sector bureaucracy, more than any other factor, could explain the existence or otherwise of extraneous costs in the land sector public bureaucracies in Ghana.

A much less charitable view of bureaucracy advocated by the public choice school (Buchanan, 1975; see further Downs, 1957; McLean, 1972; Niskanen 1971; 1973; Tullock, 1967) perceives bureaucracies, of the kind employed in land policy delivery in Ghana, as highly prone to extraneous budgets. Though deriving essentially from earlier works of Hayek (1944) and Mises (1944), protagonists such as Tullock (1965),

Downs (1957) and Niskanen (1971) have since provided a formal theoretical formulation of the public choice view. In opposition to Weberian theory, the public choice view perceives bureaus and bureaucrats as economic agents whose economic motives of self-interest maximising and rationality do not ebb away simply because they are in the realm of public sector bureaucracy (Buchanan and Tullock, 1962; 1977; Mueller, 1989). Indeed, public choice sees bureaucrats as self-interested agents acting for their own well-being (Hayek, 1944; Mises, 1944; Downs, 1957). These economic motives of bureaucrats, coupled with the fact that public bureaucracies are political (rather than apolitical), monopolistic and non-profit organisations, makes it difficult to appraise in monetary terms the services they offer (Mises, 1944; Niskanen, 1971; Page 1992; Peters, 1978). Bureaucracies such as the Ghana public land sector bureaucracies, being non-profit monopolies, receive their allocated funds from the government budget (Mises, 1944; 1962) regardless of performance (Levacic, 1987, p. 169). Thus, barring profit and loss, it is the desire and goals of the public bureaucrat, limited only by the prescriptions and budget of the central legislature or budget-approving Ministry, necessarily take control (Mises, 1944). In contrast, profit-making competitive apolitical firms save and invest their money, attempting to make profits and avoid losses; their use of funds is flexible and dependent on their profit-seeking decisions (Mises, 1944; 1962).

This creates both the opportunities and incentives for bureaucrats, as it would to any other rational economic actor, to crave to: (1) manifest machismo, enhance public reputation and prestige (Hogwood and Peters, 1985; Hogwood and Gunn, 1984; Niskanen, 1971); (2) erect formidable hedges against the diminution of their reputation, prestige, output, ease of making changes and income (Downs, 1957); (3) keep their hands on power by responding aptly to the demands of privileged groups of rent seekers, including the political sponsor who is likely to ask for advantageous government largesse or policies (Dunleavy, 1991; Lane, 1993; McNutt, 2002); and (4) protect pet policies of privileged rent seekers (Parkinson, 1957). These are achieved by expanding their budgets beyond what is required for efficient production, making extraneous budgets a natural outgrowth of public bureaucracies (see further Mises, 1962).

Bureaucrats accomplish this, it is argued, by appropriating state resources for their own use (Niskanen, 1994; Pigou, 1962), encouraging rent seeking circles (Buchanan, 1995; Krueger, 1974; Tullock, 1967), employing high cost methods of service delivery (Leibenstein, 1966), and engaging in unnecessary activities (McNutt, 2002). Capitalising on their information advantage (Lane 1993; Weber, 1964), bureaucrats obscure these extraneous costs by introducing into their budgets programmes of questionable public value. As a result Niskanen (1971, p. 64) could argue that public bureaucracies supply 'an output up to twice that of a competitive industry faced by the same demand and cost conditions'. This is achieved through excessive budget expansion. Hogwood and Peters (1985, p. 39) put the potential increase in budget sizes of bureaucracies to a level of up to twice as much as required to produce their services. This, according to Weber (1964, p. 338) is possible as bureaucrats are more likely to 'get [their] way in the long run than [their] nominal superior, the Cabinet Minister, who is not a specialist' (see also Tullock, 1965; Williamson, 1986). The result is that 'the equilibrium level of output [of public sector bureaucracy moves into] the region where the minimum achievable marginal costs ... are substantially higher than the marginal value to the sponsor' (Niskanen, 1971, pp. 47–8). This divergence between the marginal costs and marginal value of the outputs of bureaucracies imposes externalities and hence social costs on society making public sector bureaucracies socially inefficient.

Public choice theory holds further that each questionable programme approved leads to an expansion of staff positions and hence the staff roster that bears little relationship to the purpose or amount of work done by the bureaucracy (Parkinson, 1957). Each superfluous worker, according to Parkinson, generates another. Offices and bureaus multiply over time without adding value. Following this theory bureaucratic apparatuses of the developing world are often perceived as 'overdeveloped' (see further Haque, 1997). What this means is that the size of the employee rosters of public sector bureaucracies provides a good indication of the scale of possible extraneous costs.

The views expressed in the public choice theory have sparked off waves of studies. The results from these studies have been mixed with little recognised consensus. Sterne et al. (1972), Buchanan and Tullock (1977), McGuire et al. (1979), Skaggs (1980), Gist and Hill (1981) and Mbaku (1991) for instance have all tested the public choice hypothesis of excessive budgets and overproduction in specific agencies (for a comprehensive listing see (Mueller, 2004). These studies discovered results that are consistent with the propositions of social inefficiency. It is worth noting, however, that these works have often been criticised for selecting bureaucracies that have a history and reputation for 'self-serving behavior and political autonomy' (see further Lovrich and Neiman, 1984, p. 49). Studies such as Micheals and Kalish (1981) and Ruttan (1980), on the other hand, dispute the public choice hypotheses of overproduction. These dissenting studies according to Lovrich and Neiman (1984) focused on bureaucracies with high professional standards and strong commitments to task.

Many of these studies are, however, based on Western systems and hence do not cast a good view of what the situation in developing countries such as Ghana is likely to be. It is thus impossible at this stage to say whether these bureaucracies are indeed running excessive budgets, deploying excessive personnel or even overproducing. It is to this end that the current study concentrates.

7.3 The Ghana land sector public bureaucracy

In Ghana, the arrangement for land policy delivery comprises a robust and institutionally wide network of interrelated but independent civil service organisations. The Ghana Land Policy Document (GLPD, 1999) lists 18 of these government departments. In reality, however, as this study established, only six government departments in addition to their parent Ministries are directly responsible for the task. For the rest, land policy delivery is only tangential to their core functions. From the perspective of organisational forms, all the six core agencies fit the theoretical description of public bureaucracies – non-profit, non-market and hierarchical with a number of departments and sub departments carrying out their work through the application of general and impersonal rules (see further, Jackson, 1982, p. 121; Beetham, 1987, p. 1; Niskanen, 1994; Gunning, 2003, p. 226). These bureaucratic apparatuses for land policy administration have been inherited as a colonial legacy, which has been imitatively fragmented and expanded over time. The operational budgets of these agencies, traditionally classified into expenses on Services, Investments, Personnel Emoluments and Administration are fully funded by central government either directly or through donor agencies or from funds legitimately retained by the agencies from previous years' operations (see for instance MLF, 1999; 2005).

At the apex of the land services delivery framework in Ghana is the Ministry of Lands and Forestry, the main political and governing body under which all the departments, with the exception of the Town and Country Planning Department, currently operate. The departments comprise: (1) the Lands Commission – responsible for the management of public lands, certification of Stool[1] land transactions, assisting in land title registration and land policy advisory services (see further Lands Commission Act, 1994 (Act 483)); (2) the Land Valuation Board – responsible for government valuation functions including preparation of valuation lists for local authorities, assessment of compensation for state acquisitions, valuation of state owned properties and stamp duty assessment (see further, PNDCL 42 of 1986); (3) the Land Title Registry – responsible for parcel based land title registration across the country (see further Land Title Registration Law, 1986 (PNDCL 152)) (4) the Office of the Administrator of Stool Lands – responsible for the collection and disbursement of Stool land revenues in accordance with a prescribed formula (see further, Office of the Administrator of Stool Lands Act, 1994 (Act 481)); (5) the Town and Country Planning Department – responsible for physical planning, zoning and development control (see further Town and Country Planning Ordinance, 1945 (Cap 84); Local Government Act, 1994 (Act 462)); (6) the Survey Department – responsible for the surveying and mapping of land parcels (see further The Survey Act, 1962 (Act 127).

The inbuilt extraneous cost in the budgets of these bureaucracies are thus examined. In the absence of any standardised yardstick, this is examined from a comparative perspective, making pointed references to the sizes of the costs of these bureaucracies as a proportion of the overall Ghana public service budget or that of selected comparable bureaucracies.

7.4 Research method

Data for this study was gathered between July 2004 and January 2005 in Ghana. The purpose of the survey was to obtained relevant data from both the public sector and property valuation firms to enable the assessment of the scale of inbuilt extraneous costs and hence internal inefficiencies of the land sector public bureaucracies in Ghana. The main data obtained were the published approved budget outruns for these agencies together with the national budget statements for the period 2000 and 2005. Auxiliary data on employee levels of the bureaucracy were also obtained through systematic administrative records searches, observations and unstructured interviews with some staff of the agencies. In all, five of the six agencies mentioned earlier were purposively surveyed. The survey excludes the Town and Country Planning Department as the study concentrates on policies within the band of ownership acquisition and formalisation. Land use policies as implemented by the Town and Country Planning Department were essentially post ownership formalisation and hence fell strictly speaking beyond the scope of this study. Additionally, ten professional valuers were also interviewed to obtain comparables for variables such as the supervisor–employee ratios. Factor analysis as described below constituted the main statistical procedure employed in analysing the data. Descriptive statistics were also employed in places.

7.5 Factor analysis

The 'simultaneous R- and Q-mode factor analysis' (Walden et al., 1995; Booth et al., 2006) statistical procedure was employed to interrogate the data. R-mode methods are similar to principal components analysis (Kovach, 1995; Davis, 2002). This procedure starts with a raw data matrix of *n* samples by *m* parameters. The raw data are then transformed into an *m* by *m* matrix, reflecting the similarity of pairs of parameters in terms of the samples' responses to them. The technique then transforms the original parameters (some of which may display interrelationships) into a smaller number of mutually uncorrelated underlying factors. The implication is that the most significant of these factors account for more variation within the data set than any other single original parameter.

As the new factors are uncorrelated, they occupy a set of mutually orthogonal axes in a 'multidimensional factor space'. Thus, any two factors may be presented as perpendicular axes in two-dimensional space. The technique also produces 'factor loadings' for each of the original parameters on each of the new factors. The size of the factor loading is related to the amount of variance of each parameter explained by a particular factor. It is therefore possible to plot the position of the original parameters in relation to any two of the new factors as a simple scatter diagram. Parameters plotting in close proximity are generally highly correlated.

The primary aim of Q-mode methods on the other hand is very similar to cluster analysis, in that they attempt to find groups of samples that plot close together in multivariate space. In numerical terms, the technique follows a similar procedure to principal co-ordinates analysis (Kovach, 1995; Davis, 2002). Starting from the same raw data set (*n* samples by *m* parameters), this time an *n* by *n* data matrix is constructed, with each element representing the similarity between sample pairs in terms of the way they respond to all parameters. Again, factors are produced that reduce the number of dimensions needed to explain data set variance. Factor loadings for the samples allow their positions to be plotted relative to any two factors. This time, samples plotting in close proximity in factor space can be interpreted as being most similar in terms of their values on all the original parameters.

In order to perform R- and Q-mode factor analysis, it is first necessary to standardise the raw data matrix in some way to remove the effects of different parameters being measured on different scales. As shown by

Table 7.1 Procedure

Step	Procedure
1	Compile a raw data matrix of n samples (rows) by *m* parameters (columns) denoted by [X], as in conventional matrix algebra.
2	[X] is standardised to give [W]. Each element of [X] has its column (parameter) mean subtracted from it. It is then divided by the product of the column (parameter) standard deviation (s) and the square root of *n*.
3	[W]′ is created by transposing [W]. This involves turning the rows of [W] into the columns of [W]′ and the columns into rows.
4	[R] is created by matrix multiplication of [W]′.[W]. The matrix [R] represents a correlation matrix between the parameters.
5	Eigenvectors and eigenvalues are extracted from [R]. The eigenvectors are used to form a matrix [U]. The eigenvalues can be used to compute the percentage of the total variation in the original data set explained by the new 'underlying' factors.
6	The square roots of the eigenvalues are placed in the top left to bottom right diagonal elements of a matrix [^]. All other elements in this matrix are set to zero.
7	[A^R] is computed by multiplication from [U]. [^]. The matrix [A^R] contains the R-mode (parameter) factor loadings. Each column represents the loadings of the original parameters on an individual factor (column 1 on factor 1, etc.). These are the values used when plotting the parameters in 'factor space' in the form of scatter diagrams.
8	[A^Q] is computed by multiplication from [W]. [U]. The matrix [A^Q] contains the Q-mode (sample) factor loadings. Each column represents the loadings of the original parameters on an individual factor (column 1 on factor 1, etc.). These are the values used when plotting the samples in 'factor space' in the form of scatter diagrams.

Davis (2002), if a common standardisation procedure is employed on the raw data matrix prior to the R- and Q-mode analysis, a common set of factors is extracted, and both the parameter factor and sample factor loadings are relative to these same underlying factors. The loadings can therefore be plotted in the same two-dimensional factor space for any two of these factors. Table 7.1 shows the mathematical steps of the procedure (Walden et al., 1995; Davis, 2002), involving a range of basic matrix algebra operations upon the original raw data matrix (of *n* samples by *m* parameters). The procedure for simultaneous R- and Q-mode factor analysis, followed that used in Davis (2002) and Booth et al. (2006).

7.6 The data

Before delving into the results of the factor analysis, the data set is first briefly described. The main nominal time series budget data for the

Table 7. 2 Summary of budgets 2000 to 2005 in current US dollar prices grouped by expenditure items

Year	Personnel expenses	Administration expenses	Services expenses	Investment expenses	Total
2000	$2,755,734.68	$1,163,930.48	$527,842.09	$1,980,459.54	$6,427,966.79
2001	$2,521,707.72	$1,538,995.39	$1,012,097.79	$2,163,300.35	$7,236,101.26
2002	$2,058,582.95	$1,077,456.60	$1,032,551.92	$1,569,873.75	$5,738,465.23
2003	$3,001,592.57	$1,609,314.46	$865,222.83	$1,138,267.92	$6,614,397.78
2004	$2,424,026.20	$1,784,180.54	$2,586,847.83	$5,751,093.48	$12,546,148.04
2005	$3,766,706.52	$1,945,148.91	$10,638,431.52	$8,966,475.00	$25,316,761.96
Grand Total	$16,528,350.64	$9,119,026.39	$16,662,993.97	$21,569,470.05	$63,879,841.05

Source: Field survey.

Table 7. 3 Summary of budgets 2000 to 2005 in current US dollar prices grouped by agencies

Year	Lands commission	Land title registry	Land valuation boards	Office of the adm. of Stool lands	Survey department	Total
2000	$11,296,607,795.15	$14,361,195,004.72	$19,190,708,118.10	$4,557,761,966.20	$9,731,021,553.66	$59,137,294,437.83
2001	$17,541,214,419.26	$7,079,065,911.90	$18,897,951,945.52	$3,852,120,776.23	$19,201,778,545.61	$66,572,131,598.52
2002	$17,239,418,144.90	$4,354,495,823.30	$12,994,790,469.50	$3,823,035,125.00	$14,382,140,508.40	$52,793,880,071.10
2003	$23,301,189,030.00	$3,978,609,880.00	$20,706,566,510.00	$5,055,162,420.00	$7,810,931,730.00	$60,852,459,570.00
2004	$30,119,340,000.00	$3,195,425,000.00	$20,157,931,000.00	$49,173,200,000.00	$12,778,666,000.00	$115,424,562,000.00
2005	$25,380,140,000.00	$7,234,670,000.00	$16,346,200,000.00	$84,381,600,000.00	$99,571,600,000.00	$232,914,210,000.00
Average	$22,716,260,318.83	$5,168,453,323.04	$17,820,687,985.00	$29,257,023,664.25	$30,749,023,356.80	$105,711,448,647.92

Source: Field survey.

sampled bureaucracies for the period 2000 and 2005 (see Appendix 1) are compounded at a discount rate of 33 per cent, which is the average bank lending rate in Ghana for the period 2000 and 2005 (Appendix 2). These are then converted into their dollar equivalent (Appendix 3). Tables 7.2 and 7.3 below summarise the compounded budget outruns as grouped firstly by budget items or parameters (Table 7.2) and by agencies (Table 7.3) respectively. According to column-6, row-8 of Table 7.3, between the year 2000 and 2005, in real terms a total of about US$64 million was spent on government land policy service delivery in Ghana. This translates to an average annual figure of US$10.6 million. Interestingly, while bureaucracy theory anticipates that personnel costs will rise it is rather services (staff training is an example) and investments (purchases of capital goods) that are rather rising more dramatically. This may be the result of rent seeking activities, but that remains speculative at this stage as it cannot be proved from the available data.

7.7 Results of the factor analysis

The objective of this analysis is to investigate the extent to which the various budget parameters influence the growth of the budgets of the respective agencies. Following bureaucracy theory, it is expected that the respective budgets of the agencies will be heavily influenced by personnel and administrative costs even though this may be at different rates owing to the likely differences in workload.

The simultaneous R- and Q-mode factor analysis was performed using the main expense parameters (Appendix 3). The analysis reveals that factors 1 and 2 explain 39 per cent and 27 per cent respectively of the variation in all four expense parameters used. Parameter and sample loadings extracted from Factors 1 and 2 were used to generate a factor plot (Figure 7.1).

The plot shows the expense parameters of the budget outruns to have both positive and negative loadings on the factors extracted. All parameters have positive loadings on factor 1. The Investment expenses (IE), Administration expenses (AE) and the Services expenses (SE) parameters have positive loadings on factor 2. Notably, however, the personnel expenses (PE) parameter has a negative loading. The spread of these parameters indicates that they are broadly influenced by discrete gradients. These relationships suggest that a combination of factors 1 and 2 is influenced by an IE and AE gradient (horizontal, Figure 7.1) and an SE and PE expenses gradient (vertical, Figure 7.1).

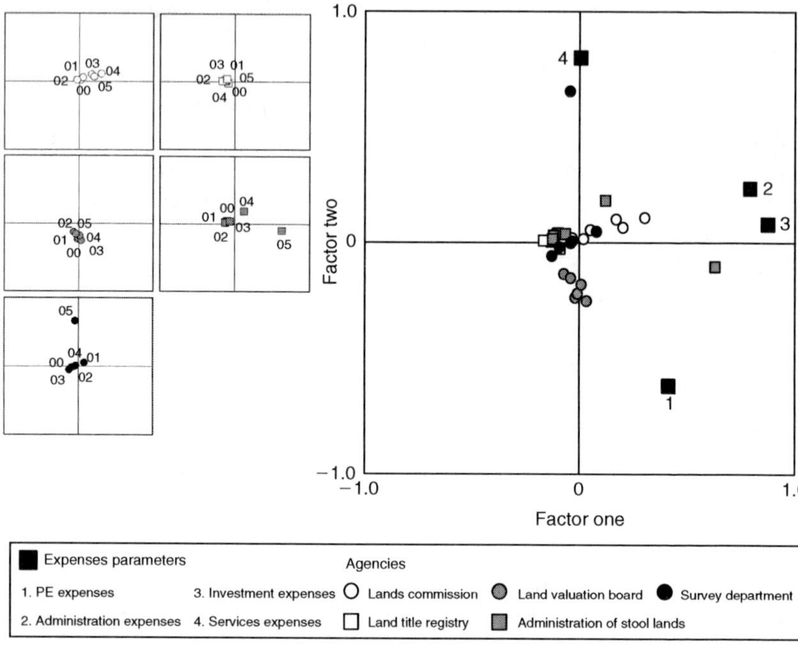

Figure 7.1 Simultaneous *R*- and *Q*-mode factor analysis plot of factor 1 versus factor 2 showing the relationship between the agency budgets

What emerges from the above spread of sample loadings is that the overall budgets for the land services delivery bureaucracies are influenced by both factors 1 and 2. However, the wide distribution of the sample points indicates that there are notable differences between some of the bureaucracies. For instance, the spread of samples along both axes has separated the Lands Valuation Board bureaucracy (negative factor 2 loadings) from the other agencies and, in doing so, indicates that PE expenses are the primary influence on the size of the budgets of the Lands Valuation Board bureaucracy. To this end the budgetary behaviours of the Lands Valuation Board appears consistent with the growing wage bill hypothesis of bureaucracy theory. But, as shall be discussed shortly, this is far from conclusive. Furthermore, both the Administrator of Stool Lands and the Lands Commission agencies have a strong factor 1 loading, which indicates that Investment expenses and Administration expenses are the main influences on the budget sizes of these agencies. With the exception of one sample point, this is also the same for the Survey Department agency. Moreover, it is noteworthy that the Land

Table 7.4 Results of the Factor Analysis of the Budgets of the Agencies

Factors	Eigenvalues	Total variance (%)	Cumulative eigenvalues	Cumulative total variance (%)
1	1.57	39.31	1.57	39.31
2	1.08	26.98	2.65	66.29
3	0.90	22.54	3.55	88.83
4	0.45	11.17	4.00	100.00

Title Registry agency is not specifically influenced by any particular expenses. Similarly, with the exception of the Administration of Stool Lands agency in 2004 and the Survey Department agency in 2005, Services expenses do not influence any of the agencies.

That said, it is noteworthy that, with time (for the analysis period 2000–5), the Lands Commission Agency (2003–5) and the Administration of Stool Lands (2004–5) are increasingly reliant on Administration expenses and Investment expenses. In contrast, the Land Valuation Board and the Land Title Registry agency seem to show no change in expenses type. Similarly, the Survey Department agency shows no obvious changes, except in one year (2005), when it is heavily reliant on Services expenses.

Table 7.4, summarises results from the Factor Analysis of the main expense parameters for each of the agencies, showing the eigenvalues, total variance (%), cumulative eigenvalues and cumulative total variance (%).

There is thus no clear consistency in the way that personnel costs in particular influence the budgets of the agencies. Indeed, with the exception of the Lands Valuation Board, the analysis show that personnel costs are not a major influence on the budgets of the remaining agencies, thereby questioning the theory that wage bills are an inevitable source of budget growth in bureaucracies.

It is worth pointing out that it is not possible to conclude from the analysis whether the bureaucrats under study actually tried to maximise budgets, or whether they were indeed successful. The results do not also tell if these budgets are excessive to provide indications of the extent to which they have been inflated with extraneous costs. That can only be detected by matching the budget provisions against actual needs. Considerations of resources and time did not allow for such detailed analysis to be carried out. The following comparative discussions are thus carried out to provide indications of the likelihood of budget maximisation and the scale of extraneous costs.

7.8 The budget growth rate pattern

The compounded annualised budget growth rate provides an index and a measure of the year on year growth rate of the budgets for the bureaucracies over the survey period. This index provides insights into the pace with which the budgets have been growing as well as their respective pattern of growth. Table 7.5 and Table 7.6 report the results of the compounded annualised growth rate. Specifically, Table 7.5 reports the indices for the respective budget items whiles Table 7.6 depicts the indices for the corresponding bureaucracies. According to the tables, in real terms the budgets for the agencies grew by an average of about 19 per cent per annum. Even so, average annual inflation in Ghana for the period was 28.5 per cent (CEPA, 2002). It follows that in real terms the bureaucracies experienced a negative annual growth rate of some 9.5 per cent. The point is that, since 1994, the mandates of the agencies have remained unchanged and, according to Hatch (2001) as corroborated by Antwi (2000) and Antwi and Adam (2003), the quality of services and executive leadership of these agencies have not changed in any significant way. This finding thus refutes the hypothesis of an excessive budget growth rate pattern.

Even barring inflation, overall the bureaucracies exhibit a rather erratic pattern of growth, oscillating from a minimum growth rate of −26.10 per cent to a maximum of 50.44 per cent (columns 6 and 7 of Table 7.5 and Table 7.6 respectively) with a typical growth rate of 19.27. The growth rate of wage bills was also quite erratic rather than consistent, ranging from a minimum deficit growth rate of −23.83 per cent in 2004 to a maximum of 25.65 per cent in 2005. Administrative expenses, the recurrent running costs according to Table 7.5 grew at an average annual rate of just some 6.53 per cent (far below the rate of inflation) ranging from a deficit growth rate of −42.84 per cent in 2002 to 80.21 per cent in 2003.

At an average wage bill growth rate of 2.29 per cent (column 2, Table 7.5), bearing the annual inflation rate of 28.5 per cent in mind, it is clear that personnel growth rate, contrary to expectations, exhibits the highest declining rate pattern. Similarly, investment expenses grew less than 10 per cent, also oscillating between deficit growth rates of −37.92 per cent in 2003 to a maximum of 80.21 in 2004. Service expenses exhibits the largest growth rate of almost 35 per cent from a minimum of −19.34 to a maximum of 75.68 per cent.

This individual pattern translates to overall budget growth rates that contradict the budget-maximising bureaucracy hypothesis. Generally,

Table 7. 5 Annualised compounded land sector budget growth rate in 2005 US$ prices by expenditure items

Year	Personnel expenses	Adm. expenses	Services expenses	Investment expenses	Total
2000	–	–	–	–	–
2001	−9.28	24.37	47.85	8.45	11.17
2002	−22.50	−42.84	1.98	−37.80	−26.10
2003	31.42	33.05	−19.34	−37.92	13.24
2004	−23.83	9.80	66.55	80.21	47.28
2005	35.65	8.28	75.68	35.86	50.44
Average	2.29	6.53	34.55	9.76	19.21

Source: Field survey.

Table 7.6 Annualised compounded land sector budget growth rate in 2005 US$ price by agencies

Year	Lands commis-sion	Land title registry	Land valuation boards	Office of the adm. of stool lands	Survey depart-ment	Total
2000	–	–	–	–	–	–
2001	35.60	−102.87	−1.55	−18.32	49.32	11.17
2002	−1.75	−62.57	−45.43	−0.76	−33.51	−26.10
2003	26.01	−9.45	37.24	24.37	−84.13	13.24
2004	22.64	−24.51	−2.72	89.72	38.88	47.28
2005	−18.67	55.83	−23.32	41.73	87.17	50.44
Average	12.77	−28.71	−7.15	27.35	11.54	19.21

Source: Field survey.

the annual budget growth rates for the respective bureaucracies oscillate erratically from a deficit growth rate of −28.71 per cent (Land Title Registry) to a maximum of 27.35 per cent (Office of the Administrator of Stool Lands) (Table 7.6). For the Land Title Registry and the Land Valuation Board in particular the trend is essentially downwards. Rather, these agencies are clearly financially malnourished and this in no doubt is resulting in a shrinking capacity to deliver. The practical consequence is that this shrinking capacity is ensuring a shortfall of supply of services to meet the existing and growing demands, leading to growing inertia, delays, inefficiencies, competitive rent seeking and corruption. Though these growth trends by themselves do not provide direct measures of extraneous costs, they show that even if extraneous costs are inbuilt in the budgets they are likely to be modest and not grow substantially.

It is now opportune to investigate the extent to which these figures represent drains on national resources as hypothesised by bureaucracy theory.

7.9 The share of the bureaucracies' budgets of national income

Table 7.7 reports a comparative analysis of the impacts of the budgets of the bureaucracies on national revenue. The two main internally generated government revenue classes in Ghana are the tax and non-tax revenues. These constitute the traditional funding sources for the budgets of public services and government bureaucracies in Ghana. The computed proportions of the budgets on the total government revenue (column 6) are an index of the respective year's budget's share of national revenue. This index helps in gauging the scale of drain that these budgets are imposing on national revenue in Ghana. As the table reports, the land sector's budget share of the preceding year's government revenue oscillates between a minimum of 0.25 per cent in 2001 to a maximum of 0.65 per cent attained in 2000. This works out to an overall average of less than 0.5 per cent (Mean = 0.49%) share of government internally generated revenue in the corresponding preceding years.

In comparison, this figure diverges starkly from the somewhat comparable forestry sector's average share of 1.5 per cent (minimum = 0.04% and maximum = 2.42%). The land sector's budget share of the total revenue is about a third of that of the forestry sector. Yet both sectors deal with land rights formalisation activities, with the land sector focusing essentially on non-forest and non-mining land transactions (covering 62.9 per cent of land area) while the forestry sector concentrates on forest land transactions (26.6 per cent of land area) (see FAO, 2004, for statistics). Such a comparatively small share does not appear to represent such a considerable drain on national resources as often imagined.

7.10 The size of the personnel roster

The evidence as analysed in Table 7.8 shows actually that the workforce sizes of the bureaucracies are shrinking in real terms. Overall, the five agencies put together employ 1,954 staff across the 10 regions of the country to serve Ghana's 22 million population, which is growing at an average annual rate of 2.14 per cent (see United Nations, 2005). Thus, if population growth is an important factor of demand for real estate as economic theory suggests, such an increasing population trend, all other demand factors notwithstanding, will engender increasing demand for real estate policy delivery services. Yet the workforce size available to meet this demand represents less than 0.3 per cent (0.24 per cent) of the total public service workforce of 800,000.00 (United Nations, 2005).

Table 7. 7 Comparison with government revenue (millions of cedis)

Year	National non-tax revenue	National tax revenue	Total internally generated revenue	Subsequent year's budget for the sampled land sector agencies		Budget share of government revenue (%)	
				Land sector	Forestry sector	Land sector	Forestry sector
1999	310,400.00	3,089,100.00	3,399,500.00	20,762.90	1,343.00	0.61	0.04
2000	961,600.00	3,731,700.00	4,693,300.00	30,596.10	74,883.00	0.65	1.60
2001	3,731,700.00	6,556,900.00	10,288,600.00	25,998.50	141,861.00	0.25	1.38
2002	252,400.00	8,547,500.00	8,799,900.00	42,029.10	212,585.00	0.48	2.42
2003	298,600.00	12,556,300.00	12,854,900.00	66,240.40	286,510.00	0.52	2.23
2004	1,136,300.00	17,403,000.00	18,539,300.00	76,652.60	251,122.00	0.41	1.35
Mean	1,115,166.67	8,647,416.67	9,762,583.33	43,713.27	161,384.00	0.49	1.50

Source: Data on non tax and tax revenue were extracted from the budget statements of Ghana (1999–2005).

Table 7. 8 Real estate sector workforce

Agency	2001				2005				Inter-census Percentage Change
	Professionals	Sub-professional	Others	Total	Professionals	Sub-professional	Others	Total	
Lands commission	52	24	211	287	39	16	209	264	−8.01
Survey department	33	29	459	521	33	35	471	539	3.45
Off. of adm. of stool lands	23	21	205	249	23	21	301	251	0.80
Land title registry	7	3	56	66	23	36	23	82	24.24
Land valuation board	36	28	773	837	35	655	128	818	−2.27
Total	151	105	1,704	1960	153	763	1,132	1,954	−0.31
Percentage	7.70	5.36	86.94	100.00	7.83	39.05	57.93	100.00	

Source: Field survey.

The distribution of this total staff level among the individual agencies is even more revealing. Lands Commission has a total workforce of 264 (0.03% of the public service), the Survey Department, 539 (0.07% of the public service), the Office of the Administrator of Stool Lands 251(0.03% of the public service), the Land Title Registry 82 (0.01% of the public service) and the Land Valuation Board, 818 (0.1%). These are indeed trivial figures relative to the 3000 staff of the Ghana Highways Authority (0.38% of public service), 800 of the Department of Urban Roads (0.1% of public service), 25,000 of the Ghana Health Service (3.13% of public service) and 240,000 of the Ministry of Education (30% of public service) respectively (see further World Bank, 2005a, p. 35).

More importantly, the workforce sizes of the land sector bureaucracies declined overall between 2001 and 2005 by some 0.03 per cent. Even the agency, the Land Title Registry, that grew significantly (24%) over the period, grew that much because of its low workforce base of 66 to only 82 staff. It is still the smallest land sector bureaucracy. This confirms further that by national standards the land policy bureaucracies are some of the smallest and declining bureaucracies in the country. Overgrowth does not thus appear to be a major source of extraneous costs, at least by national standards.

Given the failure of the bureaucracy hypothesis to provide ample explanation to the sources of extraneous costs, the ensuing section discusses other non-traditional sources.

7.11 Identified sources of extraneous costs

This study found large measures of extraneous costs in two key subtle sources. The first relates to the structure rather than the size of the workforce of the bureaucracies. The second relates to resource misallocations fostered by the existing budgeting procedures. There are other sources such as the manual land policy delivery system and the reward system. For brevity, these are discussed as part of the two key sources.

7.11.1 The acute imbalances in the workforce structure

As Table 7.8 shows, the land policy bureaucracies are manifestly bereft of professional staff (under 8 per cent of the total workforce) with major overstaffing and apparent widespread underemployment at the lower ends of the echelon-messengers, typists and clerks. These lower end employees constitute about 58 per cent of the total workforce. Owing to the continuing government freeze on employment, heads of these bureaucracies have no control over the selection of their staff mix and appointments. As a result, overall about 41 per cent of established vacancies for professional staff within the land policy bureaucracies remain unfilled. This workforce profile gives a relatively high typical supervisor–staff ratio of 1:12 for the bureaucracies relative to about 1:4 in major private survey and valuation firms in Ghana as the survey found. The practical consequences are that errant staff are not systematically and efficiently supervised while professional staff are forced to spread their efforts thinly to cover a wider range of tasks. Thus without exception, errant, secretariat, clerical and technical staff of these bureaucracies control too much of what goes on in these bureaucracies given the almost exclusively manual service delivery systems of the bureaucracies. They decide for instance when files move from one desk to the other, when correspondence, transaction documents and land certificates are typed, and the scale of preference for dealing with cases by senior officers. This has fostered an inbuilt tradition of paternalism across the bureaucracies, which tend to portray clients/customers as people seeking favors from the bureaucracies. Staff thus have the tendency to demand favours from the clients of the bureaucracies before actions are taken on their request for land rights documentation, else the cases could delay for an average of 385 days (see World Bank, 2005b). Such delays and frustrations are things that everyone would like to avoid and thus clients invariably pay these extra legal costs in addition to the official charges.

This means that these applicants have to divert resources from other productive sectors to effect these payments, not to mention the costs of the time spent in following up these documentation requests. Thus Goldsmith (1999) must be overlooking these extraneous costs in contending that because the salaries of these lower level staff are low, getting rid of them would lead to insignificant costs savings. This may be so from the government perspective but is certainly not the case from the clients' and social welfare costs' perspective. The situation is not helped by the generally poor salary structure across the civil service, which lags behind both parastatal organisations and private firms. As Hutchful (2002) puts it, these salaries hardly suffice for a minimal standard of living. As a result, heads of these bureaucracies appear to be lacking the moral courage and justification to exert control and thus seem to have, through inertia, acquiesced to these malfeasances.

Then again, professional and management staff are too involved in routine policy delivery activities and paper shuffling. The survey found that these staff strain to keep up with administrative tasks; dealing with internal and external correspondence, written evaluations of everyday staff work, preparation of staff schedules, leave approvals, preparation of reports, internal and external meetings, responding to ministerial – and often unceremonious – invitations and requests, as well as other policy delivery activities such as rent assessment and site inspections. Very little management time and capacity is thus left for business strategising, research and policy development. These conditions facilitate the accumulation of extraneous costs in terms of inefficient outputs, but these costs are largely hidden and not all empirically observable and quantifiable.

7.11.2 The extraneous costs of input control budgeting

This study found that another serious source of waste and extraneous costs is inherent in the budget preparation and implementation processes rather than the sizes of the budgets per se. The starting point for such waste is the arbitrary ceilings imposed unilaterally on the budget sizes of all Ministries and their departments by the Ministry of Finance every year. These ceilings are imposed based exclusively on financial exigencies without recourse to any critical analysis of the budgetary requirements of the ministries. Perhaps this is to address the public choice concern that, when given the opportunity, bureaucrats will inflate their budgetary requirements. In that sense some merit may exist in this approach. What emerges from this study is that after a point, however, increasing budget cuts begin to hinder the fiscal health of organisations, which invariably leads to deadweight losses through misallocation and underemployment of existing resources, a major extraneous cost.

Because the bureaucrats of the surveyed bureaucracies have little control over the size of their budgets, they show serious lack of commitment to the budget preparation process. These organisations thus do not have designated budget units or departments. What they have are budget committees mandated to be established by government. The result is that not only is budget preparation dealt with as an ad-hoc activity, the task is literally left to be handled by staff of the Accountant General's Department on secondment to the agencies or in some cases by single or very few staff as part of their long list of functions. These personnel are not professionally qualified accountants and in general have no formal training in budgeting.

The situation is compounded by the Ministry of Finance's tradition of requesting for the submission of budget estimates always at the last minute. In 2004, the survey witnessed that the bureaucracies had just a week to submit their budget statement for 2005. This under normal circumstances should not pose serious problems if a strong permanent budget unit exists within the departments. In the absence of such permanent budget units, the budget process indeed starts on receipt of the deadline for submission. Thus, behind a veil of urgency to meet deadlines and the need to keep within the ceilings, budgetary allocations are often made in haste and largely arbitrarily without any serious analysis of the fiscal and performance implications of the incorporated individual budgetary items. Under such a situation, the chances are that resources will be misallocated and this appears to be the most serious source of waste in the budgets. In retrospect, this could explain why, as observed from the survey, the agencies after all these huge budget expenditures still lack basic and appropriate equipments and resources to effectively carry out their functions.

7.12 Summary

This chapter does not and cannot tell whether the surveyed bureaucracies have attempted to or have succeeded in budget maximising. The chapter looked at the evidence, however, and found most of the suggestions by public choice on sources of extraneous costs largely wanting. The bureaucracies involved are not overgrown by national standards, and neither do they have large workforces nor budget sizes. There is a very weak incentive within the sector for bureaucrats to do so. The data showed instead that the main sources of extraneous costs are the imbalances in the workforce structure in favour of errant, secretarial and clerical staff rather than professional staff, and the input control budgeting procedures, which is inducing the widespread misallocation of budgetary items. Dealing with these two issues would remove huge sources of inefficiencies in these bureaucracies.

8
Benefits of Real Estate Policies

8.1 Introduction

If Africa wishes to prosper, it must draw insights from how the West has managed to attain and retain prosperity. There is evidence of a connection between property market efficiency and rising prosperity in the West. Earlier economists like Adam Smith (1776) and George (1912) have long detected a positive correlation between development and the performance of the property market. In comparatively recent times also, Alonso (1960), Muth (1985), Mills (1972), Ball et al. (1998), Deininger (2003) and Dam (2006) have all contributed profoundly to our understanding of the importance of landed properties to the economic development processes in both rich and poor countries. It is no wonder that all rich countries are host to active and efficient property markets. It is estimated, for example, that land and buildings 'account for between half and three-quarters of the wealth in most economies' (World Bank, 2007). Further, a developed economy like the UK derives as much as 6 per cent of its Gross Domestic Product (GDP) from its commercial property sector alone (BPF, 2006). A possible inference from this is that developed economies are rich to a degree because their property markets are well functioning. There is thus little doubt that improving the performance of property markets in the developing world is an effective and strategic means of achieving economic prosperity.

Nevertheless, property markets are imperfect economic institutions with the effect that, if left unregulated, they may reproduce errors and cause undesirable consequences. Thus, in order to secure better performance, moderate economic thinking suggests that some form of government interference into the natural workings of the market may be necessary. Such government action is needed at least to clarify property rights (Deininger, 2003), lower transaction costs (World Bank, 2008; Coase, 1960), prevent or aid the internalisation of externalities (World Bank, 2008; Antwi, 2000; Pigou, 1920) and discourage land concentration or monopolisation (Hammond, 2006). Land policies are the normal means through which governments orchestrate such actions. By way of definition, a land policy is a collection of rules that govern land use and ownership. Land policies regulate the internal workings of land markets, making provisions for the manner in which sellers, buyers and intermediaries relate to each other with respect to land. These policies dictate the courses that property markets traverse and define the outcomes they ultimately produce. As such, modern property markets are essentially creatures of land policies.

In recent years, land policies, particularly those enacted to regulate the performance of property markets in developing countries, have come under severe criticisms as being generally overdone, repressive and too costly (Hammond, 2006; Deininger, 2003; Antwi, 2000). This is not at all surprising, given the wide range of land policy types that could exist in any given country. They are also context specific in the sense that policy types that work successful in one society may fail profoundly elsewhere. These make the risk of selecting a wrong policy type for a given society very high and eminent. Additionally, the actual benefits offered by a land policy are not self-evident, and so too are their drawbacks. Thus, a policy could cause undetected damage to a given society for a considerable length of time.

Besides, the full advantages and drawbacks of land policies cannot also always be predetermined beforehand, owing to the uncertainties of the future. It is important nonetheless that the damages or benefits associated with extant land policies are always known and understood in order for the policies that are causing damages to be identified for timely reforms. The wave of criticisms mounted against land policies in the developing world has triggered a wave of land policy and institutional reforms across these countries, particularly since the early 1980s. Funding for these reforms has come from both national governments and the international development community such as the World Bank and DFID. Nevertheless, because these criticisms were preoccupied with the drawbacks of land policies and institutions, very little effort has been directed at measuring their advantages. Yet without an understanding of their benefits it is impossible to estimate their real impact on the economic development processes. With a knowledge of the downsides of developing world land policies widely discussed in the literature, the object of this chapter is to shed light and provide indications of the upsides of land policies in a developing country like Ghana in order that a more objective balancing between their cost and benefits can be fostered.

Specifically, the chapter addresses four key questions: (1) are existing land policies producing measurable and meaningful economic benefits? (2) Are the magnitudes and directions of the economic benefits, if any, uniform across the different types of land policies? (3) Are benefits from a given policy type dependent on compliance with another policy type? (4) Does the magnitude of the benefits obtained from a policy depend on which government department enforces the policy? Factorial design statistical procedure has been used to analyse empirical data obtained from Ghana to answer these questions. The justification for this method of analysis is provided shortly. To set the ensuing discussions in context, the conceptual foundations of land policies is now presented.

8.2 The place of land policies

A significant body of research demonstrates the importance of land policies (see for instance World Bank, 2008; ZLA, 2008). Even extreme liberals like Smith (1776), Hayek (1944) and Coase (1988) admit that untouched markets have blemishes that impede their ability to deliver impeccable favourable consequences. In common with other market types, the essential causes of blemishes in land markets consist of unclear property rights, a paucity and asymmetry of property market information, externalities, monopolisation of market segments and the inadequate provision for public goods. These are known collectively by economists as market failures. In exploring the practical effects of these causes in a way that affords better insights into how they affect market efficiency, it is useful to put them into reasonable categories. As such in this study, these blemishes have been grouped into precondition, omission and outcome blemishes. Different classification schema have been used by other authors.

For property markets to perform efficiently, certain basic preconditions must be met. The notable ones are: (1) clearly defined property rights or land tenure system; (2) readily available current and complete information on the essential attributes of land and relevant market condition; and (3) less onerous transaction costs. These are briefly considered in turn. To begin with, the economic function of property markets is to facilitate the interchange of property rights and money between the owners of the property rights who want money and those with money who want the property rights. For this to happen, all property rights in existing pieces of properties in any given society must be fully defined and parcelled out among individuals and institutions. Without that, land markets are bound to function less efficiently. This is because, without parcelling out the rights to specific actors, it would be impossible for the interchange to take place at all. This would, in turn, lower the economic performance of the market. It has to be emphasised that it is not sufficient for the rights to properties to be clearly defined and parcelled out. When ownership rights are clearly defined and parcelled out they must be publicly known. It should be possible for purchasers and creditors to know with a great deal of certainty whether actors purporting to sell or use a particular property as collateral for credit are indeed true owners of the property in question. Purchasers who purchase from phony owners are likely to be pushed by the market with economic losses. The purchasers/creditors must be able to know or verify who owns what land or property. This must be known together with information on relevant market events and data such as comparable prices, available land and properties for sale, the physical and environmental conditions and attributes of the property and its surroundings, and so forth.

Then again, the price people pay for a property is based on their valuation of the satisfaction/benefits they expect to gain from the property. They must thus have information about what satisfaction/benefits a given property is capable of offering. Most of the vital information about properties is not self-evident. Often, this is known only to the seller/borrower but not to the purchaser/creditor. Conversely, purchasers/creditors may know about the prices at which comparable properties are selling. Again, this information may not be available to the owner. Yet in a market based economy sellers/borrowers are not bound to disclose facts known to them that may not be known to the purchaser/creditor at the time. Such information may make the property in question less valuable than the purchaser/creditor has supposed it to be. Likewise, creditors/purchasers are not bound to disclose facts that make the property more valuable than the seller/borrower has supposed it to be. In the end, purchasers and creditors may end up paying or advancing more credit than the worth of the property. Equally, sellers and borrowers may ask for less than what the property is actually worth. Since the efficiency of markets depends on the extent to which prices agreed between parties to a transaction reflect the true satisfaction or value offered by property, it follows that, unless a means is found to ensure that all parties to a transaction are equipped with all the key information they need to reach an efficient conclusion, markets will continue to operate at suboptimal levels. Even where property rights are well defined and clearly parcelled out across actors of the society with relevant information readily available, optimal transactions may still not take place if the costs of transaction are so excessive to the point that they diminish or atrophy the potential gains from the transaction. The reason is simple. If, as a result of high transaction costs or any other market impediments, anticipated gains from transactions become unattainable or even significantly reduced, most transacting parties would most likely feel better off withdrawing from the transaction. This will, as a consequence, prevent many favourable transactions from occurring. Land markets that lack any or all of these preconditions – that is, clearly defined property rights, readily accessible information and low transaction costs – are plagued with *precondition blemishes*. Precondition blemishes are very critical for the reason that they could prevent the market from taking off at all.

The next set of blemishes is collectively described here as *omission blemishes*. Pristine land markets rely on the voluntary decisions of individuals and institutions to work efficiently. The problem with this is that, individuals and institutions engage in transactions for the sake of the anticipated gains. This means, they will keep away from transactions that are not associated with direct gains to them or for which they are not guaranteed to be the exclusive recipients of the gains. Accordingly, individuals and institutions, when behaving rationally, would avoid transactions that would lead to the production of public goods such as public roads, sewage disposal, parks, recreational areas, fire protection, waste disposal and other transactions for which they cannot be guaranteed exclusive rights to the benefits they generate. This means that while such public goods are vital for overall societal welfare, they will not be provided for in unassisted land markets.

The last are the *outcome blemishes*. Outcome blemishes refer to the adverse consequences that may follow on from the use of land in an unassisted land market. These outcome blemishes are conventionally designated externalities or diseconomies (Pigou, 1920; Coase, 1960) and they refer to the uncompensated harm or benefits that a decision maker brings onto others who are not party to the decision. For example, A's neighbour may suffer a detrimental externality when A's land is used as a landfill site or a factory. Such land uses have the tendency to reduce the economic value of adjoining properties. These adjoining properties may belong to other neighbours such as B, C and D. In a pure market based economy, the market itself has no mechanism to ensure that B, C and D are adequately compensated by A for any such losses in value of their properties that may result from A's decision to use the land as a landfill site or a factory. This shows that the outcome from free market land uses and transactions could be harmful and unfair, even unjust to others.

It is observable from the discussions above that blemishes are basically unsatisfactory and undesirable states of affairs that have to be replaced by a more satisfactory and desirable state of affairs if efficiency is to be attained; they have to be cured to bring the market to a healthy level of performance. How may this be achieved? Conventional orthodoxy, advocated by Pigou (1920), contends that since these land market blemishes are inherent in the market itself, the solution must come from external sources. The best known external source is government action in the form of land policy. This is all well and good. But, as Weimer and Vining (2004) correctly points out, there is an almost limitless list of policies from which governments could choose to deal with any given blemish. The success of these policies in curing targeted blemishes depends on the suitability of the policy selected. Even when the correct policy is selected there is still no guarantee that the correct results would be obtained. This is because land policies are in many ways comparable to drugs (or medicines). For instance, a drug that may cure an ailment may also maim or even kill the patient if inappropriately administered. Likewise a land policy that is capable of curing or suppressing a blemish is also potentially capable of aggravating a blemish or even stultifying the performance of the market altogether. So the challenge is not just about making sure that the right policy is in place; it is also about ensuring that the policies are not overdone or underdone and are efficiently administered. This balance is a delicate one to achieve. It is not uncommon to find situations in which the right policies are chosen but the blemishes remain or have even been worsened because the policies have been overdone, underdone and/or poorly administered. There are also instances whereby policies that appear superficially to be correct have turned out to be more problematic than the very blemish they were meant to cure.

There is no universally accepted way of gauging the right level of policy. The effective way to circumvent this problem is to monitor policy outcomes on a regular basis. Where the net outcomes are unfavourable, the policy is, to that degree, inappropriate, overdone, underdone and/or poorly administered. Such knowledge would then set the tone for any land policy reforms. Quite surprisingly, important as this is, the literature remains largely devoid of such measures, particularly in the context of African countries. For instance, even though Ghana is presently embarking on a comprehensive land reform programme under the ongoing World Bank-led 'Land Administration Project' at a huge cost of US$55 million, the project documents remain utterly bereft of any measures of the economic effects of the policies that are being reformed (see Hatch Associates, 2002). Even the prospects of the incoming policies are also unmeasured. If the reforms turn out to be wrongly targeted, or replace beneficial policies with poorer substitutes, the efficiency of the reform would be questionable. Further, it would leave the society with the dilemma of whether the resources spent on the reforms would not have yielded better returns had it been invested in a more productive sector. It is to provide a measure of the benefits of these land policies in Ghana that this study is directed. Measurement of the effects of land policies involves an understanding of the nature of the land policies in question.

8.3 Nature of land policies in Ghana

In most developing countries like Ghana, government interventions in property markets have taken three main routes: regulative, distributive and redistributive routes. Regulative policy types comprise those policies that impose statutory controls and requirements over the decisions and behaviours of property market dealers. In Ghana, for instance, two main types of regulative policies exist: (1) Stool[1] land certification policies (otherwise termed concurrence and consent), which insist that transactions in Stool land are void *ab initio* unless government concurs to them;[2] and (2) the general registration policies made up of deeds and Land Title Registration laws. Both registration laws give preference to land rights officially recorded in accordance with their laid-down procedures to those that are not.[3] The two laws were never meant to operate simultaneously. The Land Title Registration law, which was enacted in 1986, was, according to section 13, designed progressively to take over from the existing Deeds registration law (Land Registry Act of 1962). However, owing purely to a clash of departmental interests the takeover process stalled. As a result, the two systems of registration have operated simultaneously in the past 20 years. Contacts with the Ghana Ministry of Lands, Forestry and Mines revealed current political pressures under the instigation of the directorate of the land administration project to end the dual registration system. The duality of the registration system is, thus, unlikely to persist for long.

Nevertheless, while these policies persist, it is legitimate to enquire about their respective economic effects and hence whether they should be preferred. This can only be ascertained by providing a valuation of both types of policy. Distributive policies on the other hand are those that empower the state to acquire private lands subject to the payment of fair compensation regardless of the purposes for which the lands were acquired and how they are eventually allocated and used. The third category is the redistributive policies. These empower governments to acquire private lands without the payment of fair compensation regardless of the purposes of the acquisition and the eventual uses to which they are put. The performance of these policies is the subject matter of this chapter. Though most land policies in Ghana apply nationally, resource constraints made it impossible to carry out a national survey for the study. The study thus concentrated on Accra, Ghana.

The choice of Accra was influenced by the fact that it is a typical sub-Saharan Africa city (Antwi, 2000). Since different policies tend to be applicable to particular geographical areas of Ghana, Accra was categorised into four policy zones according to the applicable policies. Thus, the participating valuers were called upon to value four hypothetical land parcels of equal size, each located within a policy zone. For this purpose Accra, the study area, may be divided into policy zones according to the dominant policies affecting each area. Regulative policy zones were subdivided into two. These are the Stool regulative (SREG) policy zone and the general regulative (GREG) policy zone. The GREG policy zone comprises all land areas that are owned and controlled by indigenous landowners other than stools. The SREG policy zone sampled for this is the Nungua Residential Area, located within the southeastern section of Accra. Nungua is arguably the most well known SREG zone in Accra. Ajirigano is the GREG policy zone randomly selected for this study. Ajirigano is a comparatively new and fast developing residential area.

The redistributive policy (REDIS) zone sampled is the Achimota residential area located within the northwest section of Accra. The sampled redistributive zone is the New Achimota located within the Northwestern section of Accra covering about 2,870.6 acres of land, which was originally acquired by the Government of Ghana under the Executive Instrument No. 61 of 1975 for a National Sports Complex with adjacent first class residential and commercial areas. For various reasons the government did not pay compensation to the 352 claimants. This inertia on the part of government engendered a spate of encroachment in the area in 1987. Thus, though by 1979 the government had allocated all 799 plots, only 487 of the lessees were able to take possession of their plots due to resistance from the disposed owners. In all, at least 90 per cent of the area was at the time of the study under encroachment by the disposed owners. These encroachers are having difficulties obtaining formal titles to their properties.

The distributive (DIST) policy zone chosen is the East Legon Residential Area, which is located within the northeastern section of the Accra metropolis covering an area of 5.6 square miles. This zone was compulsorily acquired in 1944 by the then Government of the Gold Coast (now Ghana) under Certificate of Title No. 404/44. This was acquired as an extension to the previously acquired 1.248 square miles in 1936 for the Anti-Amaryl Aerodrome under Certificate of Title No. 252/36. While portions of the Aerodrome land were developed into the Kotoka International Airport, the acquired extension was still largely undeveloped after almost two decades. In 1960 the first postcolonial Cabinet authorised the subdivision of the extension into urban land uses for distribution to private developers. The East Legon Residential Area layout encapsulated five existing settlements: Shiashie, Abotsiman, Okponglo, La Bawaleshie and Gointe. Upon a petition to the Head of State a committee of enquiry was set up in 1975, which recommended all the settlements be retained but the residents should upgrade their structures to meet the standard of development envisaged for the area.[4] The Lands Commission commenced plot allocations for private development at East Legon, in 1975/6. It was, however, not until 1980/1 that access roads were provided in the estate (Larbi, 1994). Due to a shortage of state lands in Accra in general, re-entries have been rigorously pursued in East Legon (since 1985) and other government distributive zones of Accra to recover undeveloped lands for re-allocation (see Larbi, 1994).

An important non-policy influence on property prices is infrastructure. There are significant variations in the quality of the infrastructure provisions from the respective policy zones. Apart from the fact that the DIST zone is provided with very good infrastructure, all the other zones have very poor and unreliable infrastructure and amenities. It is thus expected that the variations in the quality of infrastructure may influence the variations in the benefits produced by the respective policies. An appreciation of existing knowledge on this subject matter is also useful for a proper understanding of the analysis presented in this chapter.

8.4 Research method

The popularity and usefulness of hedonic procedure is no longer in doubt as evidenced by the explosion of studies using the procedure

(Bailey et al., 1963; Des Rosiers et al., 2002; Grilliches, 1971; Hidano, 2002; Meese and Wallace, 1997; Mills and Simenauer, 1996; Morancho 2003; Rosen, 1974; Simon et al., 1998; Wolverton and Senteza, 2003). The hedonic procedure thus offers a good starting-point for any attempt at measuring and comparing the benefits of policies. Procedurally, the hedonic model works on the principle that commodities, like properties, consist of bundles of distinguishable attributes, each of which commands or contributes a unique fragment of the overall price of properties; the price of property is thus an aggregate measure of the unique contributions of each identifiable attribute of the property (Rosen, 1974; Saderion et al., 1994; Mills and Simenauer, 1996; Meese and Wallace, 1997; Hidano, 2002).

Economic theory also confirms that the market price of a property is a measure of the benefits that the purchaser envisages to gain from the property. The unique contributions made by each attribute to the overall price thus represent the measure of benefits associated with that attribute, viewed from the perspective of the purchaser, and this can be negative or positive. When a policy is applied to a property it becomes an additional attribute of the property in question and, hence, would also contribute its own fragment of benefits to the overall price. If the unique contribution of a policy is positive the implication is that it is having a positive economic effect (benefits); if it is zero, it is producing no benefits; and if it is negative it is producing adverse effects. The benefits of a policy summed across all affected properties represent the aggregate benefits of that policy in question, the additive effects.

For a start, the density of policies on land markets in developing countries is typically high. The institutions involved in the implementation of the policies are also generally numerous. Secondly, these interventions, in the particular case of the developing world, generally tend to co-exist with equally potent pre-existing indigenous tenure laws, regulations and practices. It is common knowledge in the social sciences that social phenomena and variables, like land policies, interact. It thus follows that land policies necessarily interact or interplay among themselves. Testing of the interaction is thus arguably at the core of any land policy analysis. The very interactions between policies may also contribute additional fragments to the overall price. Three scenarios are possible from such interplay. Firstly, the interactions of the policies may produce virtually no effect on the outcome. In that case the results from the additive hedonic procedure are complete. The interaction could, secondly, result in the policies complementing each other, in which case the effects of the interaction will be different from the aggregate effects of the individual independent variables. In that case, the effect of one policy type, for instance, depends on the magnitude of the effects of another. Thirdly, the policies could be undermining one another in which case the interaction effect may be less than the aggregate of the individual effects. Where policies are complementing or undermining each other, then they can be said to be having synergic effects. This means that the regression coefficient for the regression of the dependent variable (land price) on each of the respective policy types increases as the dependent variable increases (see Cohen et al., 2003). When the effect of one policy is low, the effect of the other policy that it interacts synergistically with also becomes low. Conversely when one is high the other becomes high also.

It is difficult to detect the interaction effects in a hedonic model unless the interactions form part of the original data set. In most developing countries existing data on property prices are not generally organised according to the policies that have affected the respective properties, let alone the interactions of the policies. In order words it is impossible to know from the existing databases which policy has been applied to which property. This makes it impossible to rely on these databases to gauge the benefits of policies. One alternative is to identify current purchasers and enquire from them the type of policies that have affected their currently acquired properties and the price at which they acquired those properties. This can prove to be expensive and time consuming. Another alternative, the approach employed here, is to enquire from professional valuers the value they are likely to put on properties that have been subjected to particular policies to generate a data set for analysis. However, this can be tested in multivariate regression analysis treating both the original policies and their interactions as nominal predictors of land prices. This technique is termed factorial design analysis.

8.5 Data collection and instrument

Sample respondents for this study were drawn from the population of professional real estate valuers in Ghana. Professional qualification is defined here as membership of the Ghana Institution of Surveyors (GIS), which is the professional body for the training and accreditation of professional valuers in Ghana. The list of professional valuers was thus obtained from the offices of the GIS in Accra, Ghana. Though the selection of sampled valuers was random, only valuers with considerable post-qualification experience (at least five years) in the sampled geographical areas were surveyed. In all, 30 experienced valuers were surveyed.

Because land policies are essentially non-market goods, stated preference (contingent valuation approach), first developed by Ciriacy-Wantrup in 1947, was employed in this study. On the practical validity of contingent valuation, see also Hanemann (1994) and Kilpatrick (2007). McLean and Mundy (1998) show that contingent valuation methodologies have a theoretical foundation in economics and are widely employed in the real estate field. The use of contingent valuation methodology to specifically value the benefits of land policies in a developing country context is not without precedent. Dowall and Leaf (1991) and Pamuk and Dowall (1998) have used the methodology to evaluate the effects of land policies on house prices in Jakarta and the East–West Corridor region of Trinidad, respectively. The detailed theoretical discussions behind the validity of this method in the valuation of land policies are presented in Dowall (1992).

Data for this research was obtained using a purposely-designed questionnaire. In Dowall and Leaf (1991), data on the valuation of policies were obtained through systematic interviews of land-brokers in their market area. Following Dowall and Leaf (1991), qualified real estate valuers were requested to value a hypothetical land covering a uniform area of 0.23 acres,[5] contingent on the assumption that the land is affected by each of the categories of the research factor *P* in turn; that is *SREG, GREG, DIST* and *REDIST* in turn. Based on the above coding, each land value obtained was classified according to the policy category to which they respectively relate. This generated 120 data points, which were analysed using the factorial design analysis. Data was collected between June 2004 and January 2005.

8.6 Analysis

As explained under the research method section, factorial design is essentially a multiple regression and correlation analysis (MRCA) of two or more nominal scaled independent variables. Statistically, the products of the independent variables represent their interaction(s) (Cohen et al., 2003). As mentioned earlier, this study aims to compare the benefits (as measured in land prices (*Y*)) of respective land policies (*P*) as well as the governmental agencies (*G*) in charge of the implementation of the respective policies. To achieve this, both the agencies and the policies involved have to be treated as independent nominal variables.

There are four categories of the research factor *P* – land policies – and three categories of *G* – the government agency. The four categories of *P* are Stool Regulative (*SREG*), General Regulative (*FREG*), Distributive

(*DIST*), and Redistributive (*REDIST*) policies. The three categories of the research factor *G* are Lands Commission (*LANDSCOM*) and the Land Title Registry (*LANDTITLEREG*)[6] and a research control (or reference) Department (*NODEPARTMENT*). It has to be mentioned again that the factors *P* and *G* are not the only variables that influence property prices in these areas. There are other non-policy influences such as infrastructure and social amenities. As the analysis stands, the effects of these other non-policy variables are captured by or built into the price effects of the respective policies. Ideally, better insights into the unique effects of the policies could be gained by segregating the effects of the non-policy variable such as infrastructure from those of the policies in particular. Unfortunately, no reliable data on the quality of infrastructure provision were available, at the time of data collection, to enable this to be done. As a result, the respective effects of infrastructure on property prices in the respective areas remain largely hidden. The same applies to the G factor. The unique effects associated with the fact that a particular agency is in charge of policies administered over an area served with very good infrastructure remains, as the analysis stands, buried in the overall effects of the particular agency including the control variable *NODEPARTMENT*. The effects of the factors *P* and *G* reported below should thus be understood as incorporating the effects of the quality of the infrastructure provided for the particular zones in which they are applicable.

That said, together these represent a 4×3 factorial design. Now, since the coefficient of the products of the nominal variables representing the respective independent variables provides a measure of possible interaction effects that may exist between them, the nominal variable of each policy type is multiplied by those of the remaining policies to test the interaction between them. Then again, the nominal variable of each policy type is also multiplied by the nominal variables representing each of the two enforcing institutions to test also for any possible interaction effects between them ($P \times G$).

The nominal variables used to represent each of the independent variable – policies and government departments – could have been derived using a variety of nominal coding techniques (see Cohen et al., 2003). Examples of the possible coding techniques include dummy, unweighted effect, weighted effect and contrast coding. However, since the aim of the research is to ascertain the comparative benefits (or effects) of respective policies and the governmental departments enforcing them respectively on an equal footing, the combination 'effect coding' method offers an appropriate way of distinguishing the

Table 8.1 Coding for the (4 × 3) factorial design

Set 1			Set 2			
G_d [Dummy coding]	**X_1**	**X_2**	**P_{ti} [Unweighted effects code] – policy zone**	**X_3**	**X_4**	**X_5**
LANDSCOM[G_{d1}]	1	0	SREG[P_{z1}]	1	0	0
LANDTITLEREG[G_{d2}]	0	1	GREG[P_{z2}]	0	1	0
NODEPARTMENT[G_{d3}]	0	0	DISTP[P_{z3}]	0	0	1
			REDISTP[P_{z4}]	−1	−1	−1

research factor *P*. With regard to research factor *G*, because of the presence of a control element in the categories, the dummy coding method offers the most effective way of distinguishing the departments. To fully represent these factors in a regression framework with a minimal risk of multicolinearity, each research factor is represented by the number of categories under the research factors minus one. Thus, *G* is coded into two comparison IVs (X_1, X_2), research factor and *P* is coded into three IVs (X_3, X_4, X_5) as indicated in Table 8.1.

The coding for Table 8.2 characterises each land parcel used in the research by the three departments for the research factor *G* and the four policies for the research factor *P*.

The data is analysed using hierarchical multiple regression and correlation analysis (HMRCA). As required by the HMRCA procedure, a decision was made on the order of entering the IVs (research factors). Since the interest of this study lies in the effects or efficacy of land policies in Ghana, there is the need to obtain the expression of the effects of these policies uninfluenced by the departments that enforce them. Thus the variance of the land prices *Y* associated with *G*, the respective departments in charge of the policies together with their overlap are first determined and then the additional contributions that each policy category makes to land prices, which is the measure of their efficacy, is determined. Thus HMRCA is conducted in the order *G*, *P* and finally (*G x P*) interactions. The main results of the analysis are reported below.

8.7 Results

Table 8.3 reports the correlation and statistical significance of the results of the HMRCA. When the land price, *Y*, is regressed on the IVs for the research factor G = X_1, X_2, the R^2 is found to equal 0.133 ($F = 8.955$, $p < 0.001$). This implies that a little over 13.3 per cent of

Table 8.2 Joint coding of the (4 × 3) factorial interaction ($G_d \times P$)

		G_d		P_z			X_1X_4	X_1X_5	X_2X_4	X_2X_5	X_3X_4	X_3X_5
		X_1	X_2	X_3	X_4	X_5	X_6	X_7	X_8	X_9	X_{10}	X_{11}
1	$P_{z1}G_{d1}$	1.00	0.00	1.00	0.00	0.00	0.00	0.00	0.00	0.00	0.00	0.00
2	$P_{z2}G_{d1}$	1.00	0.00	0.00	1.00	0.00	1.00	0.00	0.00	0.00	0.00	0.00
3	$P_{z3}G_{d1}$	1.00	0.00	0.00	0.00	1.00	0.00	1.00	0.00	0.00	0.00	0.00
4	$P_{z4}G_{d1}$	1.00	0.00	−1.00	−1.00	−1.00	−1.00	−1.00	0.00	0.00	1.00	1.00
5	$P_{z1}G_{d2}$	0.00	1.00	1.00	0.00	0.00	0.00	0.00	0.00	0.00	0.00	0.00
6	$P_{z2}G_{d2}$	0.00	1.00	0.00	1.00	0.00	0.00	0.00	1.00	0.00	0.00	0.00
7	$P_{z3}G_{d2}$	0.00	1.00	0.00	0.00	1.00	0.00	0.00	0.00	1.00	0.00	0.00
8	$P_{z4}G_{d2}$	0.00	1.00	−1.00	−1.00	−1.00	0.00	0.00	−1.00	−1.00	1.00	1.00
9	$P_{z1}G_{d3}$	0.00	0.00	1.00	0.00	0.00	0.00	0.00	0.00	0.00	0.00	0.00
10	$P_{z2}G_{d3}$	0.00	0.00	0.00	1.00	0.00	0.00	0.00	0.00	0.00	0.00	0.00
11	$P_{z3}G_{d3}$	0.00	0.00	0.00	0.00	1.00	0.00	0.00	0.00	0.00	0.00	0.00
12	$P_{z4}G_{d3}$	0.00	0.00	−1.00	−1.00	−1.00	0.00	0.00	0.00	0.00	1.00	1.00

Table 8.3 Correlation and statistical significance

Model	R	R square	Adjusted R square	Std. error of the estimate	F	Significance
1	.364(a)	0.133	0.118	$15,062.24588	8.955	.000(a)
2	.873(b)	0.763	0.752	$7,981.15299	73.300	.000(b)

Note: (a) Predictors: (constant) X_2, X_1; (b) Predictors: (constant) X_2, X_1, X_5, X_4, X_3...

the variance in land prices in Accra is attributable to the involvement of the two respective agencies in the policy enforcement process. When *Y*, was subsequently regressed on the IVs for both research factors in the order X_1, X_2, X_3, X_4 and X_5 the results revealed that the $R^2 = 0.763$ ($F = 73.300$, $p < 0.001$).

Interactions between the two research factors *G* and *P* increased the R^2 to 0.763 ($F = 73.300$, $p < 0.000$), meaning that the combined effects of the two sets of research factors account for about 76 per cent of the variances in land values, with land policies per se explaining about 63 per cent of the variance. The analysis showed rather surprisingly that interactions between the individual policies did not by themselves account for any of the variances in land values in the study area. This means that complying with more than one policy does not by itself have any additional effects on the benefits of policies received. Table 8.4 gives the regression coefficients out of which the regression equation for the effects-coded independent variables was derived.

Table 8.4 Coefficients (a)

Model		Unstandardised coefficients		Standardised coefficients	t	Significance
		B	Std. error	Beta		
1	(Constant)	11366.940	2381.550		4.773	0.000
	X1	13253.022	3368.021	0.391	3.935	0.000
	X2	2083.659	3368.021	0.062	0.619	0.537
2	(Constant)	11366.940	1261.931		9.008	0.000
	X1	13253.022	1784.640	0.391	7.426	0.000
	X2	2083.659	1784.640	0.062	1.168	0.245
	X3	−8086.614	1261.931	−0.358	−6.408	0.000
	X4	−6483.584	1261.931	−0.287	−5.138	0.000
	X5	21933.766	1261.931	0.971	17.381	0.000

Note: (a) Dependent Variable: Land Value US Dollar.

Table 8.4 produces two main regression equations: Eq. 1 and Eq. 2 together with the corresponding *t* values and significance measures of the respective coefficients.

8.7.1 Benefits of enforcement institutions

Recall that the benefit measures reported below have built into them the effects of the quality of infrastructure in the zone in which the policies implemented by the agencies apply.

$$\begin{array}{llll} Y_D = & 13{,}253.022(X_1) + & 2{,}083.659(X_2) + & 11{,}366.940 \\ t & (3.935) & (0.619) & (4.773) \end{array} \qquad (1)$$

Eq.1 gives the regression equation for the three dummy coded research factor G and the corresponding t values. From Table 8.4 it is noted that the coefficient of the Y-intercepts, \$11,366.940 and the X_1 IV ((*LANDSCOM*) = \$13,253.022) are all statistically significant ($p < 0.001$) and hence of substantive relevance. However, the coefficient for X_2 (\$2,083.659) is statistically insignificant ($p = 0.537$) at the alpha of 0.05 and, hence, of little inferential value. Nonetheless, for completeness X2 is included in the analysis. What emerges, however, from the regression equation is that the contributions of the dummy coded control variable (*NODEPARTMENT*) to the mean land price in all the policy zones put together is \$11,366.94. In other words, non-land policy attributes such as location, neighbourhood quality, streets and so forth contribute about 11 million cedis to mean land values. Further, plugging the dummy codes for the *LANDSCOM* variable, which are $X_1 = 1$ and $X_2 = 0$ (see Table 8.1), into Eq. 1 shows that the *LANDSCOM* contributes as much as \$13,200 to the mean land values in the subject policy zones. Similarly, plugging the dummy codes for *LANDTITLE*, which are $X_1 = 0$ and $X_2 = 1$, again into Eq. 1, shows that the *LANDTITLE* contributes about \$2,000 to the mean land value in the area.

8.7.2 Benefits of the land policies

Recall again that the benefits of the respective policy types reported below consist of the effects of the policy itself as well as those of the quality of infrastructure provided in the respective policy zones in which they apply. The beneficial effects of the respective policies as defined in Table 8.1 are implicit in Eq. 2, which was derived from Table 8.2 above.

$$\begin{aligned} Y_{D,P} = {} & 13253.022(X_1) + 2083.659(X_2) - 8086.614(X_3) - \\ & 6483.584(X_4) + 21933.766(X_5) + 11366.940 \end{aligned} \qquad (2)$$

These benefits are specifically estimated by plugging the effect coded variables in Table 8.1, set 2 into equation Eq. 2.

$$Y_{SREG} = 13253.022X_1 + 2083.659X_2 + 3{,}280.33$$

$$Y_{GREG} = 13253.022X_1 + 2083.659X_2 + 4{,}883.36$$

$$Y_{DIST} = 13253.022X_1 + 2083.659X_2 + 33{,}300.71$$

$$Y_{REDIST} = 13253.022X_1 + 2083.659X_2 + 4{,}003.37$$

As the four equations immediately above show, the benefits of the respective polices are as follows: Stool regulative policies (*SREG*) such as concurrence generates a positive contribution of $3,200 to the mean land values in the area. The general regulative policies (*GREG*) such as the Land Titling generate a positive contribution of $4,800 to the mean land values. But, as Table 8.4 shows, the contribution of *GREG* is statistically insignificant. Redistributive policies (*REDIST*) used to acquire private lands for which no compensation has been paid but yet allocated by the government makes a positive contribution of $4,000 to the mean land value. The biggest contributor and hence the most beneficial of all the policies is the distributive policies (*DIST*), which contributes about $33,300 to the mean land value. The entering of IVs X_9 and X_{10} yielded no effects at all and hence were not reported in the both Table 8.3 and Table 8.4.

8.8 Discussion and implications

The study reveals that land policies in Ghana make differing but positive contributions to land values with the effect that land policies tend to have varying but positive effects depending on the regulative, distributive and redistributive attributes of the policy. The policy that yields the highest benefits is *DIST*. *DIST* represents policies that grant government the mandate to acquire private land rights compulsorily subject to the payment of fair compensation and then subsequently subdivide and allocate them to individual developers and institutions. It is common knowledge that areas covered by distributive policies have the highest quality of infrastructure such as roads, water and electricity relative to the other policy zones. As stated above, it is reasonable to assume that a considerable proportion of the benefits associated with *DIST* policies may arise largely from the good infrastructure provisions in the policy zone in which they apply.

That is to say, the *DIST* benefits reported above may have very little to do with the *DIST* policies per se. This also means that to improve the benefits of other policies, lands affected by those policies must also receive similar investments in infrastructure provisions. It is interesting but not surprising to note from the results that lands within redistributive zones yielded considerably lower dividends relative to *DIST* even though they are both government compulsory acquisition policies. The next policy type is the *REDIST.* By definition these policies cover areas acquired by governments for which fair compensation had not been paid. These areas are generally subject to regular and sometimes violent land ownership contests between the government and the tenants or lessees of government on one hand and the dispossessed owners on the other. Certainly the effects of this contestation translate to relatively lower land values in the area. But more importantly, unlike the *DIST* zones, government is unable adequately to furnish these zones with good infrastructure owing to the ongoing land ownership conflicts and the risk they present to agents and staff of the governments working in the area. As a consequence, the relatively low benefits associated with *REDIST* policy may as well be as a result of the inadequate infrastructure in the area compared to those of the *DIST* policy zones.

Since the infrastructure provisions in policy *SREG* and *GREG* are practically identical, their estimated effects can be taken as a reflection of their true relative contributions. With regard to regulative policies, it is remarkable to note that the benefits of general regulative policies *GREG*, such as land title registration, are insignificant. This particular finding is consistent with findings elsewhere (see Deininger, 2003). And it actually questions the merits in devoting significant resources into the promotion and implementation of land titling in Ghana when in actual fact these resources could be yielding better dividend elsewhere. Another interesting revelation is that the two agencies involved in the implementation of land policies also make unique but differing contributions to land prices.

Again the benefit contributions of the *LANDTITLE* agency are not only smaller (about $2,000) in quantitative terms relative to that of the *LANDSCOM* ($13,200) but also statistically insignificant. This goes to buttress the earlier questioning of land titling, which is the sole policy that the *LANDTITLE* agency implements. That said, it has to be mentioned that *LANDSCOM* is making relatively high and significant contributions to land values most probably because it is involved in the management of the *DIST* zones in particular where land values are generally high as a result of their good infrastructure. Another interesting discovery is that the interactions of the policies actually yield no extra contribution. This means that there are no economic benefits in having to formalise the same land rights under more than one policy. Particularly if a land is allocated by the government within the areas affected by *DIST* policies there is no need in fact to register them under any general regulative policy such as land titling. In the same way, lands formalised under Stool regulative polices such as concurrence policies gain nothing extra by also registering under the land titling system. The same is true for other policy zones. So any extra costs incurred in complying with another policy come with no corresponding benefits.

8.9 Summary

The fundamental discovery of this study is that land titling and the land title agency in particular are yielding insignificant economic benefits. This is quite surprising considering that in the past land titling has been revered as the single most potent panacea to the poor performance of land markets in emerging markets like Ghana. This shows that, at least in the case of Ghana, more confidence is placed on land titling than it is capable of delivering in practice. Perhaps the biggest question that this finding poses is, given that land titling is generating insignificant economic benefits, what in actual fact is the Ghanaian society actually losing (opportunity costs) by not investing the monies used in implementing land titling and running the land title bureaucracies in another more productive sector or activity? Since land titling is nothing more than a means of recording land transactions onto official registers, this finding suggests the need for a more pragmatic and bespoke land information recording system that is capable of producing a much more significant benefit than the current system.

Another interesting issue is that some of these policies including the agencies analysed have been selected for reforms under the ongoing Land Administration Project. This decision was taken when the actual economic effects of the policies and agencies were unknown. This is interesting particularly because none of these policies are actually producing zero benefits. It means that if indeed they have to be replaced, the replacement policies and agencies must offer benefits significantly greater than what these are offering now. Otherwise there would be no justification for the reform. Presently the Land Administration Project has barely taken off in practical terms and discussions are afoot for its reconsideration. An ex-ante assessment of the policies that are to be put in their places would be timely given this new awareness. That said, it is important to note that though serious decisions can be made purely on the basis of the benefits that the policies are offering, a more complete decision would have to be based on the balance between the costs and benefits of the policies and not the policies alone. A study of the costs side of land policies also requires rigorous evaluation. One thing that this study makes clear is the fact that the quality of infrastructure appears to have a significant influence on the impacts of land policies. Thus without a clearer picture of variations in infrastructure provision together with other non-policy locational characteristics, the findings of this study can only be taken as indicative. Further study into the unique contribution of infrastructure and other locational attributes may help clarify the true effects of these policies.

9
Cost of Real Estate Policies

9.1 Introduction

The impact of a policy is determined by comparing its costs and benefits such that when the benefits outweighs the cost the policy is said to be having a positive economic impact; otherwise it will be having, at best, zero or, at worst, a negative impact. To determine the impacts of policies, knowledge of both its associated cost and benefits is required. The discussions in Chapter 8 have offered insights into the order of the magnitude of benefits derivable from extant sub-Saharan Africa real estate policies. With this knowledge we now need to examine the magnitude of the cost associated with these policies. We must first understand what cost means.

9.2 Cost

Cost is a highly complex and yet enormously important concept in any policy analysis. James Buchanan's[1] celebrated definition of cost is a good starting point for any exploration into the meaning and nature of cost. Buchanan defined cost as 'that which the decision maker sacrifices or gives up when he makes a choice'. This definition perceives cost as a phenomenon that is peculiar to the decision makers. In order words, non-decision makers bear no cost. Table 9.1 simplifies the nature and sources of the cost associated with real estate policies.

As the table shows, the decision makers involved in real estate policy matters fall into two main groups – government departments and market participants. The cost of real estate policy according to this definition thus is the sum total of the value of all the sacrifices made by the relevant government departments and market participants. It is unclear

Table 9.1 Real estate policy costs categories

	Real estate market participants	**Government departments**		
	Private costs	**Administrative costs**	**External costs**	**Social Costs = Private Costs + Administrative Costs + External Costs**
Direct Costs (Transaction costs)	[*Quadrant 1*] Out of pocket expenses borne by complying land purchasers: official fees and charges paid; transportation costs; unofficial fees paid; waiting time costs; speed payments.	[*Quadrant 2*] All resources employed in rendering services under the policies: time of employees of land policy agencies (measured by salaries and benefits); costs of fixed or capital assets and equipments overheads (stationery, utilities, etc,); fee subsidies.	[*Quadrant 3*] The value of all direct sacrifices made by persons and entities other than market participants and the enforcing government department occasioned by the policy.	
Indirect Costs (Opportunity costs)	[*Quadrant 4*] After-tax income forgone by complying-market participants. That is the next best alternative use of time and money spent on compliance including: earnings forgone, value of business opportunity forgone by complying market participants.	[*Quadrant 5*] Tax revenue forgone by government as a result of indirect private costs incurred by complying participants. The next best alternative uses that the direct costs used by the government to implement policies could have been employed. Rent seeking / avoidance costs. Real estate policy induced distortions of land markets.	[*Quadrant 6*] The value of all indirect sacrifices made by persons and entities other than market participants and the enforcing government department occasioned by the policy.	

from the definition the nature of the sacrifices that constitute cost. These sacrifices or costs as shown in the table fall into two categories, namely: (1) direct (or transaction) costs and (2) indirect (or opportunity costs).

The table indicates that the cost of real estate policy (transaction and opportunity costs) divides further into private, administrative and external costs. The sum total of all these costs constitutes the social costs of the policy. Private costs are the value of the policy-induced sacrifices made by market participants. Examples of these are listed in quadrants 1 and 4. Administrative costs are the value of the sacrifices necessary for the enforcement of the policy. Examples of these are listed in quadrants 2 and 5. The operation of a real estate policy may adversely affect the property rights of actors other than the main decision makers involved (Pigou, 1920). For example, the passage of a real estate policy may lead to the compulsory acquisition of the property of others for public purposes. It may also make the properties of others unsellable or much more difficult to sell because of the raised sales prerequisites that it may impose. All these, and many more besides, constitute sacrifices occasioned by real estate policies and borne by entities other than the main decision makers. These are termed external costs.

Clearly, real estate policy cost is far from simple and does not easily lend itself to full numeric or monetary quantification. It is not always possible to clearly identify all these costs. Those that could be identified may represent just a tiny tip of a possibly huge iceberg. This caveat is vital in order that the cost measured is not taken as precise figure.

While it is helpful to itemise and describe the sources of costs as we have done in the above table, it should be emphasised that a deeper appreciation of the cost of real estate policy cannot be attained from such mere itemisation of the composing elements of real estate policy costs. Though the sources of real estate policy costs may have been presented in Table 9.1 above as though they are mutually exclusive, it is crucial to recognise that in practice many of these sources are cross reinforcing; the existence of one cost type sows the seed for others to emerge and grow. Likewise the absence of one cost type makes the existence of others impossible. For this reason, it is vital that any serious inquiry into the magnitude of the cost of real estate policy exposes the nature of these interactions and their likely effects on the magnitude of the overall costs. Space limitations will not allow fuller discussions of all the possible cross interactions of these sources of costs. To illustrate the point however a few of these will be examined.

9.3 Private costs

We have already mentioned that the total private cost of a real estate policy is the sum of the private direct/transaction costs on one hand and the indirect/opportunity costs on the other. These are discussed in turn.

9.3.1 Private direct/transaction costs

Private transaction costs of real estate policy consist of all the out-of-pocket payments made by market participants in their bid to comply with a given policy. See quadrants 1 and 2 of the table for examples of transaction costs incurred by both market participants and the government departments.

Broadly, as shown in table above, private direct transaction costs may consist of service fees and charges, direct taxes, waiting time and other incidental costs such as return travel to service delivery agencies necessary to secure compliance with particular policies. These are largely readily observable and quantifiable in numeric terms. Less empirically observable are the unofficial payments ('speed payments') made by participants to officials of the delivery agencies to secure preferential treatment and expedited services.

9.3.2 Private indirect/opportunity costs

Private indirect/opportunity costs is the highest possible after-tax income that complying participants could have earned had they invested the sums of money, time and other resources used in paying for the direct/transaction costs in a more productive venture. As would be discussed shortly, this study found that, to secure compliance with a real estate policy in Ghana, for instance, market participants had to follow up the processing of their request through occasional visits to the relevant agencies at an average rate of two visits per week for an average of 76 weeks. While at the agency, the participant waited for an average of 1.5 hours per visit. The potential *after tax incomes* that participants *forgo* in order to make these follow-up visits and to pay the requisite official fees, speed moneys, taxes and other direct costs necessary to comply with a policy constitute their respective opportunity costs. The opportunity costs incurred by the complying market dealer plus the direct costs associated with a policy represent the true private costs of that policy.

9.4 The social costs

Social costs on the other hand refer to the sacrifices and burdens borne by society as a whole arising from the use of collective resources of society by governmental departments in the delivery of the policies. Like private costs, the social costs of real estate policies are the sum total of their direct and indirect social costs.

9.4.1 Direct administrative cost

Direct administrative cost of real estate policy refers to the direct expenditure of the collective resources of society to fund the set up and running of the institutional arrangements put in place to promulgate and deliver land policies. These may be classified for analytical purposes into two main parts, namely fixed and variable (or differential) costs. Fixed costs here comprise the costs of fixed assets such as land and buildings, equipment, computers, tools, infrastructure and vehicles used in the delivery of land related services. The variable costs component on the other hand comprises the expenditures on the variable resources used up in the delivery process.

These include land agencies' employee time measured in terms of salaries and benefits, the value of materials – stationery and consumables, as well as utilities, energy, interest on monies borrowed to fund the delivery, etc. Fixed costs are incurred regardless of the level of policy activities undertaken, variable costs changes with changes in the volume of policy-related activities. The direct administrative cost of real estate policy-related activities in sub-Saharan Africa are generally very steep. Toulmin and Quan (2000) report, for instance, that in South Africa the annual cost of setting up and running the institutions required by the Draft Land Bill is about US$30 million. In Uganda, estimates of the programme envisaged by the Land Bill came to US$400 million. In Ghana, a Land Administration Project, referred to previously in this book and currently underway, is estimated to cost some US$55 million (Hatch, 2002). At the micro levels, Toulmin and Quan (2000) estimates that in Niger and Ivory Coast the per hectare costs of land registration processes are the equivalent of US$1.60 and US$7 respectively.

9.4.2 Indirect administrative cost

The indirect administrative cost is perhaps the most sophisticated and difficult to measure. It arises from a wide range of disparate sources. In essence it consists of the benefits that could have been realised from the resources used up because of a real estate policy administration or activity (the direct social costs) had these been invested in other more productive alternative ventures. These may arise from innumerable sources. A few examples will suffice for this purpose. First, indirect administrative costs may arise from the opportunity costs of the fixed assets such as the land and buildings occupied and used by the government departments responsible for the administration of the policy. These are measured as the *benefits forgone* that could have been realised had the land and buildings been put to other more productive alternative use.

A second source of indirect social costs is the tax revenue lost by government as a result of the private opportunity costs (as explained above) sustained by complying participants. A third source can be traced to the aggregate demand on transport (minibuses, taxies, and drivers) and hence fuel that the frequent follow-up travelling to the agencies engenders. The resources diverted to meet this follow-up induced aggregate demand on transport could otherwise be used in more productive activities; the benefits forgone from the failure to use these means of transport in other alternative ventures constitute a land policy-induced indirect social cost to society. Fourthly, indirect administrative costs may arise from the need to postpone the development or economic use of land until the necessary policies have been complied with. In that case, profitable opportunities may be lost and with that comes tax revenue losses to the government.

As indicated in Table 9.1, indirect social costs may also arise from policy induced distortions and rent seeking (Pigou, 1962; Buchanan and Tullock, 1962; Harberger, 1964; Tullock 1967; Browning 1976; Posner 1995). In keeping with the theme of this chapter, these two indirect social costs are given a little more comprehensive treatment below.

9.4.3 Price distortions

Economic theory proceeds on the thesis that markets lead to a Pareto optimum when the marginal costs of commodities equals their marginal benefits (Connolly and Munro, 1999). This point of convergence is represented in monetary terms by the market-induced equilibrium price of the commodity in question (Smith, 1776; Farquhar and Heidensohn, 1975; Arrow, 1985; Williamson, 1986; McNutt, 2002). Economists also recognise, however, that taxes and some fees and charges associated with government interventions and policies may serve to raise the marginal costs of the affected commodity above its equilibrium price (Harberger, 1959; 1964; Browning, 1976; Harberger and Jenkins, 2002). This may lead to what economists have come to describe as deadweight losses or excess burden (Harberger, 1954).

It has to be noted, however, that not all such policy-related costs automatically lead to a rise in marginal costs above the equilibrium; some may bring the marginal costs to par or even below the equilibrium price.

In which case, deadweight losses will not arise. Relating this discussion to land policy, conventional orthodoxy suggests for instance that even though regulative policies such as land rights registration and land titling laws come with private costs, in actual fact, because land titling releases the full potential of affected properties, the private costs they bring about do not raise the marginal costs of the affected property beyond the marginal benefits. The problem with this proposition is that it is not supported by the empirical evidence, at least in the context of sub-Saharan Africa. Contemporary research shows that, in most developing societies, land title is not always beneficial and hence not always necessary (Migot-Adholla et al., 1991; Deininger and Biswanger, 1999; Payne, 2002; Antwi, 2002; Deininger, 2003; Hammond, 2006). This is because, as recently realised, indigenous land tenures of many developing societies are by themselves sufficient, with better prospects of releasing the potentials of land, in some cases better than land titling, provided they are given official recognition (Deininger, 2003). It follows that supplanting indigenous tenure systems with land title could very well be a gratuitous interference with the indigenous tenure system thereby raising the marginal costs of land above its marginal benefits (or turnover) and distorting the market.

One way in which this may arise can be illustrated by supposing that the true private costs of a land title policy that brings the marginal costs of properties at par with their marginal benefits is £20. Expectedly, all property owners who perceive a benefit of £20 or more from having their titles registered are likely to seek title registration. The problem is that the fees charged by government service agencies are not fixed by market forces and hence do not necessarily correspond to the benefits offered through the service. Most government land policy service agencies are generally monopolist in nature and hence can potentially charge any price for the services they render, as long as they can justify the charge to the legislature (see Weber, 1964; Niskanen, 1994). So if, for instance, the service providing agency decides, with the approval of the legislature, to charge £75 for a unit of the service, many consumers who do not value the benefits of land title to be beyond £20 will, if possible, withdraw their demand for land titling. In that case, the deadweight loss or indirect social costs of the land title registration policy in question will be the economic benefits that those customers who would normally have demanded the service would have gained but have had to forgo because of the rise in the price of the service. The excess burdens for those who do not find any benefits from title registration but are compelled by the law to register at that cost are much greater. Exactly the same situation will result if, as in the case of government land policy service delivery in Ghana, the actual official price for the service is equal to or even below the market price of, say, £20 but consumers are put to other extra official costs such as travel costs and 'speed payments', which together push the price of the service above its true market price.

Because in Ghana land title registration is compulsory, participants who in actual fact see no benefit in securing land title as well as those who see the benefits as falling below the associated private costs have no option but to bear the costs if they wish to remain legal. This analysis applies to all the other forms of land policy. This possibly superfluous expense constitutes a serious deadweight loss. The same logic applies to all the other extant policy.

9.4.4 Rent seeking and rent dissipation

Rent seeking and rent dissipation costs are another important regime of indirect social costs (Tullock, 1967; 1971; Krueger, 1974; Tullock, 1975; Bhagwati et al., 1985; Posner, 1995; Bhagwati, 1982; McNutt, 2002). These arise from extraneous payments such as 'speed money' and the use of other resources necessitated by the requirement to comply with land policy or to secure preferential treatment in processing requests for compliance. Speed payments (or bribes) by themselves do not represent welfare losses or social costs to society (Tullock, 1967). They are simply wealth transfers from one actor (the service user) to another (the official demanding the speed payments). As a consequence, the overall size of the wealth of society does not change.

The real problem with such extraneous payments stems from the fact that the very existence of an opportunity for such wealth transfers provides incentives for the payees in seeking to maximise their self-interest to expend vital resources to attract more of such speed payments. The act of spending productive resources to secure more of such speed payments is usually termed rent seeking, the speed money being the rent. At the same time, the service user, being conscious of these extra payments, will be seeking to avoid them, rent avoidance. They will do so by also investing resources to prevent the payment of the rent. The methods of rent avoidance may include utilisation of contacts to secure the speedier delivery of the land related services.

9.5 Measuring the social costs of land policy

The quest for a sound methodology for measuring the social costs of economic policies started as far back as the nineteenth century (Dupuit,

1844; Jenkin, 1870; Marshall, 1920) and continued into the twentieth century (Ekelund and Hebért, 1985; Hotelling, 1932; 1935; Hick, 1939; 1940; 1941; 1942; 1944; 1946; Schumpeter, 1954). Even so, the welfare costs dialogue remained, until 1954, at the conceptual level. Harberger in a seminal work (1954) moved the dialogue to a new phase, bringing in empirical measurements of deadweight losses (see also Harberger, 1964). Using the consumer surplus idea, Harberger (1954) studies the misallocation of resources associated with monopoly and argues that the deadweight loss associated with price distortions is approximately equal to the geometric area of the consumer surplus losses triangle (the Harberger Triangle). The height of this triangle is the extra marginal costs brought about by the policy and the base by the reduction in the quantity demanded of the affected product. This is explained in Figure 9.1 below. Harberger (1954) shows, using this triangle that, potential losses due to monopoly induced price distortions and market imperfections in the United States are negligible.

The studies that have followed Harberger (1954) concentrate on the deadweight losses associated with taxation on commodity, taxation on income, optimal income taxation design, non-taxation instruments, taxation and labour supply, taxation and housing largely with reference to the Western world (Vickrey, 1963; Browning, 1976; Stern, 1976; Mirrlees, 1976; Fullerton, 1991; Besley and Coate, 1991; Berkovec and Fullerton, 1992; Browning, 1976; Besley and Jewitt, 1995; Snow and Warren, 1996; Blundell, 1996; Slesnick, 1998; Robson, 2005). Many of these studies concentrate on inter-industry comparative analysis or on aggregate welfare losses in relation to Gross Domestic Product

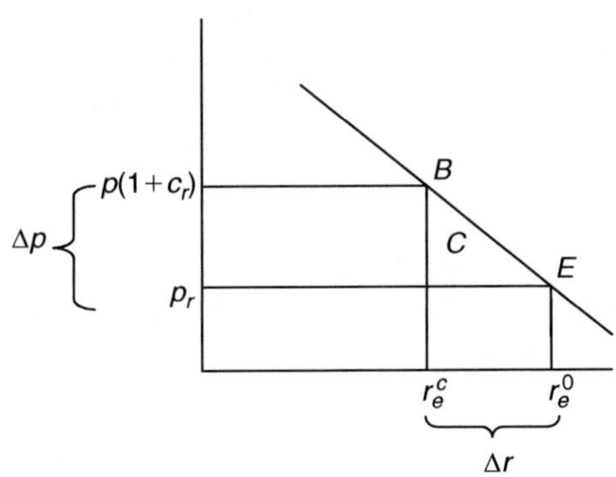

Figure 9.1 Excess burden of policy

(Björkroth, 2002). But as Geroski (1982) shows, the Harberger analysis is equally applicable to intra-industry considerations.

To date the Harberger triangle remains the cornerstone of social costs analysis. But the methodology is not without formidable criticisms. The most fundamental criticisms have come from rent seeking protagonists such as Tullock (1967), Krueger (1974) and Posner (1995) who argue that the Harberger triangle measures only a small fragment of the full social costs as it ignores a larger fragment, the rent seeking costs that are invariably associated with government interventions and the activities of monopolies as explained above. They suggests thus that the realistic approximation of social costs is the geometric area of the consumer surplus losses trapezoid made up of the triangle of lost consumer surplus (Harberger costs) plus the rectangle of monopoly profit devoted to rent seeking activities (Tullock costs) (Posner, 1995). But Fisher (1985, p. 410) has also criticised this rent seeking proposition arguing for instance that

> Unfortunately, Posner's argument, while a useful correction to the traditional proposition that deadweight loss is all that matters, is not correct as a general analysis of the costs of monopoly, and conclusions based on it about the benefits of marginal changes in antitrust activities are likely to be particularly fallacious.

Such fundamental criticism calls for some trepidation in employing the rent seeking extensions to the Harberger triangle in measuring social costs in certain fields. Browning (1976), however, suggests that a more useful way is to look at social costs as the sum of the Harberger costs (deadweight losses), the private costs and the direct social costs. This more simplified approach seems to overcome the weaknesses pointed out by Fisher. The present study has thus employed Browning's proposition to gauge the social costs of land policies in Ghana.

9.6 The model

Because the social costs model emanates and has been applied mostly in the Western context, it fails to give explicit cognisance to certain peculiarities of the developing world, particularly Ghana. To thus extend this model into the arena of land policy analysis in Ghana, certain peculiar policy-induced marginal costs, such as travel costs, waiting time costs and with speed payments (see Figure 9.1), are explicitly incorporated into the model in this study. It is worth noting, however, that economists widely agree that the requisite data for computing social costs are embedded in far too complex sources. This makes the task of compiling empirical data for their measurement overly problematic (see further Krueger, 1975; McNutt, 2002). Thus Harberger (1954, p. 77) argues 'It should be clear from the outset that this is not the kind of job that one can do with great precision'. With these methodological limitations, the best that can be hoped for 'is to get a feeling for the general orders of magnitude that are involved' (Harberger, 1954). In Figure 9.1, the assumed optimal supply of land is r_e^0 at a price p_e achieving equilibrium in the absence of land policy interferences at *E*. A linear demand curve is assumed in this analysis to simplify discussions. It is worth pointing out that a linear demand curve may be problematic when the interventions have large price effects.

As discussed above, when land policies are introduced the effect of their extra costs imposed on purchasers, say c_r, is to raise the real purchase price of land from p_r to $p_r\,(1+c_r)$. This shifts the compliance equilibrium upwards to point *B*. In this partial equilibrium framework the distortion caused by the extra costs is measured by the loss of consumer surplus, the excess burden of the policy.[2] This extra costs includes the extra official payments made privately by policy recipients to staff of the enforcement agents to expedite action on request for documentation; these are so pervasive that the costs they impose can no longer be overlooked in any policy analysis (see further Antwi, 2000; Kasanga and Kotey, 2001).

It also includes the costs of land contract, travel, lag and waiting times among others. Put formally, if the indirect compliance costs be represented by ω_1 and official charges by ω_2, then the indirect compliance costs, ω_1, is a conglomerate of a range of costs functionally represented as:

$$\omega_1 = \sum_{i=1}^{n} (\alpha_i + \beta_i + \delta_i + \lambda_1 + \ldots + \mu_i) \qquad [1]$$

In which i = the policy process and $i = 1 + 2 + \ldots + n$, α_i = costs of contract documentation, β_i = costs of site plan, δ_i = travel costs, λ_i = costs of lag time, and so on. The effective marginal costs imposed on purchasers indicated in Figure 9.1 as c_r can accordingly be computed as $c_1 = \omega_1 + \omega_2$ It is important to reiterate that only ω_2 represents a source of revenue to government from the policy enforcement activities. If the marginal costs of policy administration is represented by ϑ_g then from Figure 9.1 the social cost of land policies, which is the loss of consumer surplus over and above the revenue raised plus the costs of administering the policy can be expressed functionally as:

$$P_{rp}^{c} = \vartheta_{g} + \frac{1}{2}(\Delta p \times \Delta r) \qquad [2]$$

In which $1/2\ (\Delta p \times \Delta r)$ = the area of the triangle C in Figure 9.1. Economic theory also postulates the price elasticity of land demand ε_{r}^{p}, for instance, can be computed from the equation:

$$\varepsilon_{r}^{p} = \frac{\Delta r}{\Delta p} \times \frac{p_{e}}{r_{e}} \qquad [3]$$

This equation could be restated as:

$$\Delta r = \varepsilon_{r}^{p}\left(\frac{r_{e}}{p_{e}} \times \Delta p\right) \qquad [4]$$

From Figure 9.1 $\Delta p = c_r \times p_e$. This implies that Equation 4 can be rewritten as:

$$\Delta r = \varepsilon_{r}^{p}\left(\frac{r_{e}}{p_{e}} \times c_{r} \times p_{e}\right) = \varepsilon_{r}^{p}\,(r_{e} \times c_{r}) \qquad [5]$$

Plugging equation 5 into equation 2 above, the social costs of land policies can be estimated as:

$$P_{rp}^{c} = \vartheta_{g} + \frac{1}{2}\left(Dp \times \varepsilon_{r}^{p}\left(r_{e} \times c_{r}\right)\right) \qquad [6]$$

Since $\Delta p = c_r \times p_e$ equation 6 can be rewritten as:

$$P_{rp}^{c} = \vartheta_{g} + \frac{1}{2}\left((c_{r} \times p_{e}) \times \varepsilon_{r}^{p}\left(r_{e} \times c_{r}\right)\right) \qquad [7]$$

It is noted earlier that $c_r = \omega_1 + \omega_2$. This implies that

$$P_{rp}^{c} = \vartheta_{g} + \frac{1}{2}\left(\left((\omega_{1} + \omega_{2}) \times p_{e}\right) \times \varepsilon_{r}^{p}\left(r_{e} \times (\omega_{1} + \omega_{2})\right)\right) \qquad [8]$$

$$P_{rp}^{c} = \vartheta_{g} + \frac{1}{2}\varepsilon_{r}^{p}\left((\omega_{1} + \omega_{2})^{2} \times p_{e} \times r_{e}\right) \qquad [9]$$

In which $r_e p_e$ = price or value of land for quantity r_e. Thus the marginal social costs MS^c_{rp}, or the full excess burden of land policies, can be expressed as:

$$MS^c_{rp} = \vartheta_g + \frac{1}{2}((\varepsilon^p_r(\omega_1 + \omega_{21})^2 p_e) \qquad [10]$$

In which welfare costs are represented by the $\frac{1}{2}\left(\varepsilon^p_r(\omega_1 + \omega_{21})^2 p_e\right)$ component of the equation.

The task of this chapter is to track the costs $(\omega_1 + \omega_2)$, ϑ_g and land prices as input to be plugged into this model to approximate the social costs of respective land policies in Ghana. This research method use is discussed below.

9.7 The research method

Land policies in Ghana are delivered through a complex web of prima facie legal and administrative procedures prescribed by law, circulars, directives, orders, bulletins, gazettes and guides. Land market dealers have increasingly had to acquaint themselves to the intricacies of these formalisation procedures and to incorporate their costs incidences into their economic decisions. Thus an effective way of obtaining the requisite input data for the above model is to examine the costs of the respective documentation processes both from the perspective of market dealers and government enforcement departments.

9.8 Data collection

The data for this study was obtained in Accra, Ghana, the selected site for this study, between June 2004 and January 2005. In all 303 real estate policy recipients were surveyed. An infamous reality in land policy analyses in the developing world and in Ghana in particular is the absence of organised reliable secondary data on key variables (see for instance Antwi and Adam, 2003). This necessitated the reliance on primary sources for the data needs for this study. In all, four main approaches were employed in gathering the requisite data: (1) self administered questionnaires; (2) interviews with sampled bureaucrats in charge of policy enforcement – professional valuers and estate agents; (3) structured review of financial and administrative records obtained from sampled government departments; and (4) structured observations particularly to collect information on time spent on policy enforcement activities.

9.9 Profile of respondents

The categories of respondents surveyed for this segment of the study were the dealers – purchasers and suppliers – of land and real estate products who incidentally are the main recipients of real estate policies in Ghana. To improve the generalisability of the findings of this study the samples surveyed were randomly selected. The main impediments to this were the absence of published lists of land suppliers and purchasers from which the sample could be drawn. This made it impossible to establish the sizes of the respective population and hence denied any chance of employing rigorous selection methods such as the use of random numbers tables. Thus the size of the selected samples was determined largely by the constraints of available resources and time for the study.

In surveying these selected samples the unique permanency and conspicuousness of land made it somewhat easier to locate some of these recipients through random house to house survey. Some were also surveyed randomly when they visited the enforcement agencies to follow up on the processing of their documentation requests. The main costs information obtained from this group of recipients are the indirect costs such as the travel costs, waiting time, speed payments, etc. The use of random sampling was meant to control for likely biases by giving each potential respondent an equal chance of being selected. The samples drawn were not stratified on the basis of gender as the absence of published lists made it impossible to know the actual gender composition of the population to warrant any such gender stratification. The essential costs information obtained from this component of the survey relates to compliance costs.

The results of a cross tabulation analysis of the relationship between the policy recipients within particular policy zones and gender is summarised in Table 9.2.

In all 36.63 per cent of the respondents (total 111, male = 89 (80.18 per cent), female = 22 (19.82 per cent)) purchased land within the regulative policy zone. 15.51 per cent (total = 47, male = 35 (74.47 per cent), female = 12 (25.53 per cent) owned land or property within distributive policy zones whiles 22.44 per cent (total = 68, male = 44 (66.18 per cent), female = 23 (33.82 per cent)) owned land and property within redistributive policy zones.

9.10 The prime variables

In order to assess the social costs, using the above model, measures of the constituent variables or constructs were devised. Using Browning's

Table 9.2 Policy zone and gender of respondents

			P-zone			Total
			Regulative Policy zone	**Distributive Policy zone**	**Redistributive Policy zone**	
Gender	Male	Count	89	35	45	224
		% Within gender	39.73	15.63	20.09	100
		% Within P-zone	80.18	74.47	66.18	74
	Female	Count	22	12	23	79
		% Within gender	27.85	15.19	29.11	100
		% Within P-zone	19.82	25.53	33.82	26
Total		Count	111	47	68	303
		% Within gender	36.63	15.51	22.44	100
		% Within P-zone	100	100	100	100

Source: Field Survey.

proposition (supra), the key subordinate independent variables obtained were the administrative costs of policy enforcement and the costs of complying with applicable policies. The compliance costs independent variables were derived from two main subordinate independent variables: direct compliance costs, which depended on the subordinate variables: official fees and extra-official payments and indirect compliance costs variables which depended on some five subordinate independent variables namely; search costs, contract costs, travel costs, lag time costs and waiting time costs. The data on these variables were captured using research questionnaires as instruments, supplemented where necessary with data gleaned from other administrative records and interviews with officials of the enforcement agencies to approximate the welfare costs and subsequently the social costs.

9.11 The results

9.11.1 The indirect private costs (ω_1)

Indirect private costs are not always self evident, as only a tiny proportion of these costs are empirically observable. Thus, the costs computed in this paper are based on the observable costs only and are indications of the minimum rather than categorical private costs. At the time of the survey the currency exchange rate was US$1/¢9,200.00 and £1/US$1.9 respectively.

9.11.1.1 The contract costs

Under indigenous land tenure, there was no requirement for land transaction to be evidenced in land; only compliance with relevant customary rules regarding drink payments in the presence of witnesses was sufficient. This position was change with the enactment of regulative policies such as the Administration of Lands Act, 1962 (Act 123), The Land Registry Act, 1962 (Act 122) and the Conveyancing Decree, 1973 (NRCD 175). It became a requirement to evidence land transactions in writing.

Table 9.3 reports descriptive statistics on the unit costs data for the contract documents prepared in compliance with these regulative policies. According to the table, the marginal costs for such contract documents range from a minimum of ¢50,000.00 to a maximum of ¢500,000.00 with a mean cost of about ¢125,000.00. The study found that the majority (about 85 per cent) of these land contracts are framed and typed by typists (not solicitors) of the policy delivery bureaucracies who eventually find itinerant solicitors or barristers to endorse often without any scrutiny for a small fee. This explains why the figures are relatively manageable.

Additionally the Survey Act, 1962 (Act 127) requires such transaction documents to be accompanied by site plans prepared by licensed surveyors. As Table 9.3 illustrates, the costs of site plans in Ghana range from a minimum of ¢50,000.00 to a maximum of ¢800,000.00. The mean site plan cost in Ghana according to the survey data is about ¢130,000.00. This is manageable, again, because the site plans are not prepared by licensed surveyors as the law requires but by unlicensed cartographic

Table 9.3 Descriptive statistics on costs of land contracts (¢)

	N	Minimum	Maximum	Mean	Std. deviation
Costs of Transaction Documents	105	50,000.00	500,000.00	123,047.62	77,783.28
Costs of Parcel Plan	104	50,000.00	800,000.00	128,605.77	186,434.94
Valid N (listwise)	92				

Source: Field survey (June 2004–January 2005).

staff of the enforcement agencies and are illegally endorsed by itinerant licensed surveyors for a small fee, a process termed in Ghanaian local parlance particularly in Accra as *Gansha*.

9.11.1.2 The extra official costs

In addition to the requisite official fees, which the World Bank (2005b) estimates to be about 4.1 per cent of the land value involved, several fragments of costs are incurred by complying market dealers. Extra official cost emanates essentially because of the profound delays (average of 382 days (see World Bank, 2005b)) in servicing documentation requests, which give rise to the tradition of purchasers engaging staff of the agencies at costs to facilitate the early servicing of their documentation requests. Table 9.4 reports descriptive statistics for these extra official costs for the eight main policy strands in Ghana. Respondents were unwilling to disclose information on extra-official payments for distributive and redistributive policies, perhaps because of the sensitive nature of the information. These thus do not form part of the analysis. The extra-official payments for the rest, according to the data, range from a minimum of ¢30,000.00 (stamp duty; column 10, row 8) to a maximum of ¢5,000,000.00 (stamp duty; column 10, row 9) per documentation request. The closeness of the means and the medians of the respective extra-official costs indicate that the presence of possible outliers in the data has less considerable influence on the mean, making the means representative of the extra-official costs for the respective eight policies examined. The mean is thus relied on in computing the social costs of these policies.

9.11.1.3 The travel costs

The demand driven approach to land policy compliance, the insecurity of the postal system in Ghana and the widespread inertia of land policy enforcement agencies in Ghana necessitates frequent travel by market dealers to the agencies to follow up on their documents. This introduces two classes of costs: direct travel fare or costs and the costs or value of the travel time, both of which contribute important but distinct fragments to the marginal costs of the policies. These are thus computed separately.

9.11.1.4 The travel time

Table 9.5 reports the descriptive statistics of the duration of travel as obtained from the field survey. The table reveals that the mean travel duration to the respective agencies by market dealers is about one hour.

Table 9.4 Descriptive statistics of extra official costs

		Plotting[3]	Concurrence[4]	Stool consent[5]	State consent[6]	Land title[7]	Oath of Proof	Tax clearance certificate	Stamp duty[8]
N	Valid	74	69	70	61	71	301	68	239
	Missing	229	234	233	242	232	2	235	64
Mean		558,783.78	921,014.49	541,000.00	687,704.92	2,753,521.13	107,425.25	158,529.41	142,196.65
Median		500,000.00	800,000.00	500,000.00	600,000.00	3,000,000.00	100,000.00	150,000.00	100,000.00
Mode		300,000.00	800,000.00	300,000.00	500,000.00	3,500,000.00	100,000.00	150,000.00	100,000.00
Std. deviation		296,712.36	626,345.95	286,134.41	264,520.91	833,723.32	21,834.95	26,891.97	369,122.41
Minimum		100,000.00	100,000.00	120,000.00	450,000.00	1,000,000.00	50,000.00	150,000.00	30,000.00
Maximum		1,500,000.00	3,000,000.00	1,300,000.00	1,500,000.00	4,000,000.00	300,000.00	300,000.00	5,000,000.00

Source: Field survey (June 2004–January 2005): a multiple modes exist. The smallest value is shown.

Table 9.5 Duration (in hours) of travel to respective enforcement agencies

		Travel time to lands commission	Travel time to land title registry	Travel time to land valuation Board	Travel time to survey department
N	Valid	203	70	202	203
	Missing	100	233	101	100
Mean		1.14	1.16	1.12	1.12
Median		1.00	1.00	1.00	1.00
Mode		1.00	1.00	1.00	1.00
Std. deviation		.60	.66	.58	.58
Minimum		.25	.16	.25	.25
Maximum		3.00	3.00	3.00	3.00

Source: Field survey (June 2004–January 2005).

This coincides with the median and mode travel durations respectively, implying that the mean travel duration is not unduly affected by extreme or outlying travel durations and hence representative of travel time. The costs of this depend on the time value rate in Ghana.

9.11.1.5 *The travel time costs*

This is simply the time value rate multiplied by the average travel time. In the absence of a universally agreed time-value-rate for Ghana, the potential labour efforts lost through travels as people leave their jobs to travel to the land policy enforcement agencies or even as the leisure hours lost as people sacrifice their leisure time in pursuit of the formalisation of these contracts is adopted as a proxy for the time value rate. Knowledge of current labour wage rate in Ghana is thus required for this computation. The mean monthly wage in Ghana as at December 2003 was ¢1,220,807.00 (SSNIT, 2003). Although the minimum daily wage in Ghana has increased since then from ¢11,200.00 to ¢13,500.00, data on the current average wage in Ghana were unavailable at the time of the survey. This necessitates the adjustment of the 2003 average wage to reflect the current probable average wage in the country.[9]

The US Dollar appears to have been fairly stable in comparison to the Ghanaian Cedi during the intervening period. It is thus presumed that the increase in minimum wage compensates nearly for any depreciation of the Ghanaian Cedi against the Dollar during the period. Thus the 2003 Dollar equivalent of the wage (at US$1/¢8,204) is adopted and applied to obtain an estimate of the current average monthly wage. This gives a monthly wage of US$149. Using an average of 22 paid working days in a month and eight paid working hours in a day the mean hourly wage rate, time value rate, in Ghana approximates to US$0.85 an hour. The Cedi equivalent of this figure in today's prices (i.e. US$1/¢9,200) is ¢7,820.00 per hour. This figure is adopted as a measure of the labour or time value rate in Ghana. This implies that the time value of a typical return journey to any of the delivery agencies would be about ¢15,640.00 (¢7,820.00 × 2). The actual travel costs however depend on the frequency of visit to the agencies.

9.11.1.6 Frequency of travel

Table 9.6 reports the descriptive data on the frequency of travels or visits per week made to the respective agencies by applicants seeking compliance. The table shows that complying market dealers make an average of two visits per week to particular agencies formalising their transactions. The mean resultant time value loss or real costs of travel time to the agencies per week then works out to ¢31,280 (i.e. ¢15,640 × 2). The total real costs of travel time per contract are, however, a function of the total number of visits undertaken to complete the requisite set of formalisation procedures. This can be deduced on the average from the duration per processing procedure.

The average of 382 days for documentation requests (the longest duration in sub-Saharan Africa) works out to about 76 processing weeks.[10] This means that complying market dealers make on the average a total of about 304 trips to and from the agencies to complete their formalisation processes, 152 each way. The 152 days is derived from Table 9.6 above. This data was obtained by asking the respondents to indicate how frequently they visit the agencies to follow up on their documents.

Table 9.6 Frequency of visits per week

		Frequency of Visits to lands commission	Frequency of Visits to land title registry	Frequency of visits to land valuation board	Frequency of visits to Survey department
N	Valid	241	70	93	82
	Missing	62	233	210	221
Mean		1.89	1.99	1.42	2.40
Median		2.00	2.00	1.00	2.00
Mode		1	2	1	2
Std. deviation		1.065	.893	.798	1.110
Minimum		1	1	1	1
Maximum		5	5	5	5

Source: Field survey (June 2004–January 2005).

If this figure is applied to the real costs of travel time, ¢31,280.00, this gives an overall real marginal travel time costs of ¢9,509,120.00 (i.e. about US$1000) per documentation request. This figure excludes the actual transport fares.

9.11.1.7 Transport fare and direct travel costs

Table 9.7 reports the descriptive statistics of the transport fares. As shown in the table, the mean direct travel costs range from about ¢30,200 to ¢34,000.00. This works out to an overall average of about ¢31,300.00. The mean cost of a return trip to the agencies per visit is about ¢62,600.00. On the basis of 382 processing days duration and two visits per week, hence 152 total trips, the estimated average direct travel costs per transaction approximates to ¢9,390,000.00 (i.e. 62,600.00 × 152 trips). Again this is about eight times the average wage of Ghana (i.e. US$1000). Combining this with the costs of travelling time, the true total costs of travels associated with land policy compliance in Ghana is roughly ¢18,899,120.00 (i.e. about US$2,054.00) per typical documentation request.

9.11.1.8 The costs of lag-time

Two main variants of costs identified under this rubric are: (1) costs of waiting times at the agencies and (2) time value of delay periods.

9.11.1.9 The costs of waiting time

Table 9.8 reports the descriptive statistics on the waiting times for the surveyed respondents. When land market dealers call at the respective

Table 9.7 Travel costs

		Travel costs to lands commission	**Travel costs to Land Title registry**	**Travel costs to land valuation board**	**Travel costs to survey department**
N	Valid	186	75	177	180
	Missing	117	228	126	123
Mean		30,686.02	34,000.00	30,218.07	30,214.44
Median		20,000.00	30,000.00	20,000.00	20,000.00
Mode		20,000.00	50,000.00	20,000.00	20,000.00
Std. deviation		23,672.16	24,356.59	23,384.96	23,133.92
Minimum		4,000.00	5,000.00	4,000.00	4,000.00
Maximum		100,000.00	100,000.00	100,000.00	100,000.00

Source: Field survey (June 2004–January 2005).

Table 9.8 Waiting times (hours)

		Waiting time at lands commission	Waiting time at land title registry	Waiting time at land valuation board	Waiting time at survey department
N	Valid	228	83	106	81
	Missing	75	220	197	222
Mean		1.5450	1.6596	0.8707	1.8723
Median		1.0000	1.5000	0.7500	2.0000
Mode		1.00	2.00	1.00	2.00
Std. deviation		1.04403	1.16712	0.59479	1.00783
Minimum		0.16	0.25	0.17	0.33
Maximum		6.00	5.00	3.00	5.00

Source: Field survey (June 2004–January 2005).

agencies to follow up on their documentation requests they spend on the average between 1.5 to 1.8 hours at the particular bureaucracy. This translates to an overall average waiting time of about 1.5 hours. With an average of two visits a week over an average processing duration of 382 days, a total of 229 compliance waiting hours, equivalent to around 28 man-days (using 8 hours/ man-day), is incurred per request.

Given a time value rate of ¢7,820.00 per hour, the cost of waiting time per transaction approximates to ¢1,790,780.00. How this contributes to the overall social costs of land policies in Ghana will be established in due course.

9.11.1.10 *The costs of delays*

Perhaps the most logical of deriving this variable, the cost of delay, is to approach it from the perspective of income loss through waiting. For ease of computation this study estimates this loss to be equivalent to Ghana's average hourly wage rate of ¢7,820.00 at the time of the survey, though this figure is likely to be very conservative. This translates to an average daily wage of ¢62,560.00 (i.e. ¢7,820.00 × 8 hours). Using the compounding interest equation, the amount to which the daily wage loss (¢62,560.00) will accumulate (loss of income) at an annual discount rate of 33 per cent (being the costs of capital in Ghana) over 382 days will be:

$$\left[(1+i/360)^{n}-1\Big/_{i/360}\right]\times d_i=\left[(1+i/360)^{382}-1\Big/_{i/360}\right]\times 62{,}560.00 \quad [11]$$

$$= ¢28{,}600{,}824.67$$

The social costs implications of this cost will be examined shortly.

9.11.1.11 The costs of Act 481, 1994

The Office of Administrator of Stool Lands Act, 1994 (Act 481) imposes unique costs on suppliers of Stool lands by imposing statutory deductions on all revenue from transactions involving Stool lands. The Act in essence stipulates the following deductions: (1) 10 per cent for administration of the Act, (2) 49.5 per cent for the District Assemblies, (3) 18 per cent to the Traditional Council and (4) 22.5 per cent to the land owning stool. See Antwi (2000) for a detailed analysis of the economic merits of these deductions.

Deductions (1) and (2) are essentially revenue to government. Even though they constitute significant costs to Stool property owners, because they feature also as revenue and hence benefits to government, their effects, which are in equal magnitude but on opposite sides of the impacts equation, cancel out. They will thus have no effects on the impacts of policy and hence have to be conveniently ignored in the estimation of the social costs. Deduction (4) also counts as revenue to the particular Stool. This will reflect as a benefit to the Stool rather than cost and hence does not contribute to the social costs of the policy. Thus, deduction (3), 18 per cent of revenue or price, is more in the nature of taxation and hence is the only deduction that has non-direct compensating benefits and hence has to be incorporated into the evaluation of the social costs calculus. Using land values as indicators of Stool land revenue, the direct costs of this policy is 18 per cent of the average land values in Stool land areas. Table 9.9 presents the descriptive data on land values in the sampled Stool land area of Accra, Baatsonaa. Average land values in this area according to the data is ¢66,700,000.00.

Table 9.9 Descriptive statistics on land values

	N	Minimum	Maximum	Mean	Std. deviation
Ajirigano	10	55,000,000.00	100,000,000.00	71,500,000.00	12,703,892.66
Baatsonaa	10	50,000,000.00	82,000,000.00	66,700,000.00	10,328,493.49
East Legon	10	150,000,000.00	300,000,000.00	216,000,000.00	51,897,334.54
Sports complex	10	45,000,000.00	60,500,000.00	53,900,000.00	5,450,789.95
Valid N (listwise)	10				

Source: Field survey (June 2004–January 2005).

This implies that the average direct cost of this Act is ¢12,000,000.00 (i.e. 66,700,000 × 0.18). How this contributes to social costs is also examined shortly.

Table 9.10 below reports the summary of all the above non official compliance costs and their implications under particular policy processes. The paper turns now to the estimation of the costs of administering these policies.

9.11.1.12 *The direct administrative* (ϑ_g)

Because land policies in Ghana are administered through series of prima facie processing procedures, the costs of administering these policies turn on the costs incurred in implementing these processes. Existing data on the costs of policy administration is at the aggregate rather than the marginal level. Thus the direct labour hours spent per processing task has been relied on as the allocation base to apportion the overheads to the individual activities so the marginal costs can be derived (see Table 9.11). This is then divided by the total labour hours to arrive at the overhead per unit labour hour. Thus a way has to be found to apportion the overheads to the respective service delivery activities. The approach used here is to apportion the overheads derived from the budgets to the respective activities according to the activities' demand for labour hours.

The total overheads are assumed to be the total budgets of the respective agencies less their personnel expenses. This approach assumes that the greater the direct labour hours for a task the greater will be the overhead expenditure incurred. This may not necessarily be the case. But since what are being sought are the average costs of servicing a documentation request, this error is unlikely to contaminate the results in any significant manner. To accomplish this, a single overhead rate for the respective agencies based on their staff numbers and approved budgets for 2004 is estimated. The estimates are reported in Table 9.11. This rate is assigned to all processes handled by the corresponding agencies. Based on these established overhead rates, the costs for the respective task are established. Column 2 of Table 9.12 is a breakdown of the policy processes into the major identifiable activities. The estimated labour and overhead costs for each of the activities together with their total costs have also been estimated in columns 3, 4, and 5 respectively. It could be observed that a conservative mark-up of 15 per cent (see column 6) has been applied as provision for the incidents of costs that could not be established. The last two columns provide the equivalent costs in US Dollars and Pounds for ease of

Table 9.10 Non-official compliance costs grouped by policy processes

	State lease renewal	Concurrence	Stool consent	Plotting	Allocation	State consent	Regularisation	Land Title
Compliance Activity	Distributive	Regulative	Regulative	Regulative	Distributive	Distributive	Redistributive	Regulative
1 Transaction Documents	–	123,000.00	123,000.00	123,000.00	–	–	123,000.00	123,000.00
2 Site plan	–	128,000.00	128,000.00	128,000.00	–	–	128,000.00	128,000.00
3 Concurrence	–	920,000.00	–	–	–	–	–	–
4 Stool Consent	–	–	541,000.00	–	–	–	–	–
5 Plotting	–	–	–	558,783.78	–	–	–	–
6 State consent	–	–	–	–	–	687,704.92	–	–
7 Land title	2,800,000.00	2,800,000.00	2,800,000.00	2,800,000.00	2,800,000.00	2,800,000.00	2,800,000.00	2,800,000.00
8 Oath of proof	–	107,425.13	107,425.13	107,425.13	–	107,425.13	107,425.13	107,425.13
9 Tax clearance certificate	158,529.41	158,529.41	158,529.41	158,529.41	158,529.41	158,529.41	158,529.41	158,529.41
10 Stamp duty	142,196.65	142,196.65	142,196.65	142,196.65	142,196.65	142,196.65	142,196.65	142,196.65
11 Act 481	–	12,000,000.00	12,000,000.00	–	–	–	–	–
12 Travel time	9,509,120.00	9,509,120.00	9,509,120.00	9,509,120.00	9,509,120.00	9,509,120.00	9,509,120.00	9,509,120.00
13 Transportation	18,899,120.00	18,899,120.00	18,899,120.00	18,899,120.00	18,899,120.00	18,899,120.00	18,899,120.00	18,899,120.00
14 Waiting time	1,790,780.00	1,790,780.00	1,790,780.00	1,790,780.00	1,790,780.00	1,790,780.00	1,790,780.00	1,790,780.00
15 Delays	28,600,824.67	28,600,824.67	28,600,824.67	28,600,824.67	28,600,824.67	28,600,824.67	28,600,824.67	28,600,824.67
Total (¢)	61,900,570.73	75,178,995.86	74,799,995.86	62,817,779.64	61,900,570.73	62,695,700.78	62,258,995.86	62,258,995.86
Total (US$)	6,728.32	8,171.63	8,130.43	6,828.02	6,728.32	6,814.75	6,767.28	6,767.28
Total (£)	3,541.22	4,300.86	4,279.18	3,593.69	3,541.22	3,586.71	3,561.73	3,561.73

Source: Field survey (June 2004–January 2005).

Table 9.11 Overhead labour rate

Overheads	Lands commission	Land title registry	Land valuation board	OASL	Survey department
Administrative expenes	¢6,133,170,000.00	¢2,000,000,000.00	¢1,800,000,000.00	¢5,431,000,000.00	¢2,531,200,000.00
Service expenses	¢1,442,170,000.00	¢2,400,000,000.00	¢2,538,400,000.00	¢89,488,000,000.00	¢1,949,400,000.00
Investment expense	¢12,676,170,000.00	¢3,200,000,000.00	¢1,100,000,000.00	¢60,826,000,000.00	¢4,689,400,000.00
Total overheads	¢20,251,510,000.00	¢7,600,000,000.00	¢5,438,400,000.00	¢155,745,000,000.00	¢9,170,000,000.00
Labour force	264	82	818	251	539
Available labour hours/day	8	8	8	8	8
Number of days per year	260	260	260	260	260
Total direct labour hours	549,120.00	170,560.00	1,701,440.00	522,080.00	1,121,120.00
Overhead rate per direct labour hour	¢36,879.94	¢44,559.10	¢3,196.35	¢298,316.35	¢8,179.32
Overhead rate per direct labour hour ($)	$4.01	$4.84	$0.35	$32.43	$0.89
Overhead rate per direct labour hour (£)	GBP 2.11	GBP 2.55	GBP 0.18	GBP 17.07	GBP 0.47

Source: Field survey (June 2004–January 2005).

Table 9.12 Summary costing of policy delivery

	Policy process	Direct labour costs	Overheads	Total	15 per cent mark-up margin	Grand total	Grand total (US$)	Grand total (£)
1	Concurrence	226,064.86	522,440.00	748,504.86	112,275.73	860,780.59	93.56	49.24
2	Stool land consent	183,207.80	461,390.00	644,597.80	96,689.67	741,287.47	80.57	42.41
3	State land consent	458,004.23	723,386.53	1,181,390.76	177,208.61	1,358,599.38	147.67	77.72
4	Plotting	139,559.77	251,970.00	391,529.77	58,729.47	450,259.23	48.94	25.76
5	State land allocation	1,246,417.74	1,222,850.00	2,469,267.74	370,390.16	2,839,657.90	308.66	162.45
6	Stamp duty	51,896.08	11,168.00	63,064.08	9,459.61	72,523.70	7.88	4.15
7	Tax clearance certificate	44,308.57	102,900.00	147,208.57	22,081.29	169,289.85	18.40	9.68
8	Land title lodgment	15,503.58	142,720.00	158,223.58	23,733.54	181,957.12	19.78	10.41
9	Certificate preparation	38,298.23	347,434.00	385,732.23	57,859.83	443,592.06	48.22	25.38
10	Title certification	52,033.87	164,574.00	216,607.87	32,491.18	249,099.05	27.08	14.25
11	Regularisation	2,057,974.10	1,993,190.00	4,051,164.10	607,674.62	4,658,838.72	506.40	266.52
12	Parcel plan	377,991.64	140,958.00	518,949.64	77,842.45	596,792.08	64.87	34.14
13	Cadastral	1,895,021.73	517,092.00	2,412,113.73	361,817.06	2,773,930.79	301.51	158.69
14	Renewal lease	1,199,528.89	935,730.00	2,135,258.89	320,288.83	2,455,547.72	266.91	140.48

Source: Field survey (June 2004–January 2005).

international comparison. The average is about ¢70,263,537 (i.e. US$7,637 or £4,019). This works out to about 54 times Ghana's monthly average wage.

Table 9.13 reports the full scale of costs incurred by both the government and market dealers on account of land policies in Ghana. The costs of land documentation requests as shown in the table range from a minimum of about ¢65,359,215 (i.e. US$7,104 or £3,739) to a maximum of about ¢79,139,996 (i.e. US$8,602 or £4,527).

Specifically, requests under regulative policies cost approximately ¢69 million relative to ¢62.3 for redistributive and ¢62.2 for distributive policies. These results, however, have to be taken in the context that the data on unofficial payment for distributive and redistributive policies were not included in the calculus. Based on the above estimates, the paper now turns to analyse the social cost implications of these policies, starting with an analysis of the welfare costs.

9.11.1.13 Deadweight costs (Harberger costs)

Table 9.14 reports the resultant estimated welfare costs of the respective land policies grouped by policy type using the model devised above. Based on previous work, estimate the price elasticity of real estates in Accra to be approximately −0.5. Accordingly, since elasticity is concerned with absolute values, the negative sign is ignored and an elasticity value of 0.5 is adopted in this analysis (see Column 9).

In Column 3 of the table, the extra official compliance costs borne by market dealers are provided. Column 4 provides the mean land values for the areas affected by the respective policies. Column 5 gives the marginal compliance rate, which is the proportion of the land value expended as indirect compliance costs. The World Bank's (2005b) estimate of average costs of official payments as a proportion of land values of 4.1 per cent are adopted as the official costs of compliance and presented in column 6. Column 7 gives the effective marginal rate which is the sum total of the compliance rate (column 5) and the marginal official rate (column 6). Columns 8 and 9 give the welfare costs of indirect payments per policy process and the total welfare costs respectively. The last column is the percentage contribution of indirect compliance costs to overall welfare costs.

As shown in Table 9.14 (see column 11), on average the welfare costs consequences of land policies in Ghana per policy strand range from a minimum of ¢5,794,555 (i.e. US$630 or £331) to a maximum of ¢27,753,163 (i.e. US$2,473 or £1,302). The average welfare cost across all policy strands is ¢14,124,462 (i.e. US$1,535 or £808). Redistributive

Table 9.13 The aggregate marginal costs of land policy in Ghana

Policy process	**State lease renewal**	**Concurrence**	**Stool consent**	**Plotting**	**Allocation**	**State consent**	**Regularisation**	**Land title**
Policy category	**Distributive**	**Regulative**	**Regulative**	**Regulative**	**Distributive**	**Distributive**	**Redistributive**	**Regulative**
Compliance costs	61,900,570.73	75,178,995.86	74,799,995.86	62,817,779.64	61,900,570.73	62,695,700.78	62,258,995.86	62,258,995.86
Administration costs	5,235,478.15	3,960,999.84	3,841,506.73	4,000,737.73	5,939,877.16	4,458,818.64	7,759,057.98	3,100,219.26
Total(¢)	67,136,048.88	79,139,995.70	78,641,502.59	66,818,517.37	67,840,447.89	67,154,519.42	70,018,053.84	65,359,215.12
Total($)	7,297.40	8,602.17	8,547.99	7,262.88	7,373.96	7,299.40	7,610.66	7,104.26
Total(£)	1,533.09	2,219.82	2,191.30	1,514.93	1,573.39	1,534.15	1,697.97	1,431.44

Source: Field survey (June 2004–January 2005).

Table 9.14 Total welfare costs of land policies in Ghana

Policy process	**Policy type**	**Indirect costs (t)**	**Land value (η)**	**Marginal compliance Rate (ω_1)**	**Marginal Official costs rate (ω_2)**	**Effective marginal rate(C)**	C^2	**Price elasticity (ε)**	**Welfare cost using (ω_1): $\mu=0.5\eta$ $[\varepsilon\ (\omega_1)^2]$**	Total welfare Cost: $\mu=0.5\eta$ $[\varepsilon\ (C^2)]$	Percentage share of ω_1
State lease Renewal	Distributive	61,900,570.73	216,000,000.00	0.29	0.0410	0.3276	0.1073	0.50	4,434,815.57	5,794,551.27	76.53
Concurrence	Regulative	75,178,995.86	66,700,000.00	1.13	0.0410	1.1681	1.3645	0.50	21,183,963.34	22,753,163.43	93.10
stool Consent	Regulative	74,799,995.86	66,700,000.00	1.12	0.0410	1.1624	1.3513	0.50	20,970,912.22	22,532,342.81	93.07
Plotting	Regulative	62,817,779.64	71,500,000.00	0.88	0.0410	0.9196	0.8456	0.50	13,797,459.58	15,115,271.93	91.28
Allocation	Distributive	61,900,570.73	216,000,000.00	0.29	0.0410	0.3276	0.1073	0.50	4,434,815.57	5,794,551.27	76.53
state Consent	Distributive	62,695,700.78	216,000,000.00	0.29	0.0410	0.3313	0.1097	0.50	4,549,480.20	5,925,516.07	76.78
Regularisation	Redistributive	62,258,995.86	53,900,000.00	1.16	0.0410	1.1961	1.4306	0.50	17,978,583.33	19,277,544.22	93.26
Land title (high end)	Regulative	62,258,995.86	100,000,000.00	0.62	0.0410	0.6636	0.4404	0.50	9,690,456.41	11,008,790.83	88.02
Land title (low End)	Regulative	62,258,995.86	55,000,000.00	1.13	0.0410	1.1730	1.3759	0.50	17,619,011.66	18,918,434.83	93.13
Average	Overall	65,118,955.69	117,977,777.78	0.77	0.0410	0.8077	0.7925	0.50	12,739,944.21	14,124,462.96	90.20
	Regulative	67,462,952.62	71,980,000.00	0.98	0.04	1.02	1.08	0.50	16,652,360.64	18,065,600.77	92.18
	Distributive	62,165,614.08	216,000,000.00	0.29	0.04	0.33	0.11	0.50	4,473,037.12	5,838,206.21	76.62
	Redistributive	62,258,995.86	53,900,000.00	1.16	0.04	1.20	1.43	0.50	17,978,583.33	19,277,544.22	93.26

Source: Field survey (June 2004–January 2005).

policies incur the highest welfare costs or deadweight losses of ¢19,277,544 (i.e. US$2,095 or £1,103), followed closely by Regulative policies with welfare cost of ¢18,065,600 (i.e. US$1,963 or £1,033).

Distributive policies are the least costly with welfare costs of ¢5,838,206 (i.e. US$635 or £334).

The welfare costs of unpaid compensation for lands acquired within the redistributive policy zones have at this stage to be incorporated for a fuller picture. Based on the model above and using the average land values for the selected redistributive policy zone (sports complex area) of ¢53,900,000 (see Table 9.9) and price elasticity of 0.5 as explained above, and the percentage of direct costs imposed as 100 per cent of land value, the welfare costs of unpaid compensation per residential plot of land is estimated as: $0.5(53{,}900{,}00 \times 0.5) \times 100^2 =$ ¢13,475,000.00. When this is added to the welfare costs reported above the true marginal welfare costs of redistributive policies transposes to ¢32,753,000.00 (i.e. ¢19,277,544.22 + ¢13,475,000.00).

Bearing in mind that the welfare costs of distributive and redistributive costs are even underestimated, what emerges from the foregoing is that, as indicated in column 12 of Table 9.14, indirect compliance payments (indirect expenses), including the costs of contracts, travel, delay and extra official payments contribute, as much as 90 per cent of these welfare costs. Official payments contribute only 10 per cent in general to welfare costs. Specifically, indirect expenses accounted for 93 per cent of the welfare costs associated with redistributive policies, 92 per cent of those associated with regulative policies and 76 per cent of those associated with distributive policies. The social costs of these policies are now approximated as the sum of the welfare costs, the direct costs of compliance and policy administration.

9.12 The social marginal costs of land policies in Ghana

Table 9.15 summarises the analysis of the social cost dimensions of the respective policies. Column 6 of the table reports the marginal social costs of each policy category. As shown in the table the mean social costs of land policies in Ghana is about ¢45,347,000 (i.e. US$4,900 or £2,590) per documentation request. The minimum social cost is ¢32,600,000 (i.e. US$3,600 or £1,900) and the maximum ¢62,433 (i.e. US$6,800 or £3,600). Again, redistributive policies incur the highest mean social costs followed by regulative policies with mean social costs of about ¢49,500,000.00 (i.e. US$5,320 or £2,600).

Table 9.15 The marginal social costs of land policies in Ghana

Policy process	Policy type	Total welfare Cost: $\mu=0.5\eta[\varepsilon(C2)]$	Extra-legal compliance Costs(t)	Policy administration costs	Total social costs(¢)	Extra-legal compliance Cost as percentage of total	Total social costs (US$)	Total Social costs (£)
State lease renewal	Distributive	5,794,551.27	21,563,005.06	5,235,478.15	32,593,034.48	66.16%	3,542.72	1,864.59
Concurrence	Regulative	22,753,163.43	34,841,430.19	3,960,999.84	61,555,593.46	56.60%	6,690.83	3,521.49
Stool consent	Regulative	22,532,342.81	34,462,430.19	3,841,506.73	60,836,279.73	56.65%	6,612.64	3,480.34
Plotting	Regulative	15,115,271.93	22,480,213.97	4,000,737.73	41,596,223.63	54.04%	4,521.33	2,379.65
Allocation	Distributive	5,794,551.27	21,563,005.06	5,939,877.16	33,297,433.50	64.76%	3,619.29	1,904.89
State consent	Distributive	5,925,516.07	22,358,135.11	4,458,818.64	32,742,469.82	68.28%	3,558.96	1,873.14
Regularisation	Redistributive	32,753,000.00	21,921,430.19	7,759,057.98	62,433,488.17	35.11%	6,786.25	3,571.71
Land title (high end)	Regulative	11,008,790.83	21,921,430.19	3,100,219.26	36,030,440.28	60.84%	3,916.35	2,061.24
Land title (low end)	Regulative	18,918,434.83	25,021,650.45	3,100,219.26	47,040,304.53	53.19%	5,113.08	2,691.09
Average	Overall	15,621,735.83	25,125,858.93	4,599,657.19	45,347,251.95	55.41%	4,929.05	2,594.24
	Regulative	18,065,600.77	27,745,431.00	3,600,736.56	49,411,768.33	56.15%	5,370.84	2,826.76
	Distributive	5,838,206.21	21,828,048.41	5,211,391.31	32,877,645.93	66.39%	3,573.66	1,880.87
	Redistributive	32,753,000.00	21,921,430.19	7,759,057.98	62,433,488.17	35.11%	6,786.25	3,571.71

Source: Field survey.

9.13 Discussions

Toulmin and Quan (2000), based on data from Niger and Ivory Coast, perceives the unit direct costs of land registration to be manageable. What now emerges from this study is that the direct costs of land policies at least in Ghana are trivial relative to the associated social costs. The growth in the unofficial (not the official) and indirect compliance costs and administrative costs of land policies in Ghana, which contribute about 97 per cent of the social costs reported in this study, stems from the sheer density of land policies and complexities and profound delays in the policy administration and enforcement systems. These high compliance costs and their attendant social costs as Adam Smith (1776) argues:

> may obstruct the industry of the people, and discourage them from applying to certain branches of business which might give maintenance and employment to great multitudes. While it obliges the people to pay, it may thus diminish, or perhaps destroy, some of the funds which might enable them more easily to do so.

These high costs tend to reduce the ability of land sellers and buyers to enjoy the benefits of land policies as they create disincentive for compliance, alter choices and lead to higher rates of policy evasions and non compliance. This appears to explain, at least in part, why according to the World Bank (2005b) only 8 per cent of land transactions in Ghana have complied with these policies. Often these evasions are accomplished by diverting valuable resources from productive uses to low value or counter productive uses such as the creation of false compliance appearances in the form of the production of fictitious or even falsified documents. Some resources are even diverted from other uses to establish a physical presence on the land to ward off counter claimants or opportunistic takeovers, a protection that compliance is expected to offer. These resource diversions promote lower levels of efficient allocation of resources over time, which will lead to lower levels of productive economic activities, undermine the benefits derivable for the productive use of their resources and ultimately even lower levels of economic growth. This shows that the true social costs of each Cedi of unofficial and indirect compliance costs could go much wider and deeper than the estimates provided in this paper.

Though the sheer magnitude of these social costs by themselves gives cause for disquiet, it is not possible, exclusively on the basis of this social costs analysis alone, to reach conclusions about the suitability of these land policies in Ghana. For the presence of substantial compliance costs does not in and of itself provide evidence that the policies in question are bad or unnecessary. Adequate knowledge of the social benefits of these policies is required. This study thus provides only the baseline data against which the scale of social benefits of prospective policy reforms can be compared. However, for brevity, the social benefits of the policies have not been included in this chapter, as if the social costs estimates were included they would have to be given equal weight and space as the costs, and this would make the discussions too complex and overly long.

That said, with knowledge of the social costs of these land policies at hand, targeted policy panaceas can be defined at least to abate them or prevent them from rising, particularly when as much as 90 per cent of these costs emanate from indirect expenses. This can be approached from two angles; firstly from the level of the policy and secondly from the level of the administration of the policy. From the policy angle the question is: are the policy choices and policy mixes optimal? Table 9.16 depicts the intended goals of the policies as currently organised in practice. As can be observed from the table, virtually all the policies deal in a way with land rights formalisation and generate data for the development of databases to deal with information asymmetry.

The problem is, apart from the land titling and plotting policies, these policies are not designed specifically with the view to formalising land rights and to correct information asymmetry. Land rights formalisation and the redress of information asymmetry are mere side effects that flow from the pursuit of the main goals of the respective policies. For instance, with regard to state land allocation, the object is to assign land rights to individual and corporate developers from the centre. In the process, the rights assigned are documented and incorporated into the database. A consequence, there are at least five disparate land information databases managed separately by the Lands Commission, the Land Title Registry, the Land Valuation Board and the Survey Department. Thus rather than dealing with information asymmetry, because there is no coherent way of harmonising this information, it is not surprising that the information generated from these databases is full of anomalies. Also, a bulk of the costs result from the fact that most land market dealers have to ensure that their land rights information are formalised and recorded in all these disparate system. By selecting a more appropriate and unified land information and formalisation system so that land rights owners will not need to seek documentation at all the respective agencies will considerably reduce the costs.

Table 9.16 Intended goal and costs of policy

Policy process	Policy type	Intended goals of policy (%)				Total social costs(¢)	Extra-legal compliance Cost as percentage of total	Total Social costs (US$)	Total social costs (£)
		Externalities	Public Good provision	Information asymmetry	Land rights formalisation				
State lease renewal	Distributive			✓	✓	32,593,034.48	66.16%	3,542.72	1,864.59
Concurrence	Regulative	✓		✓	✓	61,555,593.46	56.60%	6,690.83	3,521.49
Stool consent	Regulative	✓		✓	✓	60,836,279.73	56.65%	6,612.64	3,480.34
Plotting	Regulative			✓	✓	41,596,223.63	54.04%	4,521.33	2,379.65
State land allocation	Distributive		Partly	✓	✓	33,297,433.50	64.76%	3,619.29	1,904.89
State consent	Distributive			✓	✓	32,742,469.82	68.28%	3,558.96	1,873.14
Regularisation	Redistributive			✓	✓	62,433,488.17	35.11%	6,786.25	3,571.71
Land title (high end)	Regulative			✓	✓	36,030,440.28	60.84%	3,916.35	2,061.24
Land title (low end)	Regulative			✓	✓	47,040,304.53	53.19%	5,113.08	2,691.09

Further, the Stool land concurrence and consent policies are rightly designed to deal with land use externalities by ensuring that only transactions that are in conformity with approved planning schemes are formalised and given official recognition. The trouble is, this is exactly the function performed by the Town and Country Planning department. By thus relinquishing this responsibility to the Town and Country Planning, which is the custodian of the planning schemes anyway, all the social costs associated with these two sub-policies can be avoided. This will remove the arbitrage opportunities associated with these policies that have given rise to extra legal payments and cut down on the delays in the processing times.

The second level to deal with has to do with the costs associated with the administration of the policies. Once the rights policies are selected there would be the need to strengthen the capacities of the bureaucracies in charge of the delivery of these policies with the view to cutting down the queues and waiting times.

This can be achieved through the simplification and automation of the routine procedures and activities coupled with the use of modern technologies as well as management techniques such as target setting.

It is worth mentioning that there is underway in Ghana a land reform programme under the auspices of the World Bank, DFID and other international development agencies. The danger is, this policy reform is progressing without the benefit of the true costs associated with the policies that are selected for reform. Further, the reforms are not directed specifically at reducing the density of the policies. They are aimed at harmonising the policies and strengthening the capacities of the bureaucracies involved in the delivery of the policies. So while these reforms may, if well implemented, succeed in improving the administration of the policies they may not necessarily result in a selection of optimal policy choices and mixes. Besides, this study will provide the benchmark against which the achievements of the reform can be measured.

9.14 The impacts

The aim of this book, as stated in the introductory chapter, is to examine the economic consequences of real estate policies in sub-Saharan Africa. So far we have relied on data from Ghana to offer indications of the order of the magnitude of the cost (this Chapter) and benefits (see Chapter 8) of real estate policies in a typical developing country like Ghana. It is now time to compare the costs and benefits of these policies with the view to obtaining indications of the economic impacts of these policies. We shall examine the impacts of each policy type separately beginning with the regulatory policies.

9.14.1 Regulative policies

Recall from Chapter 8 that the economic benefits of Stool regulatory policies (SREG) amountto US$3,200. General regulative policies (GREG) on the other hand generate a benefit of approximately US$4,800. The average costs of SREG policies is computed as the social cost of concurrence (US$6,690.83) and Stool consent (US$6,612.64) divided by 2 (see Table 9.15 of chapter 9). This gives an average cost of SREG of US$6,651. The estimated impacts of SREG policies in Ghana are thus negative US$3,451, computed as US$3,200–US$6,651.

The average costs of GREG policies according to Table 9.16 of the current Chapter work out as US$4,516. This is computed by dividing the estimated cost of Plotting (US$4,521.33), Land Title (High End) (US$3916.35) and Land Title (Low End) (US$5,113.08) by 3. The impacts work out as approximately positive US$280. This means that overall regulative policies in general (i.e. both SREG and GREG) are producing a negative impact of about US$3,000 per transaction.

9.14.2 Redistributive policies

We now turn to redistributive policies. According to Table 9.16 the cost of redistributive policies is approximately US$6,780. The benefits generated by redistributive policies on the other hand as estimated in Chapter 8 are approximately US$4,000. This means that redistributive policies generate negative impacts of about US$2,780, which is slightly lower than the negative impacts generated by regulative policies.

Actually, the impacts could have been worse than what was obtained for a number of reasons. Firstly, as mentioned in the current chapter, data on the extra official payments made to secure formalisation of land rights in this zone were unavailable for the analysis. Scanty anecdotal evidence suggests that extra official payments made in compliance with this policy can be up to about 50 per cent of the land value. If this data had been obtain and incorporated in the analysis, it would undoubtedly have amplified the social costs allied to this regime of policy. This would have worsened the negative impacts. Secondly, as the analysis in these chapter shows, the increase in price, attributed to this regime of policy are due to the official denial of possessory titles.

The true test of the benefits of this policy can be obtained when market dealers are allowed freely and willingly to elect to pay the extra costs to comply. Against their will, effective occupiers of land within these zones are coerced, so to speak, to pay extra for the benefit of obtaining formalised land rights. It is doubtful if such coercive price increases could rightly be classified as benefits within the meaning of economic theory. Economic principles suggest that for any increase in price to be attributed to the utilities derived by market dealers, it must flow from the willingness of the party and not by duress. It is only when consumers, on their own volition, are willing to pay a price for the policy that it is shown with certainty that they prefer to obtain that value from the policy. This is an important way of knowing whether consumers are deriving benefits as it affords them the opportunity to decide if it is worthwhile to comply with the policy. It is clear that if market dealers are not allowed the freedom, without such undue instruments of control, to decide to pay the extra price to formalise their land rights, they are not being allowed to make rational decisions on the use of their money. The extra price they are compelled to pay may not reflect the value they place on the policy. It is thus impossible under such situation of duress to know whether the policy is indeed engendering social benefits and hence impacts.

Again, owing to the tenor of this study, the costs of the inequities and injustices meted out to the displaced, dispossessed and uncompensated land rights owners were also not taken into consideration in this analysis. It is, however, not beyond questioning whether if these were to be incorporated in the analysis any merit at would be found in such policies to accord them some positive impacts.

9.14.3 Distributive policies

According to Chapter 8, distributive policies generate about $33,300 of benefits. The average cost of distributive policies on the other hand according to Table 9.16 is approximately US$3,570. This is estimated by dividing the cost of State Lease Renewal (US$3,542), State consent (US$3,558) and State Land Allocation (US$3,619) by 3. This gives an impact of about US$29,700. Really, this is reflected in the high rate of compliance and land rights formalisation in this area. Perhaps about 90 per cent of land rights in this area are formalised. The reasons for such high impacts could emanate from several sources.

Firstly because full compensation had been paid by government for all the rights acquired in the area, the potential for ownership disputes with the dispossessed as in the redistributive zones is minimal. Thus 90 per cent of allocation by government is effectively implemented on the ground. In comparison to other policy zones in the country, distributive policy zones enjoy less ownership contestations and squabbles. Besides, there are no social costs to the dispossessed landowners as they have been duly compensated hopefully at market rates.

Even if some residual social costs exist their effects on the outcome are unlikely to be substantial. Then again, because this policy zone, unlike the other policy zones, benefits from high professional management and government investment in infrastructure and such services as road networks, drains, water and electricity, they tend to attract foreign expatriates, the business community, the high standing members of society, the affluent and politicians. Demands for land in these zones are the highest in Accra and elsewhere in the country. Those who are able to acquire lands in these zones are the privileged few of society, and to avoid losing their investments they tend to show willingness to pay the extra price to comply with the policy. It is these who make the policies socially worthwhile.

9.15 Summary

The foregoing provides indications of the scale of benefits and overall economic impacts of real estate policies in Ghana. Data constraints did not enable precise estimates of these benefits and impacts to be provided. Nonetheless, the available data revealed deferring impacts of real estate policies in Ghana. As the analysis shows, regulative policies are engendering negative economic consequences while distributive policies are producing positive economic consequences. While it is clear from economic principles that redistributive policies are likely to yield negative repercussions, the data relied on showed that they are producing positive outcomes.

10 The Way Forward

10.1 Introduction

Chapter 1 laid out the main foundation for the study. It provided the background to the study and established the point that sub-Saharan Africa economies are in a dire economic state. To make progress in economic development, it was shown in Chapter 2 that three key conditions must be met. First, the society must be in possession of the right quantities and qualities of all the resources required for development, namely real estate, labour, capital and entrepreneurial skills. This makes real estate an inevitable resource in the development process. The second condition is that those resources must be used effectively. Thirdly, institutional arrangements for the productive use of these resources must be supportive of economic development.

Apart from the availability of land (the basic form of real estate), which is a gift of nature, government policies influence the two remaining conditions either for good or bad. The prevailing policy regimes do not appear to be inducing the needed efficiency. Nonetheless, due to a divergence of opinion on the true economic merits of these policies it has not been easy to point out which policies are causing harm and which ones are doing well. These divergent views persist because many of these works are qualitative in methodology, which permits value judgements to influence outcomes. This has produced stalemate in policy decisions, and progress is being sought through costly experimentations with policy reforms and ideologies. It is in the bid to break this apparent stalemate in real estate policy discussions and to move policy decisions forward in the region that this book is aimed. This was accomplished by subjecting existing government real estate policies to quantitative examination with the view to providing quantitative and objectively ascertained evidence of their true economic consequences.

To accomplish this end the focal literature on the subject was reviewed with the view to placing the study within the broad intellectual dialogue. It was established in essence that earlier land reform policies of the region launched a pattern that is thriving today. These policies commenced a regime of formal land tenure system that operated in parallel to the indigenous tenure system. This formal tenure system was achieved by the forceful takeover of large proportions of indigenous landholdings into government ownership together with a series of regulatory and registration requirements. These policies, both in terms of ideology and practice, established in essence, path dependence. This has set the framework within which these institutions function together with their lingering effects on long term state-market relation (on path dependence see North, 1990). They serve as the convenient tool by which postcolonial regimes maintained extensive control over land rights in the respective sub-Saharan Africa countries. Accordingly, they continue primarily to dictate the distribution of property rights, wealth, land endowment, inequalities and political power in these societies with long-term poverty and growth consequences. Even the current generation of land reforms appear to be threatened by these past policies. Yet little is known about the full economic impacts of these policies. This study is designed to bridge this knowledge gap.

The power to enact real estate policies in Africa, as shown in the book, have for a long while been monopolised by a few. This was reflected in the institution of colonialism, single party policy process military regimes and despotic policy process within an emergent democracy. The discussion revealed that real estate policies enacted during periods of pure autocratic rule were no different from those enacted during the democratic era because transaction costs in organising and running a viable opposition, pluralism, negotiation and consensus-seeking remained considerably high in both periods. Real estate policies were thus enacted with virtually no scrutiny and an absence of opposition to express indignation about inefficient decisions. Public opinion was of little concern, as political power was achieved not by winning of votes. Having made the transaction costs of opposition exorbitant to monopolise power, the monopolistic administrations faced very little or no transaction costs in policy formation particularly in societies where the monopolisation of power was absolute. Policies thus emerged at the whim of the monopolistic government.

10.2 The fundamental conclusions

This section outlines, based on the findings for each of the research questions, the conclusions that may be drawn from the analysis and discussions of the results. It points, with reason, to the areas of agreements or disagreement of the results of this thesis with the conventional theories and literature.

10.3 Sources of the policies

The attributes, considerations and sources of policies, whether in the field of real estate or some other economic field have attracted much attention from policy analyst as they determine the success of policies. Extant theory of policy analysis contends that a liberal policy process in which all relevant actors make informed contributions to policy formulation and implementation offers the best basis for efficient policies. This research had varied results about the basis for efficient policies. By employing insights from transaction costs theory to the policy processes of sub-Saharan Africa the study found that both monopolised and liberal policy processes offer similar potential for efficient policy formulation. Rather, what determines the attributes and efficiency of policies is the scale and pervasiveness of the transaction costs faced by respective actors in the policy process in particular societies. It is these transaction costs that also determine the attributes of the policies that are enacted and their revocability or transformation by future regimes.

On this score, this study demonstrates that real estate markets in sub-Saharan Africa have been burdened with manifold government interventions that have emerged largely from a highly government monopolised policy environment with considerably high transaction costs. This led to four classes of real estate policies: Regulative, Distributive, Redistributive and Delivery policies. Because these policies evolved from policy processes with considerably high transaction costs, as the study establishes, they are engendering particular patterns of costs and benefits distribution that have activated particular economic behavioural patterns in economic agents, politicians, bureaucrats, voters, clients and interest groups. These behavioural patterns feed back into the policy processes through lobbying for the maintenance and formation of policies that concentrates benefits on clients of incumbent governments, interest groups and bureaucrats. Whether particular real estate policies in sub-Saharan Africa will continue to remain in place under a particular regime of government or not depends on whether they afford the incumbent the opportunity to distribute favours to their clients or interest groups or quell the manoeuvres of their political opponents as opposed to the economic rationality of the policies. Yet the overriding consideration is whether the transaction costs (usually in terms of political costs) associated with reforming a policy outweighs its benefits (also usually in terms of political benefits). The calculation, this study establishes, often favours the continuous stay of policies that offer higher political benefits even if they offer lower economic benefits. This explains why policies enacted under dictatorial regimes in these countries have proved impervious to change regardless of their economic costs to society.

This striking paradox explains why while many of these real estate policies were intended as ad hoc measures by previous autocratic governments to eliminate political opposition in the policy process they have today become the key policies in sub-Saharan Africa. Many of these policies have been granted constitutional backing in the democratic era and large state bureaucracies have been established to enforce them. In Ghana, for instance, the Office of the Administrator of Stool Lands and the Lands Commission with average compounded budgets of US$2,737,600.00 and US$2,262,280.00 respectively per annum, which are growing at an annual rate of 27 per cent and 13 per cent respectively, exist essentially to enforce such policies in all the ten regions of the country. All the nine succeeding governments after Ghana's first postcolonial prime minister have adopted and continued with these policies even though some of these governments are self-confessed capitalist democratic regimes committed to the rule of law and the sanctity of private property rights.

One could understand the reluctance of these governments to recall such policies from the way these policies distribute costs and benefits on particular segments of society. The vesting policy in Ghana for instance, being a redistributive policy, concentrates benefits on the few who benefit from the allocation of this land while concentrating costs on the affected Stools, through significant reduction of their property rights and a 77.7 per cent loss of revenue. Even so, though the expropriation policy under the State Lands Act did not specifically exempt the state from compensation payments, the requirement for compensation payment under the law has been so spuriously contrived to make acquisition without compensation legally possible. Apart from the lack of interest payments on delayed compensation payments, which is a serious problem in a country where inflation is endemic, it has been possible for government particularly to place an embargo on compensation payment altogether since 1973 (Larbi, 1995). Thus while all expropriations under the colonials were paid for, there is an estimated unpaid compensation figure of at least 800 billion Cedis as at 2001 (Kasanga, 2001). All this has been possible both under liberal and monopolised policy processes. What have remained constant in both policy processes are the considerable transaction costs.

10.4 The quantitative measuring framework

The findings from this study show that existing traditional methods for evaluating the economic impacts of real estate policies are formulated based on assumptions that are largely applicable to the Western world. Most of these assumptions regarding, in particular, data availability and quality, together with the mode of operation and conventional practices within the policy environment in sub-Saharan Africa, are not applicable in sub-Saharan Africa, at least in the form presumed. Thus these methods require appropriate modifications to make them applicable to the sub-Saharan African context. This necessitated the formulation of a bespoke and portable quantitative framework for measuring the economic impacts of real estate policies in sub-Saharan Africa based on the modification and hybridisation of existing methods of impacts evaluation. This framework is largely portable across sub-Saharan African countries with some minor modifications to suit local conditions.

10.5 The quantitative dimensions of social costs of real estate policies

To date, the literature is devoid of quantitative evidence of the social costs of sub-Saharan Africa real estate policies. Studies that have sought to appraise the quantitative dimensions of the costs of real estate policies in sub-Saharan Africa and the developing world have concentrated either exclusively on the out of pocket or direct costs of these policies borne by market dealers (De Soto, 2000) or the costs of administering these policies borne by government (Toulmin and Quan, 2000; World Bank, 2003). The fundamental findings of Chapter 9 are that out of pocket costs and costs of administration of policies constitute only fragments of the real costs of real estate policies to society. In addition to these fragments, an important element of the economic costs of these policies is the welfare costs of the distortions associated with real estate policies, which are missing in current assessments of sub-Saharan Africa real estate policy costs.

Further, in the study area, other fragments of costs, such as travel costs, waiting time, travel time as well as gratuity and expediting payments, though very important, are often missing in studies investigating the costs of these real estate policies. A fuller appreciation of the costs of these policies is thus provided by focusing on their social costs, which incorporates all these as well as the traditional costs. Thus by focusing on the social costs as opposed to the out of pocket costs this thesis is able to provide more comprehensive evidence and indications of the real costs that these policies are reproducing in African societies.

A fundamental finding is that all the categories of real estate policies in sub-Saharan Africa are producing social costs or deadweight losses on society. The scale of the social costs produced by particular real estate policies in sub-Saharan Africa is dependent on the distributive or regulative attributes of the policy under consideration. The typical social cost of redistributive real estate policies per average residential building plot in sub-Saharan Africa is about ¢62.4 million, while that of regulative policies is ¢49.4 million. Distributive policies produce the least social cost of ¢33 million per average residential building plot. This discovery questions the general applicability of the conventional neoclassical and welfare economic thinking that suggests that government interventions are needed whenever market failures exist in real estate or other markets. It also contradicts the more contemporary Transaction Costs theory, which also contends that government interventions are needed when transaction costs under the price system are exorbitant and government interventions can reduce these costs significantly better than the price system. The basis for this conventional proposition is that both market failure and exorbitant transaction costs produce social costs that harm societal well-being. So, by introducing government interventions into such markets these social costs can be got rid of.

Contrary to this position, the prime insight from this finding is that neither the very existence of market failure nor exorbitant transaction costs as such offer good grounds for immediate government interventions. This is because in removing the pre-existing social costs induced by market failures and transaction costs, government interventions also invariably produce their own social costs. Government interventions will thus be economically justifiable not merely because market failures exist. But rather, when it can be guaranteed that the social costs that the intended intervention generates are smaller than the pre-existing social costs and that the intervention will be able to reduce the pre-existing social costs to a level that the sum of the remainder of the pre-existing social costs and the government policy-induced social costs will still fall considerably below the magnitude of the original pre-existing social costs. This suggests also that until the magnitude of the social costs of the market failure considerably exceed the potential maximum social costs of the intended interventions to make the above condition hold, though market failure may be apparent, the intervention will not be economically worthwhile.

Put practically, in Ghana as can be extended to other African countries, the social costs of market failures that must justify the introduction of regulative real estate policy interventions must exceed at least ¢49,500,000 (i.e. US$5,320 or £2,600) per normal residential building plot to be justified. So also should the magnitude of the social costs of market failures that require redistributive policy interventions must exceed ¢62,433 (i.e. US$6,800 or £3,600) per plot to be worthwhile. In the same way the social costs of market failures that require distributive policy interventions must exceed ¢32,900,000 (i.e. US$3,573 or £1,880) per plot to justify such policies. If these criteria is not met, then government interventions will, contrary to expectations, be amplifying the overall social costs on society to the damaging effect.

10.6 The benefits dimensions of the policies

Chapter 8 found also that all variants of real estate policies in sub-Saharan Africa offer some benefits, though at varying degrees. The scale of benefits produced by real estate policies in Ghana, as likely to be for all sub-Saharan Africa, is, however, dependent on regulative, distributive or redistributive attributes of the policy. Barring inequities and injustices in land allocations, the study found that distributive policies generate by far the most substantial benefits. These are followed by redistributive policies. Regulative policies in all their forms generate very modest benefits. Prior to this study, according to Kasanga (2001) the actual quantitative dimensions of the benefits of these policies were unknown.

10.7 Recommendations for practice

These conclusions have necessitated the following propositions for improvement in practice of policy formulation and analysis as well as recommendations for further studies.

10.7.1 The overarching policy proposition

Given that the mere existence of market failure does not imply that the introduction of real estate policies will bring success it is proposed that governments' decisions to adopt particular real estate policies must be formed on the basis of the comparative scale of the pre-existing social costs and the socials costs of the intervention. Policies should be adopted only on occasions when the pre-existing social costs of market failure are more than the potential social costs of the prospective real estate intervention. This will ensure that the potential economic impacts of prospective real estate policies are well appreciated before they are implemented and will reduce the chances of introducing harmful policies that are much more difficult to revoke and hence continue to impose greater restrictions on the functioning of these markets.

For this to work, it will be important not to be lulled into false confidence that the current democratic and liberal political order offers the right setting for efficient policy formulation. As this study concludes, it is the level of transaction costs in the policy processes that determine the level of participation and hence efficiency of policies. Thus international development agencies seeking to improve policy formulation and analysis efforts must work towards lowering the transaction costs barriers in the policy processes in these countries. This is the most plausible way by which governments could be compelled to employ the above propositions in policy formulation.

10.7.2 The regulative policy reform proposal

Since regulative policies are reproducing substantial negative economic welfare consequences in Ghana, coupled with the fact that only 8 per cent of market dealers are complying with these policies, removing these policies altogether will offer better economic prospects. Nevertheless, these would have to be replaced with a single regulative policy that is directed exclusively at compiling and supplying land information to free up the market and facilitate efficient real estate market transactions.

10.7.3 The distributive policy reform proposal

Though distributive real estate policies are producing considerable positive economic impacts, the reported instances of injustices and inequities in land allocation in the literature suggest that more could be obtained from this regime of policies if distributive equities and justices were built into the allocation of government lands. These inequities and injustices stem basically from the heavy government price subsidies on lands within these neighbourhoods. These subsidies promote competitive lobbying, bribery and rent-seeking activities for those seeking allocations. In the process, the powerful, affluent and the influential in the end price out the poor in the allocation process. What happens then is that the rich get access to these lands at government subsidised prices, while the poor are left to buy their land needs on the open market. The way forward is to create a levelled playing field for both the poor and the rich so that the poor are not cheated out of these land allocations. This can be realised by leaving land allocation within this zone to be purely market price operated. This recommendation reinforces similar propositions by such other researchers as Kasanga (2001) and Antwi (2000).

10.7.4 The redistributive policy reform proposal

At the moment government has not paid compensation for acquiring the lands in these policy zones. This is a major source of the social costs of this policy. Practically, over 70 per cent of the area has been resold and fully developed by the disposed owners. This means that the purpose for which government acquired the area cannot materialise. Thus denying these purchasers and developers official recognition of their rights appears to be suppressing the benefits from this policy. It is practically impossible or even economically unwise for government to demolish all these developments as the extant official policy stance seems to suggest. It will also be economically unwise for government to pay compensation in respect of lands that are already substantially developed by private actors. Thus to lower the social costs and increase the benefits from the real estate markets in this zone it is proposed that government ownership of the area should be handed back to the indigenous community who have already sold the area and entered into contractual agreements with the existing developers. This will mean a transformation of the area from a distributive zone to a regulative zone. The few government allocations in the area could be kept in the ownership of government and compensation paid to reduce social costs.

10.7.5 The reform of policy delivery bureaucracies

Antwi (2000) recommends that all government bureaucracies involved in policy administration should be removed for private organisations to be allowed to carry out the task of policy administration in the country. This study takes a different and opposing position on this issue. Antwi's position is based on the theoretical assumption that private firms are more efficient that public firm. But this position is not supported even by the theory. As Coase (1966, pp. 442–5) contends,

> I would not wish to imply that we fully understand the logic of pricing system or that special institutional arrangements are not necessary for its tolerable performance ... I would not argue that there should be no government regulation ... There is no industry, which is not in some way regulated.

Indeed there is evidence that government bureaucracies formed on good economic grounds are better placed to infuse trading confidence into otherwise problematic trading relations (see, for example, Goldberg, 1976; Zucker, 1986). Williamson (1996, p. 268) also notes in corroboration that, provided the regulatory framework is appropriate, both the public bureaus and the customers 'would be able to make investment in specialised asserts on better terms than they would in the absence of such regulations'.

As the study finds, the real sources of inefficiency in bureaucracies are their inbuilt irrelevant and avoidable costs. The sources for these have been identified as imbalances in the personnel rosters, misallocation in budget and lack of attention to technological changes.

It is recommended that to overcome the imbalances in the personnel rosters, the government curb on employment imposed on these bureaucracies since the launch of the structural adjustment era some 20 years ago should be removed. After all, the structural adjustment programme that this curb was intended to support has been widely found to be ill-conceived and to have worsened the conditions of Africa (see Chapter 1). The respective heads of the agencies should be given the full autonomy to decide their staff composition and as well given the full autonomy to dismiss excess or non-performing staff.

Again, strong budget analysis units would have to be set up in all the bureaucracies whose task will exclusively relate to budget preparation and detailed analysis, including performance tracking and internal auditing. The bureaucracies should be given full mandate over their budgets including the determination of salaries. There should be no government ceiling on the annual budgets of the bureaucracies. The logical limit on the budgets should be the bureaucracies' previous year's earnings. However since the services offered by these agencies are highly subsidised by government it is unlikely that their accounts for the previous year will reflect the true state of their financial achievements for the previous year on which current year's budgets can be based. To circumvent this position, government would have to credit the accounts of the agencies with the subsidies granted in respect of their services for the previous year. This will bring up their financial positions to their true state to form the basis for their current year's budgets. In this case the market will weed out the agencies that are malfunctioning but are currently hiding behind the generosity of government to survive. This will also compel managers to stamp out malfeasance and rent seeking since the full costs of such malfeasance will now bear directly on their financial position and hence very survival.

10.8 The costs of delays

It is established that the main ingredients of the social costs of real estate policies are the travelling costs and waiting times associated with following up on transactions. This means that the current highly centralised locations of the agencies are economically harmful to society. The simple but quite costly solution to this would be to set up satellite offices within the districts or localities to handle applications. Apart from reducing the costs of travel, this would also encourage market dealers to seek compliance as the services are no longer remote from them. Again the postal system would have to be utilised more often than direct travel and visits to the agencies.

10.9 Recommendations for further study

Though most writers have chastised government for inequities it remains to be established whether there is a favourable trade-off between the benefits from distributive policies and inequities, and corruptions in the distribution of government lands.

Indeed, to ascertain whether the social costs brought about by government interventions are lower than pre-existing social costs, there is the need for the formulation of a bespoke framework that will enable the measurement of pre-existing social costs and benefits under the indigenous tenure system. This is vital particularly when the current trends in policy are to hand over controls of land allocation to indigenous tenure arrangements without any objective assessment of the social costs and benefits of the indigenous tenure system.

10.10 Summary

This study has provided quantitative indications of the economic impacts of real estate policies in sub-Saharan Africa using Ghana as a case study country. This chapter outlines the major conclusions drawn from the study and provides recommendations for practice as well as for further studies.

Notes

1 Background

1. George, H. (1912), *Progress and Poverty*. Garden City, NY: Doubleday, Page & Co.
2. World Bank (2001), *World Development Report 2000/2001*. Oxford: Oxford University Press
3. World Development Indicator, 2007.
4. Sachs, Jeffrey D. (2005), *The End of Poverty: Economic Possibilities for Our Time*. New York: Penguin Books.
5. CPRC (2008), *The Chronic Poverty Report 2008–09: Escaping Poverty Traps*. Manchester: Chronic Poverty Research Centre
6. UNICEF (2006), *The State of the World's Children 2008*. New York: United Nations Children's Fund.
7. UNDP (2006), *Human Development Report 2006*. New York: United Nations Development Program.
8. Abernethy, D. (1988), 'European Colonialism and Post-Colonial Crises in Africa'. In H. Glickman (ed.), *The Crisis and Challenge of African Development*, pp. 3–23. Westport: Greenwood Press.
9. Fieldhouse, D. (1986), *Economic Decolonisation and Arrested Development*, p. 85. London: George Allen.
10. See further Menger, C. (2007), *Principles of Economics*. Auburn, AL: Ludwig von Mises Institute.

2 Primacy of Real Estate

1. Deininger, K. (2003), *Land Policies for Growth and Poverty Reduction. A World Bank Policy Research Report*. Washington: The World Bank and Oxford University Press.
2. Palmer, R. (2005), 'Oxfam GB and Land Rights: Why Does Land Matter and What is Oxfam Doing About It? A Concept Paper'. Unpublished Oxfam UK/I Memo, May 2005.
3. George, H. (1912), *Progress and Poverty*. Garden City, NY: Doubleday, Page & Co.
4. UNEP (1999) 'GEO-2000'. United Nations Environment Programme.
5. CIA (2009) 'The World Factbook'. Washington DC: Central Intelligence Agency.
6. World Development Indicators database, 2007.
7. UNEP (1999) 'GEO-2000'. United Nations Environment Programme.
8. 2003–4 FAO *State of Food and Agriculture*.
9. 2003–4 FAO *State of Food and Agriculture*.
10. United Nations (2005), *Economic, Social and Cultural Rights*. Economic and Social Council, E/CN.4/2005/48.

11. Per capita income is estimated as the national income (NI) of a society – measured by either its gross national product (GNP) or gross domestic product (GDP) – divided by the size of its population.

12. Recall that development is a much broader concept. The per capita income is only a statistical average and does not necessarily mean that each individual in the population actually earned that level of income. It does not even say anything about the fairness in the distribution of the income across the population. Besides, the well-being of an individual does not consist merely of his or her income. Well-being encompasses such other variables as levels of literacy and health. The per capita income is thus a narrower measure of the development of an individual or a nation.
13. Elkan, W. (1988), 'Entrepreneurs and Entrepreneurship in Africa'. *The World Bank Research Observer*, Vol. 3; No. 2, pp. 171–88.

3 Rationale for Real Estate Policy

1. Menger, C. (2007), *Principles of Economics*. Auburn, AL: Ludwig von Mises Institute.
2. Jevons, W. S. (1871), *Theory of Political Economy*. London: Macmillan & Co., Third Edition, 1888.
3. `Mill, J. S. (1848), *Principles of Political Economy*. New York: Prometheus Books, 2004.
4. Smith, Adam (1759), *The Theory of Moral Sentiments*. London: A. Millar, Sixth edition, 1790.
   Smith, Adam (1776), *An Inquiry into the Nature and Causes of the Wealth of Nations*, Vol. 4, the University of Chicago Edition. Available at: http://www.ibiblio.org/ml/libri/s/SmithA_WealthNations_p.pdf (accessed on 2009).
5. Mises, L. v. (1998), *Human Action: A Treatise on Economics*. . Auburn, AL: Ludwig von Mises Institute, 1998.
6. Mises, L. v., *Human Action*.
7. Locke, J. (1690), *An Essay Concerning Human Understanding*, I, pp. 331–3, edited by Fraser, A. C. (Toronto, General Publishing Company Ltd); Leibniz, G. W., 1764 [1704]. *Nouveaux essais sur l'Entendement Humain*, J. Brunschwig (ed.). Paris: Garnier-Flammarion, 1966.
8. Rothbard, M. N. (1962), *Man, Economy, and State: A Treatise on Economic Principles*. Princeton, NJ: Van Nostrand.
9. Rothbard, M. N., *Man, Economy, and State*.
10. Marshall, A. (1920), *Principles of Economics*. London: Macmillan and Co., Ltd.

4 The Political Economy of Sub-Saharan African Real Estate Policies

1. This is the policy that will drive the recipient economic system to the point where it is no longer possible to improve the well being of one individual without making at least another individual worse off.
2. The governor would, they suggested, only give his consent when he had received a report from the District Commissioner showing the area and boundaries of the proposed grant, whether the title properly belonged to the community proposing to grant it, whether the community fully

assented, whether the consideration offered was adequate and that the grant would not materially interfere with the community's requirements in the matter of agriculture, fishing, hunting and the collection of natural products.

3. Stools are a category of land owning communities that are made up of a number of families, clans and individuals. Not all families belong to Stools and even where they do there is normally a distinction between the lands owned by the family and those owned by the Stools.
4. Executive instruments or subsidiary legislation.
5. The affected Stool lands include: (1) Dormaa; (2) Nsoatre; (3) Sunyani; (4) Fiapre; (5) Odumasi No. 1; (6) Awua Dumasi; (7) Acherensua; (8) Hwidiem; (9) Kenyasi (1 & 2); (10) Ntrotroso/Gyedu Wamahinso; (11) Mehami; (12) Goaso; (13) Kukuom; (14) Mim; (15) Kasapin; (16) Akrodie; (17) Sankore; (18) Ayomso; (19) Pomaakrom; (20) Seikwa; (21) Nchiraa; (22) Manji; (23) Bredi; (24) Branam; (25) Subinso; (26) Nsawkaw; (27) Offuman; (28) Tanoboasi; (29) Booyam; and (30) Techiman.
6. Other expropriation laws such as The Lands (Statutory wayleaves) Act (Act 186) of 1963 and the Public Conveyancing Act (Act 302) of 1965 were also enacted by the regime along similar lines, though they have been used infrequently as compared to the State Lands Act.

6 Economics of Real Estate Information

1. (1) Some the judgements overlapped by this new judgement include, in particular: (1) *Owusu and Ano* v. *Mantse of Labadi* (1933), in which judgement of portions was given in favour of the La Stool by the West Africa Court of Appeal; (2) *Philip Nartey* v. *Mechanical Lloyds ltd* (1986), in which the supreme court adjudged the Agbawe family as the owner of another portion within the subject area; (3) *Peter Mensah Anteh* v. *Simeon Aryeetey* & ors, in which the appeal court also gave judgement over portions in favour of the Odai Ntow family; (4) Civil Appeal No. 16/91, in which the court of appeal gave judgement over portions in favour of the Nii Armah Sogblah family; (5) Civil Appeal No. 9/87, in which judgement was given over portions in favour of Odatei Tse We family; (6) Suit No. CCL/07/89, in which the high court gave judgement in favour of the Nii Kotey Amili family.
2. An earlier version of this chapter was published as Hammond, F. Nikoi (2006) The Social Costs of Real Estate Market Information Gaps in Ghana: Urban Policy and Research, Vol. 24, No. 3.

7 Performance of Real Estate Bureaucracy

1. Earlier version of this chapter was published as: Felix Hammond, Colin Booth and David Proverbs, (2009), The Relative Efficiency of Land Sector Public Bureaucracies in Ghana, *The American Review of Public Administration* 2009; 39; 80.

8 Benefits of Real Estate Policies

1. An earlier version of this chapter was published as: Hammond, F. (2008). Marginal Benefits of Land Policies in Ghana, *Journal of Property Research*, 25(4), 343–62.
2. See the Lands Commission Act of 1994.
3. See Land Title Registration Law (PNDCL 152) of 1986 and the Deeds Registry Act of 1962.
4. The full recommendations of the Committee of enquiry are found in the Alomatu Committee Report, Ministry of Lands and Forestry, July 1978. In all, 103 dwelling houses had either been turned into a developable plot or were affected by a road.
5. 0.23 acres is the typical size of residential land in Accra, the site for this study.
6. It is noteworthy that there are four other government departments involved in land policy administration in Ghana: the Land Valuation Board, the Administrator of Stool Lands, the Survey Department and the Town and Country Planning Department. But the activities of the first three are essentially intermediate and are ultimately fed into the activities of *LANDSCOM* and *LANDTITLEREG* surveyed for this study. Since the full impact of policies are felt only when the policy is fully applied or complied with, capturing the benefits from these intermediate agencies will only provide incomplete picture. By capturing the efficacy from the *LANDSCOM* and *LANDTITLEREG*, whose activities finalise the compliance processes, a relatively more complete impression of the ultimate efficacy of the entire land policy administration regime in the country can be gained. The activities of the sixth agency, the Town and Country Planning Department are properly speaking beyond the scope of this study as they involve the regulation of post land registration activities. This study focuses on the land acquisition and ownership formalisation phase of the land policy continuum in Ghana. For these reasons, the study concentrates on appraising the uniformity of the efficacy of the policies as administered by the selected two agencies.

9 Cost of Real Estate Policies

1. Buchanan, J. M. (1999), *Cost and Choice: An Inquiry in Economic Theory*. Library of Economics and Liberty. Available at: http://www.econlib.org/library/Buchanan/buchCv6c4.html (accessed 13 November 2008).
2. The assumption of linear demand curve in this analysis could prove problematic when the price effect of the interventions is large.
3. This is a parcel-based database system in which data is organised around the proprietary land unit. It was established with the amendment of the Stamps Ordinance (Cap 168) in 1945 (No. 29 of 1945) which introduced an internal administrative requirement to attach a 'Particulars Delivered Form' to land and real estate contracts submitted to the then Lands Department for stamp duty assessment. This afforded the opportunity for some details of the transactions together with the attached site plans to be extracted and plotted onto survey maps of the department. The essence of this was not

to build an accurate and comprehensive database for public reference and use. It was to serve as a source of comparable data for internal valuations and stamp duty assessments. Neither data recorded onto this database nor data extracted from it confer legal rights or obligations against the government or transacting parties. Notwithstanding its weaknesses, inaccuracies, incomprehensiveness, internal inconsistencies and lack of legal basis, it is currently operating as a parallel land transaction recording system to the Land Title Registration System in Accra and market dealers continue to submit their documents for recording onto this register. The public and other governmental departments including the Land Title Registry continue to conduct ownership searches and enquiries from this system.

4. This is a policy that has been in existence in its current operational form since the enactment of the Administration of Lands Act (Act 123) in 1962 even though the essence of it has been superseded by the 1992 constitutions and Lands Commission Act (Act 483) of 1994. The policy stipulates rather curiously and discriminatorily that all Stool land transactions (excluding non Stool land transactions) are invalid *abilities* unless they are certified or concurred by the Lands Commission. Thus all Stool land contract documents are to be submitted to the respective Regional offices of the Lands Commission for certification and validation.
5. This is a variant of the concurrence policy and is applicable to transactions involving previously certified Stool land transactions.
6. These are procedures prescribed for the grant of government consent to transactions involving previously allocated public lands. The Lands Commission handles this procedure, the managers of public lands in Ghana.
7. This comprises procedures under the compulsory Land Title Registration Law (PNDCL 152), 1986.
8. This is the procedure in place to enforce the provisions of the Stamp Act, 1965 (Act 311). This procedure is absolutely vital as The Stamp Act, 1965 (Amendment) decree, 1967 (NLCD 160) provides that no documents in relation to land situate in Ghana shall be 'given in evidence or be valuable for any purpose whatever, unless it is duly stamped'.
9. Admittedly the use of the average wage can be somewhat problematic, particularly if the unemployment rate in Ghana is huge. The difficulty is that unemployment figures in Ghana are fluid and largely unknown. This makes it very difficult to correct the average wage levels for unemployment among the population studied.
10. This is based on a five-day rather than seven-day week.
11. Compounding of regular series of annual payments (Amount of ¢1 p.a).

References

Achebe, C. (1967). *A Man of the People*. New York: Anchor Books.

Alchian, A. A. (1965). *Some Economics of Property Rights. Politico*, 30, 816–29.

Alden, W. (2000). *Reconstructing the African Commons*, IASCP Eighth Biennial Conference, Indiana, 2000.

Alden, W. and Hammond, D. (2001). *Land Security and the Poor in Ghana. Is There a Way Forward? A Land Sector Scoping Study*. London: DFID.

Alonso, W. (1960). 'A Theory of the Urban Land Market'. Regional Science Association, Papers and Proceedings 6, 149–57.

Alonso, W. (1964). *Location and Land Use*. Cambridge: Harvard University Press.

AMCAD (1998). *Land Records Storage and Management Study*. Accra: Government of Ghana, Ministry of Lands and Forestry and The American Cadastre Inc.

Andre Gunder Frank, *Latin America: underdevelopment or revolution* (New York, 1969), pp. x, 3–17.

Antwi, A. (1995). *An Economic Perspective of Land Policy Implementation in Developing Economies: The Case of Accra, Ghana*. London: Our Common Estate Series RICS.

Antwi, A. (1996). *Land Markets, Tenurial Structures and Economic Development: Some Ignored Aspects of Urban Land Policy Implementation in Developing Countries: A Ghanaian Example*. Edinburgh: Napier University, Department of Building and Surveying.

Antwi, A. (1998). *The Property Rights Question: The Economics of Urban Land Management in SubSaharan Africa*. London: The Royal Institute of Chartered Surveyors.

Antwi, A. (2000). 'Urban Land Markets in Sub-Saharan Africa: A Quantitative Study of Accra Ghana'. Ph.D. thesis, Napier University, Department of Economics.

Antwi, A. Y. and Adams, J. (2003). 'Rent-Seeking Behaviour and Its Economic Costs in Urban Land Transactions in Accra, Ghana'. *Urban Studies*, 40, 10, 2083–98.

Arrighi, G. (1970). 'International Corporations, Labor Aristocracies and Economic Development in Africa'. In Robert T. Rhodes (ed.), *Imperialism and Underdevelopment*. New York: Monthly Review Press.

Arrow, J. K. (1963). 'The Potential Limits of the Markets in Resource Allocation'. In George R. Feiwel (ed.), *Issues in Contemporary Microeconomic and Welfare*. London: Macmillan.

Arrow, J. K. (1969). 'Classificatory Notes on the Production and Transmission of Technological Knowledge'. *American Economic Review*, 59, 2, 29–35.

Arrow, J. K. (1985). Distributive Justice and the Desirable Ends of Economic Activity. In G. R. Feiwel (ed.), *Issues in Contemporary Macroeconomics and Distribution*. Albany, NY: State. University of New York Press.

Asante, S. K. B. (1975). *Property Rights and Social Goals in Ghana*. Accra: Ghana University Press.

Asiama, S. (1984). 'The Land Factor in Housing for Low Income Urban Settlers: The Example of Madina'. *Third World Planning Review*, 6, 171–84.

Asiama, S. O. (1990). 'Land for Housing the Urban Poor in Africa: Some Policy Implications'. In P. Amis and P. Lloyd (eds), *Housing Africa's Urban Poor* (pp. 239–51). Manchester: Manchester University Press.

Ault, D. E. and Ruthman, G. L. (1979). The Development of Individual Rights to Property in Tribal Africa. *Journal of Law and Economics*, 22, 63–182.

Bailey, M. H., Muth, R. F. and Nourse, H. (1963). 'A Regression Method for Real Estate Price Index Construction'. *Journal of American Statistical Association*, 58, 933–42.

Balchin, O. N. and Kieve, J. L. (1977). *Urban Land Economics*. London: Macmillan.

Balchin, P. N., Bull, G. H. and Kieve, J. L. (1995). *Urban Land Economics and Public Policy*. London: Macmillan Press Ltd.

Ball, M., Lizieri, C. and MacGregor, B. (1998). *The Economics of Commercial Property Markets*. London: Routledge.

Bardhan, P. (1989). 'Alternative Approaches to the Theory of Institutions in Economic Development'. In P. Bardhan (ed.), *The Economic Theory of Agrarian Institutions* (pp. 3–17). Oxford: Clarendon Press.

Bastiat, F. (1850). *Economic Harmonies*, George B. de Huszar, trans. and W. Hayden Boyers, ed. Irvington-on-Hudson, NY: Foundation for Economic Education, Inc.

Becker, L. C. (1977). *Property Rights: Philosophic Foundations*, 1st edn. London: Routledg and Kegan Paul Ltd.

Beckman, M. J. (1957). 'On the Distribution of Rent and Residential Density in Cities'. Paper presented at the Inter-Departmental Seminar on Mathematical Applications in the Social Sciences (Yale University).

Beetham, D. (1987). *Bureaucracy*. Stony Stratford, UK: Open University Press.

Berkovec, J. and Fullerton, D. (1992). 'A General Equilibrium Model of Housing, Taxes and Portfolio Choice'. *Journal Political Economics*, 100, 2, 390–429.

Berry, S. (1993). *No Condition is Permanent – The Social Dynamics of Agrarian Change in Sub-Saharan Africa*. Madison: University of Wisconsin Press.

Berry, S. (1994). 'Resource Access and Management as Historical Processes: Access, Control and Management of Natural Resources in Sub-Saharan Africa: Methodological Considerations'. Occasional Paper 13. London: IDS.

Berry, S. (1997). 'Tomatoes, Land and Hearsay: Property and History in Asante in the Time of Structural Adjustment'. *World Development*, 25, 8, 1225–41.

Berry, S. S. (1975). *Cocoa, Custom and Socio-Economic Change in Rural Western Nigeria*. Oxford: Clarendon Press.

Besley, T. (1995). 'Property Rights and Investment Incentives: Theory and Evidence from Ghana'. *Journal of Political Economy*, 103, 234–54.

Besley, T. and Coate, S. (1991). 'Public Provision of Private Goods and the Redistribution of Income'. *American Economic Review*, 81, 979–84.

Besley, T. and Jewitt, I. (1995). 'Uniform Taxation and Consumer Preferences'. *Journal of Public Economics*, 58, 73–84.

Bhagwati, J. N. (1982). 'Directly Unproductive Profit-Seeking (DUP) Activities'. *JPE*, 90, 5, 241–8.

Bhagwati, J. N., Brecher, R. and Hatta, T. (1985). 'The Generalized Theory of Transfers and Welfare: Exogenous (Policy-Imposed) and Endogenous (Transfer-Induced) Distortions'. *Quarterly Journal of Economics*, 160, 3, 697–714.

Binswanger, H. P., Deininger, K. and Feder, G. (1995). 'Power Distortions Revolt and Reform in Agricultural Land Relations'. In J. Behrman and T. N. Srinivasan (eds), *Handbook of Development Economics, Volume III*. Amsterdam, The Netherlands: Elsevier Science B.V.

Björkroth, T. (2002). 'Market Structure and Welfare in the Finnish Market for Long-Distance Telecommunications'. *Finnish Economic Papers*, Finnish Economic Association, 15, 2, 87–101, Autumn.

Blundell, R. (1996). 'Tax Reform and Welfare Measurement: Do We Need Demand System Estimation', (with J. Banks and A. Lewbel). *The Economic Journal*, 106, 438.

Booth, C. A., Fullen, M. A., Smith, J. P., Hallett, M. D., Walden, J., Harris, J. and Holland, K. (2006). 'Factor Analysis of Particle Size Specific Mineral Magnetic Measurements on Agricultural Topsoils from the Isle of Man'. *Communications in Soil Science and Plant Analysis*, 37, 249–73.

BPF (2006). *Property Development and the Community: What are the 'Hidden' Benefits of Development?* London: British Property Foundation.

Brams, S. J. (1968). 'Measuring the Concentration of Power in Political Systems'. *American Political Science Review*, 63, 2, 461–75.

Brandao, S. P. and Feder, G. (1995). 'Regulatory Policies and Reform: The Case of Land Markets'. In Claudio Frischtak (ed.), *Regulatory Policies and Reform: A Comparative Perspective* (Pre-Publication edn., pp. 191–207). Washington: Private Sector Department, The World Bank.

Bratton, M. and De Walle, N. v. (1994). 'Neopatrimonial Regimes and Political Transitions in Africa'. *World Politics*, 46.

Bretton, H. L. (1967), *The Rise and Fall of Kwame Nkrumah*. London: Pall Mall Press.

Brobbey, W. K. (1991). 'Improving Land delivery Systems for Shelter'. Final report of land policy consultancy, Accra Government of Ghana, UNDP and HABITAT.

Bromley, D. W. (1997). 'Constitutional Political Economy: Property Claims in a Dynamic World'. *Contemporary Economic Policy*, 15, 43–5.

Browning, E. K. (1976). 'The Marginal Costs of Public Funds'. *Journal of Political Economy*, 84, 283–98.

Bruce, J. W. (1986). 'Land Tenure Issues in Project Design and Strategies for Agricultural Development in Sub-Saharan Africa'. Wisconsin: Land Tenure Center, University of Wisconsin-Madison.

Bruce, J. W. (1987). 'A Perspective on Indigenous Land Tenure System and Land Concentration'. In R. E. Downs and S. P. Reyna (eds), *Land and Society in Contemporary Africa*. Hanover and London: University Press of New England.

Bruce, J. W. and Migot-Adholla, S. (1994). *Searching for Land Tenure Security in Africa*. Iowa: Kendall Hunt Pub Co.

Buchanan, J. (1995). 'Individual Rights, Emergent Social States, and Behavioral Feasibility'. *Rationality and Society*, 7, April: 141–50.

Buchanan, J. M. (1975). 'Reform in the Rent Seeking Society'. In R. D. Tollinson and R. D. Congleton (eds), *The Economic Analysis of Rent Seeking*. VT: Edward Elgar Publishing Ltd.

Buchanan, J. M. (1999). *The Limits of Liberty: Between Anarchy and Leviathan*. Indianapolis, IN: Liberty Fund, Inc. 1999. Available at http://www.econlib.com/library/Buchanan/buchCv7.html; accessed 2 March 2010.

Buchanan, J. M. and Tullock, G. (1962). *The Calculus of Consent.* Ann Arbor, MI: University of Michigan Press.

Buchanan, J. M. and Tullock, G. (1977). 'The Expanding Public Sector: Wagner Squared'. *Public Choice,* 31 (Fall), 147–50.

Buell, R. L. (1965). *The Native Problems in Africa,* vol. 1. London: Frank Cass and Co. Ltd.

Busia, K. A. (1951). *The Position of the Chief in the Modern Political System of Ashanti: A Study of the Influence of Contemporary Social Changes on Ashanti Political Institutions.* London, New York: Published for the International African Institute, by the Oxford University Press.

Byamugisha, F. and Zakout, W. (2000). 'World Bank Support for Land-Related Projects in Developing Countries: Experiences and Implications for International Cooperation'. Paper prepared for the UN Regional Cartographic Conference for Asia and the Pacific (UNRCC-AP) (Kuala Lumpur, Malaysia).

Calabresi, G. (1968). 'Transaction Costs, Resource Allocation and Liability Rules: A Comment', *Journal of Law and Economics,* 11, 67–73.

Card, E. (1975). 'The Political Economy of Ghana'. In Harris, R. (ed), *The Political Economy of Africa* (pp. 51–91). New York: Schenkman Pub. and Co.

CDD, Ghana (2000). 'Corruption and Other Constraints on the Land Market and Land Administration in Ghana: A Preliminary Investigation'. Survey Report CDD – Ghana Research Paper No. 4.

CEPA (2002). *Ghana Economic Review and Outlook.* Accra, Ghana: Centre for Policy Analysis.

Chauveau, J.-P. (1997). 'Jeu foncier, institutions d'accès à la ressource et usage de la ressource'. In B. Contamin and H. Memel-Foté (eds), *Le modèle ivoirien en crise.* Paris/Abidjan: GIDIS/Karthala.

Chen, S. and Ravallion, M. (2008). 'The Developing World is Poorer than We Thought, but no Less Successful in the Fight Against Poverty', Policy Research Working Paper 4703, World Bank, Washington DC. Available at http://econ.worldbank.org/docsearch.

Clark, C. (1980). 'Land and Food, Women and Power, in Nineteenth Century Kikuyu'. *Africa* 50, 357–70.

Cleary, S. (1989). 'Structural Adjustment in Africa'. *Trócaire Development Review,* 41–59.

Coase, R. (1972). 'Industrial Organization: A Proposal for Research'. In Victor R. Fuchs (ed.), *Policy Issues and Research Opportunities in Industrial Organization.* Cambridge, MA: National Bureau of Economic Research.

Coase, R. (1992). 'The Institutional Structure of Production: The 1991 Alfred Nobel Memorial Prize Lecture in Economic Sciences'. *Les Prix Nobel* and *American Economic Review,* 82, 713–19.

Coase, R. (1988). 'How Should Economists Choose?' In Thomas Jefferson Center Foundation (ed.), *Ideas, Their Origins and Their Consequences: Lectures to Commemorate the Life and Work of G. Warren Nutter* 63. Washington DC: American Institute for Public Policy Research.

Coase, R. H. (1937). 'The Nature of the Firm', *Economica,* 4, 386–405.

Coase, R. H. (1960). 'The Problem of Social Cost'. *Journal of Law and Economics,* 3, 1–44.

Coase, R. H. (1966). 'The Economics of Broadcasting'. *American Economic Review,* 56, 440–7.

Cobb, R. W. and Elder, C. D. (1972). *Participation in American Politics: The Dynamics of Agenda Building*. Boston: Allyn and Bacon.

Cohen, J., Cohen, P., West, S. G. and Aiken, L. S. (2003). *Applied Multiple Regression/Correlation Analysis for the Behavioral Sciences*, 3rd edn. London: Lawrence Erlbaum Associate Publishers.

Coldham, S. (1987). 'The Effect of Registration of Title upon Customary Land Rights in Kenya'. *Journal of African Law*, 22, 91–111.

Connolly, S. and Munro, A. (1999). *Economic of the Public Sector*. Harlow: Prentice Hall Europe.

Cousins, B. (2000). 'Tenure and Common Property Resource in Africa'. In C. Toulmin and J. Quan (eds.), *Evolving Land Rights, Policy and Tenure in Africa* (pp. 135–50). London: DFID/IIED/NRI.

CPRC (2008). *Chronic Poverty Report: 2008–2009*. Manchester: Chronic Poverty Research Centre.

Creswell, J. W. (2003). *Research Design: Qualitative, Quantitative and Mixed Methods Approaches*. London: Sage Publications.

Daddieh, C. (2001). 'Beyond Governance and Democratization in Africa: Toward State Building for Sustainable Human Development'. Available at: http:// www.kzoo.edu/africa/SUSFINAL2.html.

Dahl, R. (1961). *Who Governs?: Democracy and Power in an American City*. New Haven, CT: Yale University Press.

Dahl, R. (1989). *Democracy and its Critics*. New Haven: Yale University Press.

Dahl, R. and Lindblom, C. E. (1953). *Politics Economics and Welfare*. New York: Harpers.

Dahlman, C. J. (1979). 'The Problem of Externality'. *The Journal of Law & Economics*, 22, 1, 141–62.

Dam, K. W. (2006). 'Land, Law and Economic Development'. Chicago, John M. Olin Law & Economics Working Paper No. 272 (2D Series).

Danquah, J. B. (1928). *Gold Coast: Akan Laws and Customs and the Akim Abuakwa Constitution*. London: Routledge.

Davis, J. C. (2002). *Statistics and Data Analysis in Geology*. Chichester, UK: Wiley.

Davis, L. and North, D. C. (1971). *Institutional Change and American Economic Growth*. New York: Cambridge University Press.

De Soto (1989). *The Other Path: The Economic Answer to Terrorism*. New York: Basic Books.

De Soto, H. (2000). *The Mystery of Capital: Why Capitalism Triumphs in the West and Fails Everywhere Else*. London: Bantam Press, Black Swan Edition.

Decalo, S. (1992). 'The Process, Prospects and Constraints of Democratisation in Africa'. *African Affairs*, 91, 7–35.

Degnbol, T. (1996). 'The Terroir Approach to Natural Resource Management, Panacea or Phantom? – The Malian Experience'. Working Paper 2. Roskilde: Roskilde University; International Development Studies.

Deininger, K. and Binswanger, H. (1998). *The Evolution of the World Bank's Land Policy*. Washington DC: World Bank.

Deininger, K. and Binswanger, H. (1999). 'The Evolution of the World Bank's Land Policy: Principles, Experience and Future Challenges'. *World Bank Research Observer*, 14, 247–76.

Deininger, K. (2003). *Land Policies for Growth and Poverty Reduction*. Washington DC: World Bank and Oxford University Press.

Delville, L. P. (2000). 'Harmonising Formal Laws and Customary Land Rights in French-Speaking West Africa'. In C. Toulmin and J. Quan (eds), *Evolving Land Rights, Policy and Tenure in Africa* (pp. 97–122). London: DFID.

Delville, L. P. H., Ouedraogo, H. and Toulmin, C. (2002). 'Land Tenure Dynamics and Government Interventions'. In *Making Land Rights More Secure: International Workshop for Researchers and Policy Makers.* Ouagadougou: GRAF/GRET/IIED.

Demsetz, H. (1967). 'Towards a Theory of Property Rights'. *American Economic Review*, 57, 347–59.

Denyer-Green, B. (1998). *Compulsory Purchase and Compensation*, 5th edn. London: Estates Gazette.

Des Rosiers, F., Theriault, M., Kestens, Y. and Villeneuve, P. (2002). 'Landscaping and House Values: An Empirical Investigation'. *The Journal of Real Estate Research*, 23, 1/2, 139–61.

DFID (1997). 'Eliminating World Poverty: A Challenge for the 21st Century – White Paper on International Development' (Rep. No. Cm 3789). London: Department for International Development.

Dickerman, C. (1987). 'Urban Land Concentration'. In R. E. Downs and S. P. Reyna (eds), *Land and Society in Contemporary Africa.* Hanover and London: University Press of New England.

Dixon, C., Simon, D. and Närman, A. (1995). 'Introduction: The Nature of Structural Adjustment'. In D. Simon, W. V. Spengen, C. Dixon and A. Närman (eds), *Structurally Adjusted Africa: Poverty, Debt and Basic Needs.* London: Pluto Press.

Doebele, W. (1983). *Why Cadastral Systems are Important for Less Developed Countries.* Water Supply Urban Development Department, New York, World Bank.

Domar, E. (1957). *Essays in the Theory of Economic Growth.* Oxford: Oxford University Press.

Doner, P. (1972). *Land Reform and Economic Development.* Harmondsworth: Penguin.

Dowell, E. D. (1991). 'The Land Market Assessment – A New Tool for Urban Management'. Urban Management Programme Discussion Paper No. 4, Washington DC: The World Bank.

Dowall, E. D. (1992). 'A Second Look at the Bangkok Land and Housing Market'. *Urban Studies*, 29, 25–37.

Dowall, E. D. and Leaf, M. (1991). 'The Price of Land for Housing in Jakarta'. *Urban Studies*, 28, 707–22.

Downs, A. (1957). *An Economic Theory of Democracy*. New York: Harper and Row.

Downs, A. (1967). *Inside Bureaucracy*. Boston: Little, Brown and Company.

Drobak, J. N. and Nye, J. (eds) (1997). *The Frontiers of the New Institutional Economics*. New York: Academic Press.

Dunleavy, P. (1991). *Democracy, Bureaucracy and Public Choice*. Hemel Hempstead, UK: Harvester Wheatsheaf.

Dupuit, J. (1844). 'On the Measurement of the Utility of Public Works'. In *Annals des Ponts et Chaussées*, 2nd series, Vol. 8, reproduced in D. Munby (ed.) (1968). *Transport*. Middlesex: Penguin Books Ltd.

Dye, T. R. (1998). *Understanding Public Policy*, 9th edn. Upper Saddle River: Prentice Hall.

Eicher, C. K. and Baker, D. C. (1982). *Research on Agricultural Development in Sub-Saharan Africa: A Critical Survey*. MI: Department of Agricultural economics, Michigan State University.

Ekelund, R. Jr. and Hebert, R. (1985). 'Consumer Surplus: The First Hundred Years'. *History of Political Economy*, Fall, 17, 419–54.

Falloux, F. (1987). 'Land Management Title and Tenancy'. In T. J. Davis and I. A. Schirmer (eds), *Sustainability Issues in Agricultural Development – Proceedings of the Seventh Agriculture Sector Symposium* (pp. 190–208). WA: World Bank.

FAO (2004). 'FAOSTATS, Food and Agriculture Organization of the United Nations'. Available at: http://faostat.fao.org (December 2008).

Farquhar, J. D. and Heidensohn, K. (1975). *The Market Economy*. Oxford: Philip Allan Publishers Ltd.

Farvacque, C. and MacAuslan, P. (1992). *Reforming Urban Land Policies and Institutions in Developing Countries*. Washington DC: The World Bank.

Feder, G. and Feeney, D. (1991). 'Land Tenure and Property Rights: Theory and Implications for Development Policy'. *The World Bank Economic Review*, 5, 1, 135–53.

Feenan, R. (1998). 'Property Data and Market Development Issues and the Future'. In P. Wyatt and P. Fisher (eds), *Property Information Today: Geographic and Land Information Management*. London: RICS Business Services Ltd.

Fieldhouse, D. K. (1986). *Black Africa 1945–1980: Economic Decolonization and Arrested Development*. London: Unwin Hyman.

Field-Juma, A. (1996). 'Governmance and Sustainable Development'. In C. Juma and J. B. Ojwang (eds), *In Land We Trust: Environment, Private Property and Constitutional Change* (pp. 9–39). Nairobi: Initiatives Publishers; London: Zed Books.

Finer, H. (1945). *The president's cabinet*. Cambridge, MA: Harvard University Press.

Firmin-Sellers, K. (1996). *The Transformation of Property Rights in the Gold Coast: An Empirical Analysis Applying Rational Choice Theory*. Cambridge: Cambridge University Press.

Fisher, F. M. (1985). 'The Social Costs of Monopoly and Regulation: Posner Reconsidered'. *Journal of Political Economy*, 93, 410–16.

Fisher, I. (1930). *The Theory of Interest*. New York: The Macmillan Co.

Frank, A. G. (1969). *Latin America: Underdevelopment or Revolution*. New York: Monthly Review Press.

Freenan, R. and Dixon, J. (1992). *Information and Technology Application in Commercial Property*. London: Macmillan.

Friedman, L. S. (2002). *The Microeconomics of Public Policy Analysis*. Oxfordshire: Princeton University Press.

Friedmann, J. (1987). *Planning in the Public Domain: From Knowledge to Action*. New Jersey: Princeton University Press.

Fullerton, D. (1991). 'Reconciling Recent Estimates of the Marginal Welfare Cost of Taxation'. *American Economic Review*, 81, 302–8.

Geertz, C. (1978). 'The Bazaar Economy: Information and Searching Peasant Marketing'. *American Economic Review*, 68, 28–32.

George, H. (1879). *Progress and Poverty*. Garden City, NY: Doubleday, Page & Co.

George, H. (1912). *Progress and Poverty*. Garden City, NY: Doubleday, Page & Co.

Geroski, P. A. (1982). 'Simultaneous Equations Models of the Structure-Performance Paradigm'. *European Economic Review*, 19, 145–58.

Gist, J. R. and Hill, C. R. (1981). 'The Economics of Choice in the Allocation of Federal Grants: An Empirical Test'. *Public Choice*, 36, 63–73.
Glickman, H. (1988). 'The Present and Future of the African State in an Age of Adversity'. In Harvey Glickman (ed.), *The Crisis and Challenge of African Development*. London: Greenwood Press.
GoG (1973). Conveyancing Decree, 1973 (N.R.C.D. 175). Accra: Assembly Press.
GoG (1999). 'Ghana Land Policy Document'. Accra: Ministry of Lands and Forestry.
Goldberg, V. (1976). 'Towards an Expanded Economic Theory of Contract'. *Journal of Economic Issues*, 10, 45.
Goldsmith, A. A. (1999). 'Africa's Overgrown State Reconsidered: Bureaucracy and Economic Growth'. *World Politics*, 51, 4, 520–46.
Gordon, H. S. (1954). 'The Economic Theory of a Common Property Resource: The Fishery'. *Journal of Political Economy*, 62, 124–42.
Gough, K. V. and Yankson, W. K. (2001). 'Land Markets in Africa Cities: The Case of Peri-Urban Accra, Ghana'. *Urban Studies*, 37, 2485–500.
Government of Ghana (1958). *Parliamentary Debates*. Accra: Assembly Press.
Government of Ghana (1959). *Parliamentary Debates*. Accra: Assembly Press.
Government of Ghana (1998). *Land Records Storage and Management Study*. Accra: Ministry of Lands and Forestry.
Grilliches, Z. (1971). *Price Indexes and Quality Change: Studies in New Methods of Measurement*. Cambridge: Harvard University Press.
Grindle, M. and Thomas, J. W. (1990). 'After the Decision: Implementing Policy Reforms in Developing Countries'. *World Development Report*, 18, 8, 1163–81.
Grindle, M. and Thomas, J. W. (1991). *Public Choices and the Policy Change: The Political Economy of Reform in Developing Countries*. Baltimore and London: The John Hopkins University Press.
Gunning, J. P. (2003). *Understanding Democracy: An Introduction to Public Choice*. Taipei, Taiwan: Nomad Press.
Gurr, T. (1993). 'Why Minorities Rebel: A Global Analysis of Communal Mobilization and Conflict since 1945'. *International Political Science Review*, 14, 2.
Gurr, T. (2003). *Why Men Rebel?* Princeton: Princeton University.
Gyekye, K. (1998). 'Person and Community in African Thought'. In P. H. Coetzee and A. P. J. Roux (eds) *Philosophy from Africa*. Johannesbourg: ITP.
Hallett, G. (1979). *Urban Land Economics*. London: The Macmillan Press Ltd.
Hameso, S. (2002). 'Issues and Dilemmas of Multiparty Democracy in Africa'. *West Africa Review*. 2(2).
Hammond, F. (2006). *The Economic Impacts of Sub-Saharan African Urban Real Estate Policies, in School of Engineering and the Built Environment* (p. 360). Wolverhampton: University of Wolverhampton.
Hanemann, W. M. (1994). 'Contingent Valuation and Economics'. Berkeley: Department of Agricultural and Resource Economics, University of California.
Haque, M. S. (1997). 'Incongruity between Bureaucracy and Society in Developing Nations: A Critique'. *Peace & Change*, 22, 432–62.
Harberger, A. (1954). 'Monopoly and Resource Allocation'. *American Economic Review Proceedings*, 44, May, 77–87.
Harberger, A. C. (1959). 'Monopoly and Resource Allocation'. *American Economic Review*, 49, 134–46.

Harberger, A. C. (1964). 'Taxation, Resource Allocation, and Welfare'. In *The Role of direct and Indirect Taxes in the Federal Revenue System*. Princeton: Princeton University Press for Na. Bur. Econ. Res. and Booking Inst.

Harberger, A. C. (1972). 'Cost-Benefit Analysis of Transportation Projects'. In *Project Evaluation: Collected Papers* (pp. 248–79). London and Basingstoke: Macmillan.

Harberger, A. C. (2002). 'Chapter 23: Cost-Benefit Analysis of Transportation Projects'. In A. C. Harberger and G. P. Jenkins (eds) *Cost-Benefit Analysis*. Cheltenham: Edward Elgar Publisher.

Harberger, A. C. and Jenkins, G. P. (2002). 'Introduction'. In A. C. Harberger and G. P. Jenkins (eds), *Cost-Benefit Analysis* (pp. xiii–xv). Cheltenham: Edward Elgar Publishing Ltd.

Hardin, G. (1968). 'The Tragedy of the Commons'. *Science*, 162, 1243–8.

Harris, R. (1975). 'The Political Economy of Africa – Underdevelopment or Revolution'. In R. Harris (ed.), *The Political Economy of Africa*. London: Shenkman.

Harrison, P. (1987). *The Greening of Africa: Breaking through in the Battle for Land and Food*. London: Paladin, for IIED/Earthscan.

Harrod, R. F. (1948). *Towards a Dynamic Economics*. London: Macmillan.

Hartley, K. and Tisdell, C. (1981). *Micro-Economic Policy*. London: John Wiley and Sons Ltd.

Harvey, J. (1987). *Urban Land Economics*. Basingstoke: Palgrave Macmillan.

Hatch Associates (2001). *Ghana Land Administration Project*. Accra: Ministry of Lands and Forestry.

Hatch Associates (2002). 'Project Preparation Report: Ghana Land Administration Project'. Ghana: Ministry of Lands, Forestry and Mines.

Haveman, R. H. (1976a). 'Evaluating the Impact of Public Policies on Regional Welfare'. *Regional Studies*, 10, 449–63.

Haveman, R. H. (1976b). 'Policy Analysis and the Congress: An Economist's View'. *Policy Analysis*, 2, 235–50.

Hayek, F. A. (1945). *The Road to Serfdom*. London: Routledge.

Hick, J. R. (1939). 'The Foundations of Welfare Economics'. 49, 696–712.

Hicks, J. R. (1940). 'The Valuation of Social Income'. *Economica*, 105–24.

Hicks, J. R. (1941). 'The Rehabilitation of Consumers' Surplus'. *Review of Economic Studies*, 8, 108–16.

Hicks, J. R. (1942). 'Consumers' Surplus and Index Numbers'. *Review of Economic Studies*, 9, 126–37.

Hicks, J. R. (1944). 'The Four Consumers' Surplus'. *Review of Economic Studies*, 11, 31–41.

Hicks, J. R. (1946). 'The Generalised Theory of Consumer's Surplus'. *Review of Economic Studies*, 13, 68–74.

Hidano, N. (2002). *The Economic Valuation of the Environment and Public Policy: A Hedonic Approach*. Cheltenham: Edward Elgar Publishing.

Hobbes, T. (1651). *Leviathan*. New York: Collier.

Hodgson, G. (1988). *Economics and Institutions*. Cambridge: Polity Press.

Hogwood, B. W. and Gunn, L. A. (1984). *Policy Analysis for the Real World*. Oxford: Oxford University Press.

Hogwood, B. W. and Peters, G. B. (1985). *The Pathology of Public Policy*. Oxford, UK: Clarendon Press.

Hotelling, H. (1932). 'Edgeworth's Taxation Paradox and the Nature of Demand and Supply'. *Journal of Political Economy*, 40, 577–616.

Hotelling, H. (1935). 'The Most Predictable Criterion'. *Journal of Educational Psychology*, 26, 139–42.

Hutchful, E. (2002). *Ghana's Adjustment Experience: The Paradox of Reforms*. New York: United Nations Research Institute for Social Development.

IIED (1999). 'Land Tenure and Resource Access in West Africa: Issues and Opportunities for the Next Twenty Five Years'. London: International Institute for Environmental and Development.

Isard, W. (1956). *Location and Space Economy*. Cambridge: MIT Press.

Jackson, P. (1982). *The Political Economy of Bureaucracy*. London: Phillip Allan.

Jenkin, H. C. F. (1870). 'The Graphic Representation of the Laws of Supply and Demand, and Their Application to Labour'. In A. Grant (ed.), *Recess Studies*. Reprinted in S. Colvin and J. A. Ewing (eds) (1887). *Papers, Literary, Scientific, &c. by the late Fleeming Jenkin*, Vol. 2, pp. 76–106. London: Longmans Green.

Jenkins, W. I. (1978). *Policy Analysis: A Political and Organisational Perspective*. London: Martin Robertson.

Jenkins, G. P. (1999). 'Evaluation of Stakeholder Impacts in Cost-Benefits Analysis'. *Impact Assessment and Project Appraisal*, 17, 87–96.

Jenkins-Smith, H. C. (1990). *Democratic Politics and Policy Analysis*. New York: Harcourt Brace and Company.

Jevons, W. S. (1972–81). *Papers and Correspondence of William Stanley Jevons* ed. by R. D. C. Black. London: Macmillan.

Johnson, O. E. G. (1972). 'Economic Analysis, the Legal Framework and Land Tenure Systems'. *Journal of Law and Economics*, 15, 1, 259–76.

Kaldor, N. (1939). 'Welfare Propositions of Economics and Inter-Personal Comparison of Utility'. *Economic Journal*, 49, 549–52.

Kaniki, M. H. Y. (1985). 'The Colonial Economy: The Former British Zones'. In A. Adu Boahen (ed.), *General History of Africa: VII* (pp. 383–4). CA: UNESCO.

Kasanga, K. R. (1990). 'Institutional/Legal Arrangements for Land Development – Case Study of Three Secondary Cities of Ghana'. Final report to HABITAT Urban Management Programme.

Kasanga, K. R. (2001). 'Ideology and Land Policy in Ghana'. Paper presented at the USAID and World Bank-Sponsored Side Event to the World Summit on Sustainable Development: Property Rights: Reflections on Governance, Assets, and Stewardship. The Export House, Johannesburg, South Africa.

Kasanga, K. and Kotey, N. A. (2001). *Land Management in Ghana: Building on Tradition and Modernity*. London: International Institute for Environment and Development.

Kasanga, K. (2002). 'Land Tenure Resource Access and Decentralization in Ghana'. In C. Toulmin, P. L. Delville, and S. Traoré (eds) (2002). *The Dynamics of Resource Tenure in West Africa*, Oxford: James Currey, pp. 25–36.

Kathryn Firmin-Sellers, *The Transformation of Property Rights in the Gold Coast: An empirical analysis applying rational choice theory*, Cambridge University Press, 1996.

Keohane, R. (1988). 'International Institutions: Two Approaches'. *International Studies Quarterly*, 32, 4, 379–96.

Killick, T. (1978). *Development Economics in Action: A Study of Economic Policies in Ghana*. London: Heinemann.

Kilpatrick, J. A. (2007). 'Valuation of Brownfields'. In M. Gerrard (ed) *Brownfield Law and Practice*. London: Lexis Nexis.

Kitching, G. (1980). *Class and Economic Change in Kenya: The Making of an African Petite Bourgeoisie 1905–1970*. New Haven and London: Yale University Press.

Kivell, P. (1993). *Land and the City*. London: Routledge, Chapman and Hall Inc.

Klein, P. G. (1999). *New Institutional Economics*. Available at: http://encyclo.findlaw.com/053book.pdf, retrieved on 4th April 2002.

Kovach, W. L. (1995). 'Multivariate Data Analysis'. In D. Maddy and J. S. Brew (eds), *Statistical Modelling of Quaternary Science Data* (pp. 1–38). Technical Guide Series No. 5. Cambridge, UK: Quaternary Research Association.

Krueger, A. O. (1974). 'The Political Economy of the Rent-Seeking Society'. *American Economic Review*, 64, 291–303.

Krueger, A. O. (1975). *The Benefits and Costs of Import Substitution in India: A Microeconomic Study*. Minneapolis: University of Minnesota Press.

Lane, J. E. (1993). *The Public Sector: Concepts, Models and Approach*. London: Sage.

Larbi, O. W. (1994). 'Urban Land Policies and Delivery of Developable Land in Ghana'. Ph.D. Thesis, Department of Land Management and Development, University of Reading, UK.

Larbi, O. W. (1995). *The Urban Land Development Process and Urban Land Policies in Ghana*. London: The Royal Institution of Chartered Surveyors.

Larbie, W. O., Antwi, A. and Olomolaiye, P. (2003). 'Land Valorization Processes and State Intervention in Land Management in Peri-Urban Accra, Ghana'. *International Development Planning Review*, 25, 4, 355–71.

Larbi, W. O., Antwi, A. and Olomolaiye, P. (2004). 'Compulsory Land Acquisition in Ghana: Policy and Praxis'. *Land Use Policy*, 1, 2, April, 115–27.

Laswell, H. D. (1956). *The Decision Process: Seven Categories of Functional Analysis*. College Park: University of Maryland.

Leftwich, R. H. (1973). *The Price System and Resource Allocation*. Hinsdale, IL: The Dryden Press, Oklahoma State University.

Leibenstein, H. (1957). *Economic Backwardness and Economic Growth*. NY: John Wiley & Sons.

Leibenstein, H. (1966). 'Allocative Efficiency vs. "X-Efficiency"' *American Economic Review*, 56, 3, 392–415.

Le Roy, É., Karsenty, A. and Bertrand, A. (1995). *La sécurisation foncière en Afrique. Pour une gestion viable des ressources renouvellables*. Paris: Karthala.

Levacic, R. (1987). *Economic Policy Making*. Brighton, UK: Wheatsheaf.

Lewis, A. W. (1954). *Economic Development with Unlimited Supplies of Labour*. Manchester: Manchester School of Economic and Social Studies.

Lindblom, C. E. (1959). 'The Science of Muddling Through'. *Public Administration Review*, 19, 78–88.

Lindblom, C. E. (1980). *The Policy Making Process*, 2nd edn. New Jersey: Prentice Hall Inc.

Lindblom, C. E. and Woodhouse, E. J. (1993). *The Policy Making Process*, 3rd edn. Englewood Cliffs: Prentice-Hall.

Lindblom, I. C. (1977). *Politics and Markers*. New York: Harper.

Lipsey, R. G. (1993). *An Introduction to Positive Economics*, 7th edn. Oxford: Oxford University Press.

Lonsdale, J. (1985). 'The European Scramble and Conquest in African History'. In R. Oliver and G. N. Sanderson (eds), *Cambridge History of Africa, Vol. VI*. Cambridge: Cambridge University Press, pp. 680–766.
Lovrich, N. P. and Neiman, M. (1984). *Public Choice Theory in Public Administration: An Annotated Bibliography*. New York: Garland.
Lund, C. (2001). 'African Land Tenure: Questioning Basic Assumptions'. In T. A. Benjaminsen and C. Lund (eds), *Politics, Property and Production in the West African Sahel: Approaches to Natural Resources Management*. Uppsala: Nordic Africa Institute/Transaction Publishers.
Mabogunje, A. L. (1980). *The Development Process: A Spatial Perspective*. London: Hutchinson.
Mabogunje, A. L. (1989). *The Development Process: A Spatial Perspective*. London: Unwin Hyman Ltd.
Mabogunje (1992). 'Perspectives on Urban Land and Urban Management Policies in Sub-Saharan Africa'. Washington DC: World Bank.
Mack, R. (1971). *Planning and Uncertainty*. New York: John Wily.
Marshall, A. (1920). *Principles of Economics*. London: Macmillan and Co., Ltd.
Mattingly, M. (1993). 'Urban Management Intervention in Land Markets'. In N. Devas and C. Rakodi (eds), *Managing Fast Growing Cities*. Harlow: Longman.
Mbaku, J. M. (1991). 'Military Expenditures and Bureaucratic Competition for Rents. *Public Choice*, 71, 19–71.
McAuslan, P. (2000). 'Only the Name of the Country Changes: The Diaspora of 'European' Land Law in Commonwealth Africa'. In C. Toulmin and J. Quan (eds), *Evolving Land Rights, Policy and Tenure in Africa* (pp. 75–96). London: DFID/IIED/NRI.
McGuire, T., Coiner, M. and Spancake, L. (1979). 'Budget-Maximizing Agencies and Efficiency in Government'. *Public Choice*, 34, 333–57.
McKean, R. (1965). 'The Unseen Hand in Government'. *American Economic Review*, 55, 496–505.
McLean, I. (1972). 'The Scientific Status of Political Science – a Comment'. *British Journal of Political Science*, 2, 383–4.
McLean, D. G. and Mundy, B. (1998). 'The Addition of Contingent Valuation and Conjoint Analysis to the Required Body of Knowledge for the Estimation of Environmental Damages to Real Property'. *Journal of Real Estate Practice and Education*, 1, 1, 1–19.
McNutt, P. A. (2002). *The Economics of Public Choice*. 2nd edn. Cheltenham, UK and Nothampton, MA, US: Edward Elgar.
Meek, C. K. (1949). *Land Law and Custom in the Colonies*. London, New York and Toronto: Oxford University Press.
Meese, R. A. and Wallace, N. E. (1997). 'The Construction of Residential Housing Price Indices: A Comparison of Repeat Sales, Hedonic Regression and Hybrid Approach'. *Journal of Real Estate Finance and Economics*, 14, 11–32.
Megarry, R. and Wade, W. (2000). *The Law of Real Property*, 6th edn. London: Sweet and Maxwell.
Menger, C. (1871). *Principles of Economics*, translated by J. Dingwall and B. F. Hoselitz, with an introduction by Friedrich A. Hayek (1981). New York: New York University Press.
Micheals, R. and Kalish, L. (1981). 'The Incentives of Regulators: Evidence from Banking'. *Public Choice*, 36, 187–92.

Migot-Adholla, S., Hazell, P., Blarel, B. and Place, F. (1991). 'Indegenous Land Rights System in Sub Saharan Africa: A Constraint on Productivity'. *World Bank Economic Review*, 5, 155–75.

Mills, E. S. (1972). *Studies in the Structure of the Urban Economy*. Baltimore: Johns Hopkins University Press.

Mills, E. S. and Simenauer, R. (1996). 'New Hedonic Estimates of Residential Constant Quality House Prices'. *Journal of Property Research*, 39, 209–15.

Ministry of Lands and Forestry (MLF) (1999). Budget Statement. Accra, Ghana.

Ministry of Lands and Forestry (MLF) (2005). Budget Statement. Accra, Ghana.

Mirrlees, J. A. (1976). 'The Optimal Structure of Incentives and Authority within an Organization'. *Bell Journal of Economics*, 7, 105–31.

Mises, L. V. (1944). *Bureaucracy*. New Haven, CT: Yale University Press.

Mises, L. V. (1962). *Bureaucracy*. Westport, CT: Arlington House.

Mises, L. von (1996). *Human Action: A Treatise on Economics*. Irvington-on-Hudson, NY: The Foundation for Economic Education.

Miyao, T. (1981). *Dynamic Analysis of the Urban Economy*. New York: Academic Press.

Mol, P. W. and Wiersum, K. F. (1993). 'Common Forest Resource Management'. In D. A. Messerschmidt (ed.), *Common Forest Resource Management: Annotated Bibliography of Asia, Africa, and Latin America*. Rome: FAO.

Morancho, A. B. (2003). 'A Hedonic Valuation of Urban Green Areas'. *Landscape and Urban Planning*, 66, 35–41.

Morgan, G. (1985). Land information systems: Design considerations for the organization of supporting technologies. Cartography Division, World Bank.

Morgan, W. T. W. (1992). 'Tropical African Colonial Experience'. In W. B. Gleave (ed.), *Tropical African Development: Geographical Perspectives*. New York: John Wiley and Sons Inc.

Mueller, D. (1989). *Public Choice II*. Cambridge: Cambridge University Press.

Mueller, D. C. (2003). *Public Choice III*. Cambridge: Cambridge University Press.

Mueller, D. C. (2004). *Public Choice III*. Cambridge, UK: Cambridge University Press.

Munro, F. J. (1984). Studies in Economic and Social History. London: Macmillan Press.

Muth, R. F. (1985). Models of Land-Use, Housing, and Rent: An Evaluation, *Journal of Regional Science*, 25, 593–606.

Mutt, R. R. (1969). *Cities and Housing: The Spatial Pattern of Urban Residential Land Use*. Chicago: University of Chicago Press.

N'Diaye, M. (2000). *International Policies, African Realities: Democracy in Africa*. Dakar: Forum of African Voluntary Development Organisations.

Nakamura, R. (1987). 'The Textbook Policy Process and Implementation Research'. *Policy Studies Review*, 7, 142–54.

Niskanen, W. (1973). *Bureaucracy: Servant or Master*. London: Institute of Economic Affairs.

Niskanen, W. A. (1994). *Bureaucracy and Public Economics, The Locke Institute*, UK and Brookfield: Aldershot, US: Edward Elgar.

Niskanen, W. A. Jr. (1971). *Bureaucracy and Representative Government*. Chicago: Aldine-Atherton.

Noronha, R. (1985). *A Review of the Literature on Land Tenure Systems in Sub-Saharan Africa*, vol. 43. Washington: Research Unit of the Agriculture and Rural Development Department, World Bank.

North, D. C. (1981). *Structure and Change in Economic History*. London: W. W. Norton and Company.

North, D. C. (1990). *Institutions, Institutional Change, and Economic Performance*. New York: Cambridge University Press.

North, D. C. (1997). 'The Contribution of New Institutional Economics to an Understanding of the Transitional Problem'. WIDER Annual Lectures 1, Helsinki, Finland: World Institute for Development Economics Research.

North, D. C. and Thomas, R. P. (1973). *The Rise of the Western World: A New Economic History*. Cambridge: Cambridge University Press.

Nurkse, R. (1953). *Problems of Capital Formation in Underdeveloped Countries*. Oxford: Blackwell.

Nzongola-Ntalaja, G. (1997). 'The State and Democracy in Africa'. In G. Nzongola-Ntalaja and M. C. Lee (eds), *The State and Democracy in Africa*. Harare: AAPS Books.

Ohimen v. *Adjei and Another*. 2 WALR 275, 1957.

Okoin, J. R. M. (1999). 'Côte d'Ivoire's Rural Land Plan'. Contribution to the workshop on land tenure policies in Sub-Saharan Africa, 16–19 February 1999, Berkshire, UK, IIED, London.

Okoth-Ogendo, H. W. O. (1982). 'The Perils of Land Tenure Reforms'. Paper prepared for workshop on Land Policy and Agricultural Production in Eastern and Southern African Countries (Gaborone, Botswana).

Okoth-Ogendo, H. W. O. (1994). 'Land Tenure, Agrarian Legislation and Environmental Management Systems'. In R. J. Bakema (ed.), *Land Tenure and Sustainable Land Use* (pp. 21–30). Amsterdam: Royal Tropical Institute.

Okoth-Ogendo, H. W. O. (1998). 'Implementing Land Legislation in Uganda: Drawing on Comparative Experiences'. Paper for a DFID Technical Workshop on Uganda's Land Act (Jinja, Uganda).

Okoth-Ogendo, H. W. O. (2000). 'Legislative Approach to Customary Tenure and Tenure Reform in East Africa'. In C. Toulmin and J. Quan (eds), *Evolving Land Rights, Policy and Tenure in Africa* (pp. 123–34). London: DFID/IIED/NRI.

Ollenu, N. A. (1962). *Principles of Customary Land Law in Ghana*, Law in Africa Volume 2. London: Sweet and Maxwell.

Ortiz, A. and Bertaud, A. (2001). 'Land Market and Urban Management: The Role of Planning Tools'. In M. Freire and R. Stren (eds), *The Challenge of Urban Government: Policies and Practices*. Toronto: The World Bank Institute and The Centre for Urban and Community Studies.

Page, E. C. (1992). *Political Authority and Bureaucratic Power: A Comparative Analysis*, 2nd edn. New York: Harvester Wheatsheaf.

Palmer, R. (2000). 'Land Policy in Africa: Lessons from Recent Policy and Implementation Processes'. In C. Toulmin and J. Quan (eds), *Evolving Land Rights, Policy and Tenure in Africa* (pp. 267–88). London: DFID/IIED/NRI.

Pamuk, A. and Dowall, D. E. (1998). 'The Price of Land for Housing in Trinidad: Implications for Affordability'. *Urban Studies*, 35, 2, 285–99.

Parkinson, N. C. (1957). *Parkinson's Law and Other Studies in Administration*. Boston, MA: Houghton Mifflin.

Parsons, W. (2001). *Public Policy: An Introduction to the Theory and Practice of Policy Analysis*. Cheltenham: Edward Elgar Publishing Ltd.

Parsons, W. (2003). *Public Policy: An Introduction to the Theory and Practice of Policy Analysis*. Northampton: Edward Elgar Publishing Ltd.

Payne, G. (1989). *Informal Housing and Land Subdivisions in Third World Cities: A Review of the Literature*. Oxford: Oxford Polytechnic (now Oxford Brookes University).

Payne, G. (1997). *Urban Land Tenure and Property Rights in Developing Countries: A Review*. London: IT Publications/ODA.

Payne, G. (2002). *Land Rights and Innovation: Improving Tenure Security for the Urban Poor*. London: Intermediate Technology Publications.

Pejovich, S. (1990). *The Economics of Property Rights: Towards a Theory of Comparative Systems*. Dordrecht, Boston: Kluwer Academic Publishers.

Pejovich, S. (1997). 'Introduction' to Chapters 2, 3, 4 and 5. In S. Pejovich (ed.), *The Economic Foundation of Property Rights* (pp. 3–6). Cheltenham: Edward Elgar.

Peters, B. G. (1978). *The Politics of Bureaucracy: A Comparative Perspective*. New York: Longman.

Pigou, A. C. (1920). *A Study in Public Finance*, 3rd edn. London: Macmillan.

Pigou, A. C. (1962). *The Economic of Welfare*, 4th edn. London: Macmillan and Co. Ltd.

Platteau, J.-P. (1992). *Land Reform and Structural Adjustment in Sub-Saharan Africa: Controversies and Guidelines*. Rome: Policy Analysis Division, FAO.

Platteau, J.-P. (1996). 'The Evolutionary Theory of Land Rights as Applied to Sub-Saharan Africa: A Critical Assessment'. *Development and Change*, 27, 29–85.

Platteau, J.-P. (2000). 'Does Africa Need Land Reform'. In C. Toulmin and J. Quan (eds), *Evolving Land Rights, Policy and Tenure in Africa* (pp. 51–74). London: DFID/IIED/NRI.

Pogucki, R. J. H. (1950). 'Report on Land Tenure in Native Customary Law of the Protectorate of the Northern Territories'. Accra: Lands Department.

Polanyi, K. (1944). *The Great Transformation: The Political and Economic Origins of Our Time*. New York: Amereon Ltd.

Posner, R. (1977). 'The Social Costs of Monopoly and Regulation'. *Journal of Political Economy*, 83.

Posner, R. (1995). *Overcoming Law*. Cambridge: Harvard University Press.

Posner, R. A. (1975). 'The Social Costs of Monopoly and Regulation'. *Journal of Political Economy*, 83, 4, 807–27.

Posner, R. A. (1993). 'The New Institutional Economics Meets Law and Economics'. *Journal of Institutional and Theoretical Economics*, 149, 1, 73–87.

Principal Voices (2005). 'Economic Development – Smaller World Greater Wealth, Growing Divide'. Available at http://www.principalvoices.com/economy.html. Accessed on January 2006.

Przeworski, A. (1991). *Democracy and the Market*. Cambridge: Cambridge University Press.

Quan, J. F. (1997). 'The Importance of Land Tenure to Poverty Eradication and Sustainable Development in Sub-Saharan Africa'. In *Background Report for the 1997 UK Government White Paper on International Development*. London: DFID.

Quan, J. F. (2000). 'Land Tenure, Economic Growth and Poverty in Sub-Saharan Africa'. In C. Toulmin and J. Quan (eds), *Evolving Land Rights, Policy and Tenure in Africa* (pp. 30–50). London: DFID/IIED/NRI.

Rao, P. K. (2003). *The Economics of Transaction Costs, Theory, Methods and Application*. Basingstoke: Palgrave Macmillan.

Reyna, S. P. (1987). 'The Emergence of Land Concentration in the West African Savanna'. *American Ethnologist*, 14, 3, 523–41.

Reyna, S. and Downs, R. (eds) (1988). *Land and Society in Contemporary Africa*. Durham, US: University Press of New England.

Richard, B. 1996. Tax Reform and Welfare Measurement: Do We Need Demand System Estimation',(With J. Banks and A. Lewbel.), *The Economic Journal*, Vol.106, No.438, 1996.

Richardson, G. B. (1960). *Information and Investment*. Oxford: Oxford University Press.

Rimmer, D. (1992). *Staying Poor: Ghana's Political Economy, 1950–1990*. Oxford, New York, Seoul and Tokyo: Pergamon Press.

Robson, A. J. (2005). 'Complex Evolutionary Systems and the Red Queen'. Economic Journal, Symposium 'Markets as Complex Adaptive Systems' 115, F211–F224.

Rochefort, D. A. and Cobb, R. W. (1994). *The Politics of Problem Definition*. Lawrence, KS: University Press of Kansas.

Rodney, W. (1985). 'The Colonial Economy'. In *General History of Africa: VII Africa under Colonial Domination 1880–1935*. UNESCO: University of California Press.

Rose, M. (2002). 'Implications of Costly Information'. 22 April, Library of Economics and Liberty. Available at http://www.econlib.org/library/Columns/Teachers/information.html, accessed 2 March 2010.

Rose, R. (1986). 'Comparing Public Policy: An Overview'. *European Journal of Political Research*, 1, 67–94.

Rosen, S. (1974). 'Hedonic Prices and Implicit Markets, Product Differentiation in Pure Competition'. *Journal of Political Economy*, 82, 1257–78.

Rostow, W. W. (1960). *The Stages of Economic Growth*. Cambridge: Cambridge University Press.

Ruttan, V. W. (1980). 'Bureaucratic Productivity: The Case of Agricultural Research'. *Public Choice*, 5, 529–47.

Ruttan V. W. and Hayami, Y. (1984). 'Toward a Theory of Induced Institutional Innovation'. *Journal of Development Studies*, 20, 203–23.

Sabatier, P. and Jenkins-Smith, H. (1993). *Policy Change and Learning: An Advocacy Coalition Approach*. Boulder, CO: Westview Press.

Sachs, J. D. (2005). *The End of Poverty: Economic Possibilities for Our Time*. New York: Penguin Books.

Saderion, Z., Smith, B. and Smith, C. (1994). 'An Integrated Approach to the Evaluation of Commercial Real Estate'. *Journal of Real Estate Research*, 9, 151–68.

Sarbah, J. M. (1897). *Fanti Customary Laws*. London: Clowes.

Sawyer, M. C. (1994). 'The Nature and Role of the Market'. In C. Pitelis (ed.), *Transaction Costs, Markets and Hierarchies*. Oxford: Basil Blackwell Ltd.

Schtaz, S. P. (1988). 'Africa Capitalism and African Economic Performance'. In H. Glickman (ed.), *The Crisis and Challenge of African Development*. London: Greenwood Press.

Schumpeter, J. A. (1954). *History of Economic Analysis.* New York: Oxford University Press.

Scott, J. C. (1955). 'Patron-Client Politics and Political Change in Southern Asia'. *American Political Science Review*, 66.

Sender, J. and Smith, S. (1986). *The Development of Capitalism in Africa.* London/ New York: Methuen.

Shillington, K. (2005). *History of Africa*, Rev. 2nd edn. New York: Palgrave Macmillan.

Shipton, P. (1987). 'The Kenyan Land Tenure Reform: Misunderstandings in the Public Creation of Private Property'. In R. E. Downs and S. P. Reyna (eds), *Land and Society in Contemporary Africa.* Hanover and London: University Press of New England.

Simon, H. A. (1957). *Administrative Behaviour*, 2nd edn. New York: Free Press.

Simon, H. A. (1979). 'Rational Decision Making in Business Organization'. *The American Economic Review*, 69, 493–513.

Simon, R. A., Quercia, R. G. and Marice, I. (1998). 'The Value Impacts of New Residential Construction and Neighbourhood Disinvestment on Residential Sales Price'. *Journal of Real Estate Research*, 15, 1/2, 148–61.

Sjaastad, E. and Bromley, D. W. (1997). 'Indigenous Land Rights in Sub-Saharan Africa: Appropriation, Security and Investment Demand'. *World Development*, 25, 549–62.

Skaggs, N. T. (1980). 'An Analysis of Federal Reserve Behavior: A Public Choice Approach'. Unpublished doctoral thesis, Duke University.

Slapper, G. and Kelly, D. (2001). *The English Legal System*, 5th edn., London: Routledge-Cavendish.

Slater, D. (1993). 'The Geopolitical Imagination and the Enframing of Development'. Paper presented at the Trilateral Conference on Global Change, University of Amsterdam.

Slesnick, D. (1998). 'Empirical Approaches to the Measurement of Welfare'. *J. Econ. Lit.*, 36, 4, 2108–65.

Smith, A. (1776). 'An Inquiry into the Nature and Causes of the Wealth of Nations'. In E. Cannan (ed.) (1904), *Library of Economics and Liberty.* London: Methuen and Co., Ltd.

Snow, A. and Warren, R. (1996). 'The Marginal Welfare Cost of Public Funds: Theory and Estimates'. *Journal of Public Economics*, 61, 289–305.

Social Security and National Insurance Trust (SSNIT) (2003). 'Research Report Quarterly Digest. Benefits Dept. and Area. Ops. Depts'. Available at: http://www.ssnit.com/corpDetails_n.cfm?EmpID=30&CorpID=13. Accessed on February 2004.

Stamm, V. (2000). 'Land Tenure Policy: An Innovative Approach from Côte d'Ivoire'. IIED Drylands Issue Paper, No. 91.

Stern, N. (1989). 'The Economics of Development: A Survey'. *Economic Journal*, 99, 597–687.

Stern, N. (2002). 'A Strategy for Development'. In B. Pleskovic and N. Stern (eds), *Annual World Bank Conference on Development Economics 2001/2002.* New York: World Bank/Osford University Press.

Stern, N. H. (1976). 'On the Specification of Models of Optimum Income Taxation'. *Journal of Public Economics*, 6, July–August, 123–62.

Sterne, R. S., Rabushka, A. and Scott, H. A. (1972). 'Serving the Elderly: An Illustration of the Niskanen Effect'. *Public Choice*, 13, 81–90.

Stigler, G. J. (1961). 'The Economics of Information'. *J. Polit. Econ.*, 69, 213–25.

Stigler, G. (1966). *The Theory of Price*, 3rd edn. New York: Macmillan.

Stone, D. A. (1989). 'Causal Stories and the Formation of Policy Agendas'. *Political Science*, 104, 281–300.

Stone, D. (1996). *Capturing the Political Imagination: Thin Tanks and the Policy Process*. London: Frank Cass and Co.

Sutton, R. (1999). *The Policy Process: An Overview*. London: Overseas Development Institute.

Tisdell, C. A. (1974). *Economics of Markets: An Introduction to Economic Analysis*. Australia: John Wiley.

Tom Björkroth, 2002. "Market Structure and Welfare in the Finnish Market for Long-Distance Telecommunications," Finnish Economic Papers, Finnish Economic Association, vol. 15(2), pages 87–101, Autumn.

Toulmin, C. and Quan, J. (2000). 'Evolving Land Rights, Policy and Tenure in Sub-Saharan Africa'. In C. Toulmin and J. Quan (eds), *Evolving Land Rights Policy and Tenure in Africa* (pp. 1–30). London: DFID/IIED/NRI.

Tullock, G. (1965). *The Politics of Bureaucracy*. Washington DC: Public Affairs Press.

Tullock, G. (1967). 'The Welfare Costs of Tariffs, Monopolies, and Theft. *Western Economic Journal*, 3, 224–32.

Tullock, G. (1971). 'The Costs of Transfers', *Kyklos*, 4, 629–43.

Tullock, G. (1975). 'Competing for Aid'. *Public Choice*, 21, 41–52.

Turvani, M. (1997). 'Illegal Markets and the New Institutional Economics'. In C. Mernard (ed.) *Transaction Cost Economics*. Cheltenham: Edward Elgar.

UNDP (2006). *Beyond Scarcity: Power, Poverty and the Global Water Crisis: Human Development Report 2006*. New York: UNDP.

UNICEF (2006). *The State of the World's Children 2007*. New York: The United Nations Children's Fund.

United Nations (2000). *Basic Facts about the United Nations*. New York: United Nations.

United Nations (2005). *World Population Prospects: The 2004 Revision, Highlights*. New York: United Nations.

Valenzuela, J. S. (1992). 'Democratic Consolidation in Post-Transitional Settings: Notion, Process, and Facilitating Conditions'. In Scott Mainwaring, Guillermo O'Donnell, and J. Samuel Valenzuela (eds), *Issues in Democratic Consolidation* (pp. 57–94). Notre Dame: University of Notre Dame Press.

van den Brink, R. (2003). *Land Policy and Land Reform in Sub-Saharan Africa: Consensus, Confusion and Controversy*. Washington: World Bank.

Vickrey, W. S. (1963). 'General and Specific Financing of Urban Services'. In Howard G. Schaller (ed.), *Public Expenditure Decisions in the Urban Community*. Baltimore: Johns Hopkins Press.

Von Thunen, J. H. (1826). 'Der isolierte staat in Beziehung auf landwirtschaft und national ekonomie'. In E.t.C.M.W.1.P.G.Hall (ed.), *VonThunen's Isolated State*. Oxford: Pergamon Press.

Wardham, E. A. (1989). 'Structural Adjustment Programmes for Socio-Economic Recovery and Transformation'. *Indonesia Quarterly*, XVII, 207–17.

Warriner, D. (1964). 'Land Reform and Economic Development'. In C. Eichner and C. De Witt. (eds), *Agriculture in Economic Development.* NY: McGraw-Hill.
Weber, M. (1964). *The Theory of Social and Economic Organisation,* edited by T. Parsons and A. M. Henderson. The Free Press.
Weimer, D. L. and Vining, A. R. (2004). *Policy Analysis: Concepts and Practice,* 4th edition. Upper Saddle River, NJ: Prentice Hall.
Williamson, O. (1996). *The Mechanisms of Governance.* New York: Oxford University Press.
Williamson, O. E. (1971). 'Markets or Government: Framework and Implications'. In R. N. Langlois (ed.), *Economics as a Process-Essay in the New Institutional Economics* (pp. 171–202). Cambridge: Cambridge University Press.
Williamson, O. E. (1979). 'Transaction Cost Economics: The Governance of Contractual Relations'. *Journal of Law and Economics,* 22, 233–61.
Williamson, O. E. (1981). 'The Economics of Organization: The Transaction Cost Approach'. *American Journal of Sociology,* 87, 3, 548–77.
Williamson, O. E. (1986). 'The Economics of Governance: Framework and Implications'. In Richard N. Langlois (ed.), *Economics as a Process: Essays in the New Institutional Economics.* New York: Cambridge University Press, pp. 171–202.
Williamson, O. E. (1991). 'Economic Institutions: Spontaneous and Intentional Governance'. *Journal of Law, Economics, and Organization,* 7 January, 159–87.
Williamson, O. E. (1994). 'Evaluating Coase'. *Journal of Economic Perspectives,* 8, 2, 201–04.
Wily, A. (2000) 'Reconstructing the African Commons'. Indiana: IASCP Eighth Biennial Conference.
Wolverton, M. L. and Senteza, J. (2003). 'Hedonic Estimate of Regional Constant Quality House Price'. *Landscape and Urban Planning,* 19, 3, 236–53.
Woodman, G. (1998). *Customary Land Law in the Ghanaian Courts.* Accra: Ghana Universities Press.
World Bank (1975). *Land Policy Reform Paper.* Washington DC: World Bank.
World Bank (1981). *Annual Report.* Washington DC: World Bank.
World Bank (1988). *Adjustment Lending – An Evaluation of Ten Years of Experience. (Report Prepared under the Leadership of Stanley Fischer).* Washington DC: Country Economics Department, World Bank.
World Bank (1989). *Sub-Saharan Africa: From Crises to Sustainable Growth.* Washington DC: World Bank.
World Bank (1993). *World Development Report.* Washington DC: World Bank.
World Bank (2001). 'Attacking Poverty: World Development Report 2000/2001 Published for the World Bank'. Washington, New York: Oxford University Press.
World Bank (2002). *Global Development Finance: Financing the Poorest Countries.* Washington DC: World Bank.
World Bank (2003). 'Land Policies for Growth and Poverty Reduction'. A World Bank Policy Research Paper. Washington: World Bank.
World Bank (2005a). *An Independent Review of World Bank Support to Capacity Building in Africa: The Case of Ghana.* Washington DC: World Bank.
World Bank (2005b). *Doing Business in 2005: Removing Obstacles to Growth.* Washington DC: World Bank.
World Bank (2007). *World Development Indicators.* Washington: World Bank.

World Bank (2007). *POVCAL*, World Bank, [Online] available at http://iresearch.worldbank.org/PovcalNet/povcalNet.html, Retrieved on 3rd March, 2009.

World Bank (2008). *Land Policy: Securing Rights to Reduce Poverty and Promote Growth*. Washington DC: World Bank.

Wunsch, J. S. and Dele, O. (1990). *The Failure of the Centralised State: Institutions and Self-Governance in Africa*. Boulder: Westview Press.

Wyatt, P. and Fisher, P. (1998). 'Property Information Today: Geographic and Land Information Management'. In P. Wyatt and P. Fisher (eds), *Property Information Today: Geographic and Land Information Management*. London: RICS Business Service Ltd.

Young, C. (1996). 'Africa: An Interim Balance Sheet'. *Journal of Democracy*, 3, 53–68.

ZLA (2008). *Land Policy Options for Development and Poverty Reduction: Civil Society Views for Pro-Poor Land Policies and Laws in Zambia*. Lusaka: Zambia Land Alliance.

Zolberg, A. R. (1968). 'The Structure of Political Conflict in the New States of Tropical Africa'. *The American Political Science Review*, XLII, 70–87.

Zucker, L. G. (1986). 'The Production of Trust: Institutional Sources of Economic Structure, 1840–1920'. In B. M. Staw and L. L. Cummings (eds), *Research in Organizational Behaviour*, 8 (pp. 53–111). Greenwich, CT: JAI Press.

Author Index

Subject Index